CLASS SIZE
AND
INSTRUCTION

Research on Teaching Monograph Series

PUBLISHED

Student Characteristics and Teaching by Jere E. Brophy and Carolyn M. Evertson

Pygmalion Grows Up: Studies in the Expectation Communication Process by Harris M. Cooper and Thomas L. Good

The Invisible Culture by Susan Urmston Philips

Active Mathematics Instruction by Thomas L. Good and Douglas Grouws

Cooperative Learning by Robert E. Slavin

Class Size and Instruction: A Field Study by Leonard S. Cahen, Nikola Filby, Gail McCutcheon, and Diane Kyle

FORTHCOMING

Staff Networking in Secondary Schools by Philip Cusick

CLASS SIZE AND INSTRUCTION

Leonard S. Cahen
ARIZONA STATE UNIVERSITY

Nikola Filby
THE FAR WEST LABORATORY FOR
EDUCATIONAL RESEARCH AND DEVELOPMENT

Gail McCutcheon
OHIO STATE UNIVERSITY

Diane W. Kyle
UNIVERSITY OF LOUISVILLE

Longman
New York & London

CLASS SIZE AND INSTRUCTION: A Field Study

Longman Inc., 1560 Broadway, New York, N.Y. 10036
Associated companies, branches, and representatives
throughout the world.

Developmental Editor: Nicole Benevento
Editorial and Production Supervisor: Ferne Y. Kawahara
Manufacturing Supervisor: Marion Hess
Composition: Vail-Ballou Press, Inc.

Library of Congress Cataloging in Publication Data
Main entry under title:

Class size and instruction.

  Bibliography: p.
  Includes index.
    1. Class size—United States—Case studies.
2. Teaching—Evaluation—Case studies. I. Cahen,
Leonard.
LB3013.2.C56 1983   371.2′51   82-20376
ISBN 0-582-28325-6

Manufactured in the United States of America

Contents

Preface   vii

Part I   1

  1 Introduction   3
  2 Methods Used to Study Class Size
      and Instruction   9

Part II: Virginia   33

  3 Pine Springs School   35
  4 Miss Anderson's Classroom   44
  5 Mrs. Hopkins' Classroom   71
  6 Mr. Jameson's Classroom   91
  7 Class Size and Instruction
      at Pine Springs School: What Did
      and Did Not Change?   111

Part III: California   125

  8 Harrison School   127
  9 Ms. Taylor's Classroom   134
  10 Mrs. Monroe's Classroom   156
  11 Discussion of California Site   175

Part IV   183

  12 Quantitative Data   185
  13 Conclusions   201

Part V   209

  14 Implications for Conducting Research 211
  15 Implications for Teaching and Schools 218

References   222

Appendix A Instructions for Rating Student Engagement/
           Interaction 224

Appendix B Median Percent of Observations Where
           Target Student Displayed Categorized
           Behavior 233

Index   235

Preface

This book is the culmination of three years of collaborative research. Our team, Nikola Filby, Gail McCutcheon, Diane Kyle, and I, started working together in the summer of 1978. At that time, Cahen and Filby were at the Far West Laboratory in San Francisco, and McCutcheon and Kyle were at the University of Virginia. Parallel studies were carried out at the two sites during the 1978–79 school year. After our intensive year of field study, the team scattered with the winds: Cahen went to Arizona State University, and Kyle went to the University of South Carolina as a visiting professor. A year later, Kyle accepted a professorship at the University of Louisville, and McCutcheon moved to Ohio State University. Dr. Filby remained at the Far West Laboratory, conducting an intensive study on instructional grouping practices in reading and mathematics—the latter serving as a continuation and extension of our work on class size and instruction. Other efforts on the issue of class size and instruction have continued at the Far West Laboratory under the direction of Dr. Steven Bossert.

The research reported in this book reflects a long-term research commitment by the Far West Laboratory and the National Institute of Education (NIE). The field study reported here has its roots in the Beginning Teacher Evaluation Study (BTES—Phase II and beyond), begun in 1974. Following BTES, the Class Size and Instruction Program was initiated in 1978. This program included the field study reported here, in addition to other activities. The project also supported two research syntheses on the research literature on class size. They are reported in Glass, Cahen, Smith, and Filby, 1982. The National Institute of Education, through its Teaching and Learning Division, has supported and fostered this continuing research program for the past seven years. We gratefully acknowledge the support of Drs. Virginia Koehler and Joseph Vaughan.

Because two teams wrote the studies reported here, the reader will undoubtedly find some unevenness in the book. This is due primarily to some initial philosophical and background differences between the Virginia team (McCutcheon and Kyle) and the San Francisco Bay Area team (Cahen and Filby). McCutcheon brought an extensive experience in classroom-based observational research, combined with a "point of view" style, referred to as educational criticism. Using this approach, a researcher enters the classroom with explicit values and opinions, gained through experience, about the nature of healthy educational environments. Evidence gathered through observations and other means are "tested" against this a priori and explicit statement of values.

This is not to say that Cahen and Filby entered their classrooms without value structures and opinions. However, the latter research team was far less experienced in qualitative techniques. Their frame of reference was heavily influenced by their five-year experience with the Beginning Teacher Evaluation Study, which examined classrooms in the light of a model called Academic Learning Time (ALT). This model defines productive learning time as a function of time allocated to instruction, modified by variables called engagement or attention rate of the pupil and the appropriateness of the tasks as reflected in differential levels of student success. These initial site-team differences provide strength and breadth to the study. Different methods of gathering evidence undoubtedly improved the study. Whenever possible, we attempted to blend our strengths. At other times, the research teams worked primarily through their special strengths. These techniques, we believe, provide adequate levels of consistency without destroying the uniqueness of individual contribution.

In the drafted chapters, we immediately became aware that the reports generated from the research in the two sites differed greatly regarding the issue of appraisal of what was seen and reported. This is not to be interpreted that the Virginia team was innately more harsh or critical; rather, to appraise was an integral part of the Virginia writing endeavor. The difference is evident in writing style and organization, in what the two teams chose to observe and interpret and in what issues they raised. Yet the studies are parallel for the themes of class size, especially regarding instruction in classrooms. Communication between the teams enhanced the research performed at both sites. While critical differences can be seen between the teams, it is important to point out that we shared many similar points of view. These included a commitment to understanding and fostering high-level, quality schooling; to research involving teacher–researcher collaboration; and to classroom-based research focused on instructional problems of importance to schooling generally.

As we move to the final phases of publishing our research, the team looks upon the experience as an interesting and profitable one for us professionally. We have learned from each other new points of view and capacities for conducting research. We had many profitable hours of discussion, which included many hours of arguing points of view and hammering out differential approaches to the gathering of evidence. As data and information emerged from the two field sites, we met to discuss the findings. Similarities and differences in the information, and in our interpretations, served as the catalyst for a continued commitment to a better understanding of the complexities of instruction in classrooms, and schooling in general. Some information led to new insights. Other evidence led us to expand our investigation at one site from what was just learned at the other. At other times we found recent experiences confirming what we ourselves and other researchers believed about schooling. In the work we present here, some readers may respond with a comment that "we found the obvious." For some of the team, a finding was confirming; to others, the insight was new. In all cases, we developed a deeper and more personal appreciation of fundamental issues. Our conclusions include some statements of the obvious (i.e., that schooling is a complex process). It is important, however, to provide evidence that obvious and commonsense notions have empirical grounding. The study provides evidence of some commonsense notions about class size. Perhaps most important is a commonly shared opinion that research on teaching must be translated into professional teaching programs—both pre-service and in-service.

The running of field research sites is expensive. On one hand, we wish we had been able to increase the generalizability of our findings by including more classrooms, pupils, and teachers. On the other hand, anyone who has gotten involved in case-study or ethnographic approaches to the understanding of instructional processes in classrooms knows that one cannot conduct research in a great many classes without paying heavily in the form of not being able to interpret in depth the "thickness" of the phenomenon underlying the evidence. The researcher must decide how best to allocate research resources. One can expect to learn different things from studying four classes extensively, as we did, than from studying, say, 40 classes with less extensive observation.

In closing, we would like to acknowledge some of the people who contributed to our research. Dr. Rob Moore, of San Francisco State University, participated actively as a field observer. In addition to serving in this role, he served as an informal on-the-spot consultant to the teachers in the Oakland, California site. The secretarial help of Sharon Hansen, at the Far West Laboratory, Christy Betonti, at Arizona State University, and Jackie Richardson, at the University of South Carolina is gratefully acknowledged. Anne Paige Ewing and Dr. Dorene Ross collected data in the California and Virginia field sites. Teachers in Virginia, Ohio, South Carolina, Kentucky, and California read drafts of the case studies. Their reactions and suggestions have been incorporated in the final version of the studies appearing in this book.

Lastly, we extend our acknowledgments to the pupils, field teachers and principals. Because we are protecting the anonymity of the school sites, the pupils, and the teachers, they must remain unnamed.

As we bring this research to press, we share a feeling that the process of teaching and learning is a very complex one. Collectively, we have seen many fine teachers. We hope that the report of our field research can be used in a positive way to support the position that teaching is a very difficult and complex profession; that simple solutions exist only for simple questions, of which there are few in education; and that the public must understand the complexities of schooling—an understanding which, we hope, will help the public to see that the country generally receives great value from its public school system. Schools cannot be unjustly used as a target for frustration about high taxes and the culture in general. We must learn about the good that schools do and learn how to support public education efficiently.

Leonard S. Cahen

Part I

1

Introduction

> There's more space; everyone can breathe . . .
> I can give more individual instruction time . . .
> There's more of *me* left at the end of the day!
>
> *Second-grade teacher*

Teachers of all grade levels, of all content areas, and from every type of school system would undoubtedly echo the sentiments of this second-grade teacher reacting to the advantages of reduced class size. "Smaller is better" is a well-established notion among teachers, a notion generating heated discussion as professional associations and school boards struggle to provide quality education, yet find that budget restrictions may make it difficult to justify the expense of smaller class sizes.

Unfortunately, 60 years of research on class size have failed to provide conclusive answers to such questions as: Do students learn more in smaller classes? Do reduced class sizes increase the likelihood of positive schooling outcomes? Does instruction improve when teachers work with a smaller number of students? Are smaller classes more enjoyable places for teachers and students to work? The research findings suggest that smaller seems better in some cases but not in others. Consequently, school board policy makers have not received strong enough evidence to justify the costs of massive reductions in class size.

The research reported in this book has been an attempt to shed new light on the class-size issue by going beyond the primary question of *whether* class size has an effect to the question of *how* class size influences teaching and learning. Our focus has been on understanding class size as one of several factors influencing what takes place in classrooms. Although we recognized that reduced class size wouldn't guarantee a better quality of schooling, we felt it would provide the potential for teachers to create or modify learning environments. Understanding what changes did and did not occur and possible reasons for these might help to explain why achievement gains have been found in some studies of class-size effects but not in others. Furthermore, evidence of the benefits of smaller class size might reveal effective practices that could have potential for larger classes, too.

The Research Plan

The class-size field study took place during the 1978–79 school year. Four second-grade teachers participated, two from a rural school in Virginia and two from an urban, inner-city school in California. (The overview chapter for each site elaborates details about the schools and classrooms.)

In order to understand how the same teachers and students responded to different class-size conditions, we used a design allowing us to reduce class size in the middle of the year. We accomplished this by adding one extra teacher in each school, thus reducing class size by one-third. Each classroom then became a case study of "larger" versus "smaller" class-size comparisons.

Some key questions framing the study included: What characteristics describe the classrooms, and what transpires there before and after the class size change? What factors appear to influence teachers to make some instructional changes as a function of class size, but not others? What factors appear to limit or constrain teachers from taking advantage of the potential of a smaller class? (Chapter 2 includes a more extensive discussion of research questions.)

To understand the complexities and nuances of the classrooms and to answer the many questions related to class-size effects, we incorporated a variety of research methods in this study. These included extensive, naturalistic observations, field notes, and interviews as well as systematic behavioral observations and some achievement test data. Additionally, the teachers had the opportunity throughout the study to be active collaborators in the research enterprise. They speculated with us about class-size effects and considered what changes to make in their classes. They kept journals of their experiences, recording first their plans and later their observations and reactions. Their observations are an important form of evidence reported in the case studies.

As researchers, we attempted to provide a climate of support for teacher change by encouraging them to think about what changes might be possible with smaller classes. Although we responded to teacher interests with instructional materials, suggested resources, and classroom demonstrations, we did not advocate or require any particular changes or provide any in-depth professional development activities. Throughout the study, the focus remained on understanding the naturally occurring changes related to class size.

Background and Perspectives

The field study is one of several projects sponsored by the Class Size and Instruction Program at the Far West Laboratory for Educational Research and

Development. To provide a context for the field study, the following section describes other research conducted at the Far West Laboratory and other research on class size.

Two of the authors participated in the Beginning Teacher Evaluation Study (BTES) conducted at the Far West Laboratory in San Francisco (Fisher, Berliner, Filby, Marliave, Cahen, and Dishaw, 1980). This project involved studying 25 second-grade classrooms and 22 fifth-grade classrooms in northern California in an attempt to understand the complex relationships between what teachers do and pupil improvement in reading and mathematics. The central concept in the BTES research was Academic Learning Time (ALT), a measure of the amount of time a student spends successfully engaged in classroom work. More ALT generally means more learning is taking place, as shown by higher gains on achievement tests. One advantage to the ALT concept is that one can analyze how instructional processes influence components of the measure. For instance, one component of ALT is student attention (engagement) to academic tasks. Some BTES students and some classes showed higher rates of attention than others, and these differences reflected greater learning. The frequency of student contact with the teacher seemed to influence student attention rates; students paid attention more often when they spent time in group work *with* the teacher or when the teacher monitored more frequently during seatwork. Smaller classes may increase the likelihood of work in small groups or individual contact with the teacher and thus may foster greater student attention to tasks.

A second component of ALT is student success rate. Students who were observed to be more successful in their work on daily assignments showed greater learning during the year. Success reflects, in part, the appropriateness of the match between assigned tasks and student competence. If students are given tasks which they do not understand well enough to work on with reasonable success, they will not learn. The concern for individualization reflects this issue. Studies of class size suggest that the teacher may be able to monitor student performance and assign tasks more appropriately with fewer students in the class.

Formal and informal observations in BTES revealed the management skills teachers need to provide appropriate tasks and maintain student attention. The BTES study (Filby and Cahen, 1977, 1978) further documented teacher awareness of pupils' skills and achievement levels as an important factor in providing tasks of appropriate difficulty. Also, the teachers who were able to provide more feedback to students about their performance had classes that improved academically. These findings suggested that teachers might be able to do a more thorough job of assessment, diagnosis, prescription, and feedback if they had fewer pupils in their charge. This perception guided the development of the Class Size and Instruction Project. Our experience with many second- and fifth-grade classes convinced us to work in depth in only a few classes.

Another matter concerned the inconclusive evidence about the relationship of class size and achievement. Drs. Gene V. Glass and Mary Lee Smith of the

University of Colorado agreed to synthesize the literature on the relationship of class size to achievement and on the relationship of class size to classroom processes, teacher satisfaction, and pupil attitude. Their technique, sometimes called "meta-analysis," is relatively new and needs to be described in some detail. In most reviews of the literature, for example, in the area of comparing two approaches to teaching reading, the summarizer reports his or her personal conclusions about the consistency of the findings reviewed across single studies. The meta-analysis approach developed by Glass (1976) numerically synthesizes data across studies. This approach creates a single data point from each study reviewed and does not discard data because the given study failed to reach classical levels of significance. Glass and Smith incorporated into their meta-analysis various studies containing data from dissertations, and published and unpublished research reports. For each study reporting data (such as an achievement mean for a large class and achievement mean for a small class, and a measure of variability called the standard deviation) an effect size was calculated. The effect size was defined as the difference between the achievement means for the large and small classes divided by the standard deviation. Glass and Smith (1978, 1979) plotted effect sizes against class size.

The meta-analysis of the relationship of class size to achievement is summarized in the graph shown in Figure 1.1. The graph is slightly modified from one appearing in Glass, Cahen, Smith, and Filby (1982). An examination of this graph shows clearly that on the average, smaller classes achieve higher achievement scores than larger classes, and that the advantage of reducing classes

FIGURE 1.1 The Glass-Smith Curve

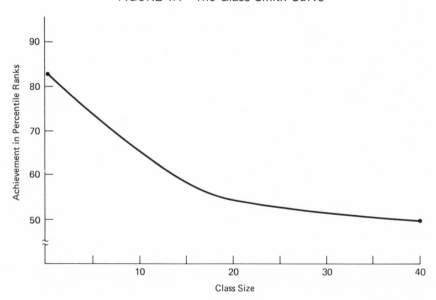

is not strong until class size is reduced below approximately 15 students. If a student in a class size of 40 has an "average" achievement score on a normed test (the 50th percentile), then a student in a class size of 20 can be expected to score at the 55th percentile, while a student in a class of 10 can be expected to score at the 65th percentile. As the graph also shows, the expected difference in achievement between a class size of 25 and a class of 30 is much smaller than the difference between class sizes of 10 and 15.

In a second meta-analysis, Smith and Glass (1979) examined the relationship of class size to teaching processes, teacher satisfaction, and pupil attitude. While fewer studies have been done in each of these areas than in the area of achievement and class size, the relationship of teacher satisfaction to class size appeared to be very strong. Teacher satisfaction or morale dropped dramatically as class size increased. Pupil attitudes were also less favorable as class size increased. Classroom or teaching processes were also associated with class size; as class size decreased, an increase was observed in individualization of instruction, student participation, and quality of instruction. The research synthesis of teaching processes cannot provide a very detailed picture of the changes in instruction occurring with a reduction in class size. One study exemplifies this research.

A major recent study of class size was carried out in Toronto (Wright, Shapson, Eason, and FitzGerald, 1977). In this study, class size was controlled, and detailed observation and testing was done for students in grades 4 and 5. In some cases the same teachers could be compared teaching a small class (16 or 23 students) and a large class (30 or 37 students). In smaller classes, students had more questions addressed to them individually, and participated more fully in classroom activities. Small classes were quieter than large classes, and there was some indication that student attitudes might be more positive in the smaller classes.

Many studies on the quality of instruction were done at Teachers' College, Columbia University, where there was a long tradition of research on class size (see Newell [1943], McKenna [1955], Richmond [1955], Coble [1968] and Olson [1970]). In later work, researchers developed an observation instrument called "Indicators of Quality." The work done with this observation instrument was critiqued along with other class-size studies in a major review by Ryan and Greenfield (1975). The reader may also wish to locate the class-size research review by Porwoll (1978).

In addition to attending to the new findings from the meta-analyses provided by professors Glass and Smith, we examined the literature about class size and found it to be confusing. In this literature, one could find cases where larger classes were better than smaller classes, but a greater number of cases where there was no obvious advantage to smaller over larger. However, the literature contained repeated comments, hypotheses, and insights about the relationship of class size to educational outcomes. These remarks included severe warnings about the complexity of the class-size issue. Perhaps these warnings meant that the number of students did not necessarily reflect the varied sorts of problems teachers face in different situations. Clearly, reducing class size was no guarantee that educational environments or instructional strategies would necessarily change. Indeed, the field studies reported in this book support the notion that reducing class size does not guarantee other changes.

The second meta-analysis was completed concurrently with the field study reported in this book. Evidence and information, then, are building from two roads of inquiry—the meta-analyses and the field studies presented here. The meta-analyses of Glass and Smith have already received wide attention and circulation. The two meta-analyses and a series of reaction papers examining the policy implications of the two meta-analyses have been completed and published (Glass, Cahen, Smith, and Filby, 1982).

The findings and implications from the field study reported in this book complement those from the meta-analyses; these two sources of information and evidence clarify some of the questions related to class size, and perhaps future studies will further expand our knowledge about these matters.

Outline of the Book

This book is organized in several parts. Part 1 includes a chapter on methodology, describing in detail our approach to the study. Part 2 describes the school year in Virginia, beginning with a description of the school setting, continuing with a chapter about each of the classes, and concluding with a discussion of what happened at the Virginia site. Part 3 presents this same sequence of chapters for California. In Part 4 we synthesize and discuss results across the two schools. One chapter reports numerical data, providing details about the collection and analysis of these data and a comparison of data across sites. The other chapter reviews what we know about class size and its role in the schooling process. Finally, in Part 5, we discuss the implications for conducting research and for teaching and learning. Throughout the book we portray what we saw in classes, how teachers felt about the experiences, the evidence we have about how class size influences the experiences of children, and our understanding of social context as it shapes what teachers do and believe they may do.

2

Methods Used to Study
Class Size and Instruction

This chapter discusses methods used in our study of class size and instruction and processes involved in working together as a team. How did we gather evidence about various matters? How did we decide that those matters were important? How did we work together despite the distance separating us? The chapter also discusses logistics such as locating schools and teachers to be involved in the study and dividing the classes to reduce their sizes.

DEVELOPMENT OF THE RESEARCH TEAM

One of the primary difficulties facing the research team concerned how to work together although we were conducting research in Virginia and California— two sites separated by much distance. We believed it was important to study class size in two very different locations to enable us to examine the influence of policies and the social milieu on what happened in classrooms. The problem of communication was important for us to deal with because we wanted to keep the studies parallel, permitting comparisons and allowing us to make interpretations across both sites. In other words, we wanted to be sure we were studying the same matters in essentially the same ways. The team—Gail Mc-Cutcheon and Diane Kyle in Virginia, and Len Cahen and Nikki Filby in California—met several times, sent one another project notes, and communicated frequently by telephone.

While the telephone calls and project notes informed us of one another's concerns and findings and renewed our enthusiasm about the study, the meetings contributed more to building a cohesive team spirit. Whether meeting on a front porch in Charlottesville, or walking along a street to a delicatessen in San Francisco, discussing research findings in a conference room at the Far West Laboratory, or conferring around a picnic table in Ohio, we explored issues in great depth and our confidence in one another grew. Early in our collaboration, we "brainstormed" about matters we wanted to study and possible ways of gathering evidence about them. We taught one another about research techniques and called to attention certain issues not previously considered. In later phases of the process, everyone critiqued each other's early chapter drafts. While each of us was responsible for particular chapters, the chapters are actually a composite of the group's views.

Several considerations influenced our decision about how many classrooms we should observe. Our questions called for us to study classrooms intensively—a time-consuming endeavor. Because the four researchers had other obligations in addition to research, we realized we had to limit the number of classrooms to be observed. Our time, then, was limited due to other obligations; yet we wanted to gather evidence about many facets of classroom life and its relation to class size, and to understand how those facets affected one another. As a result, we chose to study two schools—one in Virginia and one in California—and two classrooms (later three) in each state.

While intensive studies of a few classrooms have the potential for providing a rich, deep understanding of a problem, studying only a few cases also has its drawbacks. In our study, we considered few teachers and their teaching styles, and saw only two settings (with each one's accompanying traditions, policies, physical facilities, several student populations, and so on). We invite readers to compare what we portray in parts II and III to what they know of schools elsewhere.

GENERATING THE QUESTIONS

As individuals and as a team we conceived of lists of questions to guide our study. These questions concerned the nature of instruction and the possible influence of class size. Before we selected schools, we had developed many themes and questions, but some of these emerged as we observed particular situations. For example, the Virginia researchers became interested in classroom interruptions. In California, Ms. Taylor, one of the teachers, became convinced that her students' attendance was better in a smaller class, even accounting for inclement weather. Many questions arose because of our knowledge and beliefs about instruction, schools, children, and ways to conduct research. At one early meeting, we developed the following list of questions that served to focus our research efforts:

A. Instruction
  1. Subjects taught
     a. What is the daily/weekly schedule?
     b. What is its origin?
  2. Nature of activities
     a. What do children generally do in the classroom?
     b. When the teacher is working with one group, what are the other children doing?
     c. Why these activities? System or state mandates?
     d. What is the pattern of supervision of seatwork?

e. What does the teacher believe/say about instructional activities?

f. How does class size appear to influence these activities?

3. Use of materials
   a. What use does the teacher make of instructional materials?
   b. After the class size change, does the teacher cover more pages? Use more of the enrichment activities? Supplement the text with other materials? Cover more material or study materials in a more in-depth manner? Individualize?

4. Organization—groups, time, space
   a. How is classroom space used?
   b. How are groups formed? Who's in each group? Why?
   c. What organization of time occurs?
   d. Does this change when class size is reduced? If so, in what ways? What reasons do teachers give for the changes?

5. Planning
   a. What information does the teacher use when planning?
   b. Does planning change after the split? Does the teacher take individuals into account more?

6. Pupil assessment
   a. How does the teacher assess students' needs and progress?
   b. How much/what types of evidence does the teacher collect?
   c. What sorts of feedback do students receive—conference, papers passed back? What is said or written on a paper or in a conference?
   d. When are papers and workbooks corrected? By whom? How long do students wait? What happens then—does the student take it home, change wrong answers, look at it, throw it away, show it to peers, etc.?
   e. How does this change with class size? In what ways?

B. Interactions

1. Teacher–student
   a. Do teachers interact with students both in formal and informal encounters? Some students more than others?
   b. What is the nature of these interactions? Who initiates them?
   c. What opportunities exist for teachers to learn about their students? What do they seem to learn? How do they use the information?
   d. Do teachers spend more time talking about the subject matter, procedures, or behavior?
   e. How does this change with class size? In what ways?

2. Student–student interactions
   a. Do students interact with each other as well as with their teachers during instructional periods?
   B. How does this change with class size? In what ways?

C. Interruptions
  1. With a smaller number of students, do fewer in-class interruptions occur?
  2. What is the nature of these interruptions?
  3. Why do they seem to occur? What is their origin?
  4. Does this change with class size? In what ways?

D. External Factors
  1. What mandates from the principal, district, state affect instruction?
  2. What external factors seem to encourage or inhibit change? What do teachers know of them and say about them?

These questions became part of our project notes. In other project notes, we discussed general themes of the study, ways we might document our questions, and their possible relation to class size. For example, we discussed individualization in one set of notes from Virginia to California:

> One would think that individualization would increase with fewer students, where the teacher suited the approach and materials to the interest and needs of a particular child. Here, a record of what children are doing in the classroom, along with the teachers' reasons for presenting those activities and materials to children could be evidence. Is there variation? Does the teacher take into account individuals' strengths, needs, and interests? If not, is this due to division-(system-)wide mandates, or some other factors?

Such notes served to keep our studies parallel and provided an occasion for us to consider themes, questions, and variables worthy of study. We discussed similar matters over the telephone.

THE RESEARCH APPROACH

As we conceived questions, we speculated on reasonable ways to gather evidence about the questions and selected techniques for doing so. It seemed reasonable to collect information from various sources regarding the goings-on in classrooms before and after class size was reduced, in addition to information about the setting and students' learning. We collected some information through coded observation instruments and from tests. Other information was collected through observing, discussing matters with the teachers and students, and by examining students' work, teachers' journals, teachers' lesson plans, documents such as school-wide memoranda, agendas for teachers' meetings, report cards, and policies.

We conceived of the enterprise as an attempt to document what transpired, to describe, interpret, and appraise events for those who did not accompany us to these classrooms at Pine Springs School and at Harrison School. Descriptions provide, for the benefit of readers, an understanding of the nature of those classrooms; interpretations provide patterns and a conceptual context for the descriptions; appraisals critique—positively and negatively—what happened. The aim of such work is to permit readers to have a rich understanding of what transpired.

It should be noted that these studies are not automatically generalizable to all situations, since various factors influence each classroom situation differently. Some policies at work in the Virginia school, for example, may not be in force elsewhere. For this reason, readers are encouraged to be active, selecting from the studies what is relevant to their settings or what is particularly illuminative. Descriptions provide evidence of the character of the Virginia and California settings and the teaching and learning occurring there, enabling readers to decide what applies to their situations. Interpretations and appraisals provide patterns, concepts, considerations, concerns, and visions which may be appropriate to consider in the readers' settings as well. For example, researchers or teachers who read this study might be intrigued by how a particular context inhibits or encourages change, or how culture is reproduced in settings in which they observe or teach as well as in the Virginia and California schools.

The approach, then, is based on collecting evidence about the questions and themes we developed before we began the study and while the research was underway. The studies presented here describe, interpret, and appraise what we observed. Reading the studies necessitates the readers' personally generalizing from these cases to their own particular situations. The following section describes our logistical arrangements for the study.

Logistical Arrangements

Selecting schools for the study. In both Virginia and California, difficulties arose with regard to locating schools for the study. In Virginia, the difficulty lay in locating a school with sufficient space to house the third class when we reduced class size in January. Although enrollment was declining, former classrooms became reading resource rooms, science laboratories, and other rooms with specific purposes. Our problem in Virginia may have been exacerbated, in part, by some administrators' perceptions of the potential political implications of our study. In other words, some administrators may have been concerned that if we discovered that reducing class size improved instruction and achievement, teachers might demand smaller classes. We located one county-wide school system in rural Virginia where administrators appeared to be interested, and three principals attended a meeting where we discussed the project and our needs. One school was having a new wing constructed; contractors promised completion by Thanksgiving. Another school had two possible small rooms to use, and the principal, Mrs. Fleming, appeared to be very supportive of the study. The third school was fully departmentalized throughout; reducing class size in two teachers' homerooms might not necessarily have decreased their class size substantially because the students were regrouped across classes for particular subjects. Because the Virginia team was skeptical about the promised completion date of the wing in the first school, and because of the third school's organization, we chose to work at Pine Springs School, where space, although small, was available and Mrs. Fleming was supportive.

The Virginia team met with the teachers during lunch to outline the project and to discuss its potential benefits to the school, teachers, and students. The assistant superintendent called us a few days later to inform us that the central office had approved Pine Springs School as the school in which we were to work.

The California team's difficulties also concerned space. Contacts were made with several schools. A school being used to develop instruments for the study was a strong possibility, for space was available. However, it was a long commute and contained only one second grade. Finally, through a local teachers' center, the California team contacted the principal at Harrison School. Harrison School had one second-grade classroom, and a combination second- and third-grade class. Two meetings were held with the teachers and principal at Harrison. At the meetings, the California researchers described the nature of the project, its benefits for teachers and pupils, and what would be required of teachers and of the school. A one-page handout summarized this information. A longer document described what we discussed in the meetings. This latter document was given to the teachers and principal to read before they made a final decision about participation, and to ensure that everyone understood the specifics of the agreement. Once the principal and two teachers at the Harrison School agreed to participate, the necessary paperwork was sent to the district office for official approval.

Selecting target students. Early in our planning, we decided to select twelve target students in each site for more intensive observation and study. Four were to be students who were to remain in each of their original classrooms after we reduced class size, and four would be students who were to be transferred to the new classroom.

In Virginia, Miss Anderson and Mrs. Hopkins (the two second-grade teachers) and Mrs. Fleming (the principal of Pine Springs School) met with the Virginia researchers to divide the classes and to select target students. In California, this process was a joint venture between teachers and researchers. In both sites, we discussed with the teachers the reasons for choosing target students and the need for selecting students of different types. We suggested that target students might be those who would be thought to benefit greatly from the smaller class; they might also be students who would not necessarily benefit from reducing class size, but who might be interesting to watch for various reasons. We discussed balancing the target students in terms of achievement level, gender, and race, and those who were shy as opposed to those who were outgoing. In some cases a teacher suggested a particular student to include; in other cases, we made a suggestion and the teacher accepted it or suggested a change.

Dividing the classes. In both Virginia and California, decisions about select-ing students for the third class were made cooperatively by teachers and re-searchers. The principals participated as well.

In Virginia, the teachers and principal read the original class rosters, dis-cussed individuals, and nominated some for the new class or suggested that they should remain where they were. During the meetings, held in October, teachers expressed concern about matters such as whether the three classes appeared to be balanced in terms of high and low achievers, troublemakers and placid children, race, and gender. Teachers also voiced their opinion that sev-eral children should remain with them because they appeared to have difficulty in adjusting to new situations; a mid-year shift might be detrimental. The teach-ers further hoped to separate children who seemed to get into trouble when they were together. When school resumed after December vacation, Mrs. Fleming informed the students about their assignments to the rooms and sent letters home.

In California, one teacher suggested creating a list by the random selection of each third student from the class list. The researchers also created a ''bal-anced'' list by choosing some students from each reading group. The teachers examined the lists and suggested changes. Specifically, they were urged to consider students who should not be moved because they might suffer unduly from the shift, such as a low-achieving student who had formed a positive and productive relationship with his or her current teacher. Teachers were also re-quested to identify any students whose parents might be expected to object strongly to the shift. The principal was invited to indicate students who should not be moved. Individual meetings were held with Mrs. Monroe and Ms. Tay-lor, the two teachers, to review the list and agree on substitutions. The final list was given to the principal for his approval. A change in plans had to be made at the last minute; the split of classes in California had to be made a month ahead of schedule, due to an immediate district order to reduce class size. This change in schedule made it impossible to meet with the parents ahead of time. Instead, the principal sent a letter to parents only two days before the new class was to start, explaining that a new class had been created. Also at this time, the principal decided not to move any third-graders to the new room. Nikki Filby and Mrs. Monroe met at noon to revise the list quickly, substituting second-graders for the third-graders who had been on the list.

Hiring a third teacher. In Virginia, hiring the new teacher was left in the hands of Mrs. Fleming, the principal. She reviewed recent applications and interviewed Mr. Jameson, a newly arrived, experienced teacher who resided in the community. She asked if he would agree to be part of the research, and he expressed interest in it as well as in teaching second grade. Mrs. Fleming hired him mostly because he was the only male applicant for the position, and she believed children at Pine Springs School needed more contact with male teach-ers; at the time, no males taught at the school. She also believed he was highly competent. In California, Nikki Filby assumed the position of the third teacher. The district also provided an additional teacher who had just returned to the school system from a medical leave; this teacher functioned as Nikki Filby's associate.

Collecting Evidence

As mentioned earlier, our research questions implied that we had to use many methods for gathering evidence about different facets of the class-size issue. We used coded observation instruments, maintained field notes of observations of classes and discussions with principals and teachers, and collected school memoranda and students' work. Teachers kept journals about their own observations and reactions.

Coded observation. The California researchers provided several instruments developed for earlier studies which seemed appropriate to the study of class size and instruction. As discussed in Chapter 1, these instruments were developed for the Beginning Teacher Evaluation Study (BTES).

On one of these instruments, we coded whether students appeared to be engaged in what they were doing. This instrument required researchers to observe both target students and the entire class. The seven specific categories of student behavior appearing on the instrument were: engaged–academic, engaged–procedures, engaged–rules, waiting for help, off–task (quiet), misbehaving, and "down time," which meant that students had no assignment. The category engaged–academic meant that the student was paying attention and working on an academic task. Included in this category might be activities such as doing a math worksheet, reading a book, measuring the size of a desk top, listening to the teacher explain phonics rules, listening or participating in a class discussion about a story, or even asking another student how to work on a problem. In all cases, students were attending to academic content or to skills. These categories and use of the instruments are described more fully in Appendix A.

Two different procedures using this same instrument recorded data about students' attention. One procedure was to take a whole-class measure. Every 15 minutes the observer recorded the time, looked around the room, and counted the number of children whose behavior fell into each of the seven categories. For instance, at 10:15 one morning, nine out of 13 children might be sharpening pencils or getting their workbooks (engaged–procedure). The second method of measurement involved more frequent observation of each target student. The researcher looked at the first target student, noted behavior, and marked it on the coding sheet, then looked at the second student, noted and recorded behavior, and so forth for each target student. Each target student was observed once approximately every three minutes during mathematics or reading class.

When observing target students, researchers noted additional information along with students' attention. If the student was in a group for a lesson, the researcher recorded whether or not the student had a chance for active participation. Four categories of participation were identified—choral response, individual turn, hand raised but not called on, and no turn. This information could be used to check the possibility that each student might have a chance to participate more frequently in a class with fewer students.

For target students involved in independent seatwork, observers also recorded information about whether the student was in contact with another person. The student might be in contact with the teacher, another adult, a student, or no one at all. Several features of evidence collected through this instrument relate to our speculations about class size. With fewer students, the teacher (or aide) might be able to get around to each student to check work or to help individuals more often. This would be reflected by the evidence from the instrument if we found more frequent contact with the teacher (or another adult). Also, the teacher might be more inclined to allow students to work together in a smaller class, since fewer problems might exist with noise and overall discipline problems. Students working together would be recorded as student contact on an academic task. A "notes" section of the observation form allowed the observer to describe unusual situations and to include additional information to facilitate understanding the numbers recorded.

Training in using this observation instrument was carried out in Virginia by conducting paired observations in classrooms not involved in the study. Two researchers would observe for about half an hour, then leave the classroom to compare records and discuss questions or discrepancies. Modifications in categories and directions were made during the training period, and the two teams reached agreement over the telephone about how to code common classroom events likely to be observed in both schools. Following the training period, researchers observed in pairs in the Virginia and California classrooms to assess reliability. Paired observation was carried out in December and again in May. Single observations were made more frequently. Results indicated high inter-observer agreement, with some discrepancies due to collecting data at different moments when observing each student. Reliability data and results of these observations are presented in Chapter 12.

Achievement tests. As discussed in Chapter 1, the relationship between achievement test scores and class size has already been documented in the meta-analysis by Glass and Smith. While performance on achievement tests was not the focus of this study, a few short achievement tests were administered and analyzed.

Four achievement scales from the BTES test battery were administered in December and May, because these two testing times corresponded to the dates when the "B" and "C" tests were administered in BTES. This would permit us to compare the data to BTES data. All students in each class were tested. Testing time was about 50 minutes in December. In May, there were two sessions—one of 40 minutes and one of 30 minutes. Teachers administered the tests. Additional details and results of the testing are discussed in Chapter 12.

Field notes. In addition to these instruments, we collected evidence by observing in classrooms; while observing, we maintained field notes. In Virginia, Diane Kyle and Gail McCutcheon observed classes, beginning in the autumn, shortly after selecting the school. Visits averaged three or more times weekly and lasted from two hours through the entire day. Len Cahen, Rob Moore, and Nikki Filby observed classrooms shortly after selecting their school, and usually visited classrooms at least once a week for several hours each time.

Rob Moore, who was helping with observations in California, and Len Cahen found dictating quietly into a small tape recorder to be a helpful way of maintaining field notes. They later edited the transcripts of those notes. Virginia researchers kept notes in small books. Examples of field notes from Virginia and California follow.

Virginia Field Notes

Gail McCutcheon   Mr. Jameson's Room
May 23

9:35, 12 students for math (low group).

Mr. J: You don't need your books right now, and everybody turn and face this way. This morning we're going to start carrying. Okay, ladies and gentlemen, today we're going to start doing something important. We've *been* adding problems like this: (writes on board)

827   (While he writes, Rachel Lee says,
$+132$ "Oh, thass easy!")

Mr. J: This is harder (writes on board).

827   (Clifford calls, "Carry the one!)
$+256$

9:38
Mr. J: I'm going to start with a simpler problem today. Writes

$47 =$ _____ tens, _____ ones
$+28 =$ _____ tens, _____ ones

This is where our work with tens and ones will come in handy. Any guesses about the number of tens in 47? (Guesses from kids: 5, 4, called out). Emmet says, "five," pauses, corrects himself—"No, it's four. I'm positive." Folds his hands.

[¹ Continuity with last week's work!]

Together they work the problem—Emmet's at board, writing answers. Rachel Lee and Clifford coach him.

1. Gail McCutcheon circled or boxed her tentative interpretations or questions for further study.

$$47 = 4 \text{ tens, } 7 \text{ ones}$$
$$+28 = 2 \text{ tens, } 8 \text{ ones}$$
$$6 \text{ tens, } 15 \text{ ones}$$

9:42

Mr. J: Is there a ten in 15 ones?

Clifford: Yeah, one.

Mr. J: How many tens do we have altogether in this problem? Six tens plus one ten?

Sarah Ann: Sixteen

Mattie: Six? Seventy?

(Mr. J seems frustrated—sighs, smiles.) ''Let's take this simple problem and do it like regular people do. Everybody watch this now, it's important. Mattie! You have to pay attention!''

He writes

53   [²I wonder why he gives up—what was going through his mind—
+58   when he decided to show them this way instead of the book's
          way; finding answers as opposed to math theory?]

Says, ''Ronald, what's $3 + 8$?'' Ronald puts down a 1 below the one's place. ''Where does the other 1 go?''

9:45

Ronald: On top of the 5.

Mr. J: (To class) You've gotta know how to do this. I'm not going to tolerate your not listening. If you don't pay attention, there'll be trouble all along.

Passes out paper, and they work one problem—5 of 12 have it right. Next problem, after reteaching, 9 of 12 have it right.

9:50   He circulates and reteaches Sarah Ann, Mattie and Cynthia.

Observer: Diane Kyle   Miss Anderson's room

(The Teacher sits on the table in front of the room waiting for the class to settle down for spelling. Twenty students—several talking, moving around room, sharpening pencils, finding books, papers.)

1:05

T: OK, page 36. Take your spelling books out so we'll all be ready. Everybody should be in their seats. Mike, what are you doing? Page 36.

Mike: We did this.

2. After class, Mr. Jameson reported they ''seemed confused by the math theory, so I decided to show them how to get the answer instead.''

T: We haven't done the bottom part. Page 36. C'mon, Rachel Lee, Robert. Come on, Albert.

Albert: What page?

T: Shh, shh Robert. If you need to sharpen your pencils, sharpen them now, but one at a time, please. Roy, what are you doing? Keith, do you see somebody up there? Sit down. Come on, Clarence, that's enough. Quickly sharpen your pencils. Those in your seats need to get quiet. I'm waiting. I'm not going to talk over noise.

(Low murmuring still goes on; two out of their desks; about seven or eight look through books, papers, instead of being ready to start—six minutes have gone by.)

[Does it always take this long to start a lesson? The pencil-sharpening routine seems to be disruptive and takes so *long*—usual? What about other routines?]

1:13

T: Number one at the bottom of page 36. Turn around in your seat, Roy, Robert. What is picture A? Robert?

Robert: Black.

T: Ok, spell *black*.

Robert: B–l–a–c–k

(T writes words on board as students spell them.)

T: Robert, how do you spell the *k* sound in *black?*

Robert: *ck*

(Repeats procedure for each picture. What is picture ___? Spell it for me. How do you spell *k* sound? Words: black, block, sock, lock, stick, kick.)

1:18

T: Ok, Adelina, Mike, it's time for you to go to Mrs. Wilson. All right, I'm not going to talk over this noise. (Several have turned around to talk; others whisper to one another across the aisles.) What do these words have that's the same? Ronald?

Ronald: *ck*

T: Yes. Now, if I start with this word (writes *back* on board), and I want to change it to this word (draws a picture of a sack), what letter needs to change?

Gladys: Change *b* to *s*.

(Class goes through remaining four pictures in same way).

1:22

T: Ok, I'm going to give you some paper. I want you to do what we've just gone over. Shh. Put your name and date on the paper. Start on page 36 with number 1 and go through page 37. (Noticing Rachel Lee's lost tooth), Rachel Lee, you can go rinse your mouth out in the bathroom.

[Do they always go over the answers before doing the seatwork? Why? Does everyone do the same spelling even if they're in different reading groups? True for other subjects? Rationale?]

T: Put your name and date on the paper where it should go. Please be quiet; some are trying to work. Valerie, come on.

(T moves around room, has erased answers from the board. Keith goes to get help.)

T: OK, you'll have to stay in your seats so I can come help you.

(As I move around, I find: Gladys finishes quickly then draws and erases smile faces. Randolph finishes before most start and concentrates on drawing a truck. Ronald thinks stick picture is a stem. He goes through all the other pictures and agrees they have *ck* sound, but not number 5 because it's stem. Vernon seems to be having great difficulty; Cynthia falls asleep.)

1:40

T: Ok, if you've finished, put your papers on the front table neatly. I'll call rows to get coats to go outside.

(The noise level increases as students move to turn in papers, talk to one another, and get ready for leaving the room.)

T: Shh. If you expect to go outside, you know what you should be doing.

(Ms. Lindley enters—needs reading folders for learning disabled students. Four students sent to work on unfinished morning work instead of going outside. Students wait with heads down to be dismissed.)

1:45

Spelling class over.

[How often is not going outside used as time to finish morning work? Why couldn't the four go outside? What will happen to the spelling work? Will the T find out why Ronald missed *stick?*][1]

California Notes

January 25, 1979
Mrs. Monroe's Class (Before Split)
Len Cahen (Observer)

9:05   Today is Friday, January 25. Gail McCutcheon is visiting the class, along with Nikki, Rob Moore, and myself.

9:08   The a.m. reading groups start working. Mrs. Willis has five children working with her.

Mrs. Monroe works with another group consisting of four boys.

1. Diane Kyle put parentheses around potential interpretations and questions worthy of further study or speculation.

A third group (7 pupils) works independently of the 2 other groups.

Mrs. Willis' group is at the one o'clock table;[1] Mrs. Monroe's low group is at the seven o'clock table; and the third group of 7 pupils is at the nine o'clock. I note Mrs. M. moves all the way to the front board to put some words on to teach phonics. She is a long way from the presence of the group.

Group 1 with 5 pupils are all engaged (100 percent). This is attributable to the fact that they are working directly with Mrs. Willis. The fast group is working independently. This group has eight pupils. Four out of the eight (50 percent) are engaged. A new student has just joined the fast-working group, making group size nine. In the small group (slow) working with Mrs. Monroe, two out of the three students are constantly engaged. Kevin is engaged at times, but usually is not engaged.

9:14   A buzzer sounded, and Mrs. Monroe had to respond to a communication from the office. *Let's find out how often this takes place and the nature.*[2]

9:15   Mrs. M. moves to the fast group of 8 pupils.

The slow group of 3 students is given seatwork to do. Two of the students (67 percent) start to work immediately. Thirty seconds later all three students in this group are engaged.

Mrs. Willis continues to work with her five pupils in the group. She is correcting paperwork for the students. *The engagement rate goes down as the students sit and wait for her.* She says to one student, "I can only correct one paper at a time."

Observation No. 1
Mrs. Monroe
Thursday, January 25, 1979
Rob Moore (Observer)

9:00 a.m.—The children enter the classroom with a minimum of confusion. They go directly to their seats. Then, Mrs. Monroe gives a direction that they are to get out their books. When a child doesn't, she calls the child's attention to the task directly; for example, she will say, "Get out your book, Scedric." The next direction after she's given the page number is "Put your fingers on the words as I read them." Mrs. Monroe was referring to a box in the one corner of the workbook page which contained the vocabulary words. After she had read the words, Mrs. M. asked, "What do they all start with?" When this question was answered, she then went back to the words and showed the children how structural analysis could be used to decode the words. For example, with the word "aside," she called attention to the fact that "side" was a part of the word and all that had to be done was to blend the sound of

1. Len Cahen mapped actions by conceiving of the geography of the room as a clock.

2. Len Cahen underlined questions for further study as well as his tentative interpretations to indicate their difference from his observation notes.

"a" with "side" and get "aside." Another example she used was "shore" in "ashore." She called attention to 'ashore" and showed that in it was "shore" and all one had to do was blend the sound of "a" with "shore" and get "ashore."

Mrs. Monroe then called the attention of the class to the sentences which appeared below the box of vocabulary words. When a child was not following her direction to follow along as she read the sentences, Mrs. Monroe would say for example, "Kevin can hear me and follow directions." Mrs. Monroe would say such a sentence authoritatively. Mrs. M. then read the sentences.

Mrs. Monroe then reminded the class that no one talks unless he or she is called upon. When one child tries to get help in finding the page, Mrs. Monroe says, "Let her find the page herself." Then there is "round robin" reading of the sentences. One child reads a sentence, then another child reads another and so forth as each child takes his/her turn.

Included in such notes, then, were both observations and tentative interpretations or questions in need of further study. For example, in the first excerpt, Gail McCutcheon noted continuity between the May 23 mathematics lesson and one observed the previous week, and wondered why Mr. Jameson changed his approach to regrouping for addition in the middle of the lesson.

Discussions with teachers. We also maintained notes and transcripts about our discussions with teachers. These sometimes occurred informally with an individual teacher during a free moment between classes or during lunch. Virginia teachers had common planning time for an hour weekly, arranged for by the principal. California teachers and researchers met together after school or at lunch time. Several full-day meetings were held with the teachers by hiring substitutes. During these meetings, issues related to the project were discussed, such as:

What changes will you plan for when class size is reduced?
What do you think might happen anyway, whether you plan for it or not?
What changes have you seen in Ronald? What about Mattie?
Do you think that separating Keith from Albert has helped them?

In Virginia, these all-day meetings were audiotaped and later transcribed to provide evidence of the teachers' views of what occurred and their plans for changes when we reduced class size.

Teachers also raised some questions or points in meetings. For example, Ms. Taylor believed attendance rose when class size was decreased, and she obtained attendance records to check this. Miss Anderson believed she was able to teach more skills and content when she had fewer students, and analyzed her planbook to see whether she progressed through material more rapidly than when she had a larger group. Other discussions focused upon questions teachers had about their teaching. For example, Mr. Jameson had difficulty teaching phonics as presented in the Houghton Mifflin guide and children did not appear to be learning phonics. He was obligated to teach phonics, however, since assessment tests were keyed to phonics, and the tests were required in the school system (see Chapter 3). Upon examining some of the lessons, we found that several vowel sounds were to be presented in one lesson. Perhaps this was the source of confusion. Mr. Jameson and Gail McCutcheon planned to teach the sounds separately, with more examples in each lesson than appeared in the guide. On another occasion, Mrs. Hopkins wondered what to do with her high mathematics group, since they were almost finished with the mathematics book. Materials and a book of mathematics activities were shared with her. Ms. Taylor expressed concern about a student who was having difficulty with spelling. Several activities were discussed and resource materials shared in response to such problems. Rob Moore, in California, also presented several demonstration lessons early in his visits, based on teachers' questions about how to teach regrouping for subtraction and about mathematics games.

Primarily, though, discussions with teachers concerned questions about their perceptions of changes and lack of changes after class size was reduced. Teachers also volunteered their own ideas, rather than merely responding to our questions. Less frequently, discussions provided an opportunity for teachers to seek advice and ask about the practice of teaching.

Documents and students' work.   In order to understand the setting in which the study was undertaken, we collected and read memoranda, policies, and other school documents that might have affected what teachers believed they could do or were supposed to do. In Virginia, for example, we noticed that many memoranda and faculty notices contained references to controlling students. Also, target students' work and workbooks were collected to note how teachers evaluated students' work, what the children were required to do, and what learning appeared to be taking place.

Teachers' journals.   Teachers maintained journals to respond to our questions and write on their own as they observed and thought about the project. Through the journal, for example, Virginia researchers asked about the teachers' backgrounds and experiences. We asked teachers to speculate about how they thought a class might be different with fewer students, what sorts of things they thought would be the same regardless of class size, and what changes they actually observed. Journals differed somewhat. For example, Mrs. Monroe included more entries about her planning, while Ms. Taylor included more specific observations about individuals. Ms. Taylor began using a tape recorder in early February, as did Mr. Jameson. These recordings were transcribed. Researchers read the journals three times during the year, so we could understand the teachers' points of view as we progressed, and so we could share the teachers' observations with the team on the other side of the country. This understanding was further facilitated by our informal discussions and meetings with the teachers.

Through discussions and journal entries we tried to involve the teachers in collecting evidence. Teachers' observations were important for two reasons.

First, we hoped to understand teachers' perspectives—what they wanted to accomplish and their beliefs about why particular things happened. Second, researchers could not be present every day, so the teachers' observations could help present a more complete record. In Ms. Taylor's view:

> [As the project progressed], the importance of the teacher in this project began to emerge. The concept of the role broadened and deepened. It became obvious in meetings and discussions that our observations were an integral part of the research. Because we had not been trained as "research observers," we had the impressions that what we saw would be of minimal value when compared with the observations made by the research team. As we became aware, through discussion with the team, of the value of our observations, we began to observe in a more meaningful manner because what we saw was being used and we were being listened to. Journal entries became valuable tools for the teaching team in understanding and planning for students as well as for the research team in gathering observational data. As the teaching team interacted with various observers in the classroom, they were able to fill in the gaps created by limited observation time. This interaction sparked ideas to be used in instruction and broadened understandings of the educational process. We saw that observations made when no team observer was present were needed in order to bring continuity to their observations.

The instruments, notes, journal entries, documents, and students' work were later indexed according to our research questions to facilitate locating evidence illustrating, supporting, or calling into question a particular research question or interpretation. With so much evidence—boxes full—this sort of indexing by theme and interpretation was crucial in locating salient evidence.

Reflection

Before we began to observe, we reflected upon what to study. What themes associated with class size and instruction seemed important? How might we collect evidence about them? And while we observed, and afterwards, we reflected on what we saw, collected, and discussed. What did it all mean? This activity continues from a project's beginning on past its being reported. When we met, whether as separate teams within California or Virginia, or when the two teams got together, we discussed what we were learning. We essentially told one another stories about what we saw and what it seemed to mean. We pondered, speculated, argued, chatted. In Virginia, sessions often lasted into the wee hours of the morning. The California team had more difficulty getting together, for Nikki Filby was teaching second grade all day. Rob Moore had no office at the research headquarters and had many responsibilities associated with his university teaching, and Len Cahen was managing the entire project. Private reflection allowed us to make meaning out of what we saw; reflection in public permitted us to begin constructing interpretations aloud in a safe environment, and when the two teams met, this exchange also facilitated our keeping the studies in California and Virginia parallel.

WRITING ABOUT THE STUDIES

Writing requires the researcher to consider what facts, interpretations, concepts, and appraisals to provide to the audience, and the best way of rendering the experience into prose in order to permit the audience to understand the nature of what happened and the relation of the setting to the research questions. Active, evocative narrative, interwoven with concepts and vision, does not typify reports of educational research, yet this sort of writing may make a setting more accessible to readers. Questions guiding the reflection phase were: "What was it like to be there?" and "What did we think about it?" In the writing phase, we wondered how to convey the answers to readers to help them understand our experiences.

An important difference between the two teams concerns the writing phase of the project. The California team chose to report the cases in fairly straightforward prose and not to appraise explicitly, or not to judge the merits of an activity or how well it was performed. This choice of prose, in the California team's view, is intended to enhance communication through objective, commonly agreed upon words and meanings, as well as to leave to readers the task of judging the merits of an activity or practice. The Virginia team wrote in more evocative prose, at times employing metaphor and imagery. This style is also intended to enhance communication, but in a different way, through helping readers to envision events, discussions, the general atmosphere of classrooms, and so forth. The Virginia team appraised what was seen, for we were there and believed we should critique what occurred.

Readers are encouraged to read these studies actively. The California cases require readers to generalize to their own situations when appropriate and to appraise for themselves what happened. The Virginia studies also require readers to make personal generalizations and to agree with or dismiss appraisals, based upon their own philosophies, theories, values, and experience.

PROCESSES OF THE RESEARCH

Three highly related processes in this type of research are description, interpretation, and (for the Virginia studies) appraisal. The processes are essential in two ways. First, they are related to the reflection process and to the writing of the reports for others to read. They are also interrelated in that descriptions provide the facts about which interpretations are constructed, while those facts also provide evidence corroborating or negating the interpretations. In other words, descriptions provide evidence for interpretations but interpretations provide form, order, and coherence to the descriptions. Appraisals and interpretations provide a conceptual context into which readers might place the descriptions. It is not enough, in our view, to provide picturesque descriptions of what transpired in relation to our questions; descriptions must also be set within a context in order to render them understandable. This context is provided through interpretation and appraisal.

Description

Major questions of the descriptive enterprise are: "What was seen and heard?" and "What's it like to be there?" Our notes primarily recorded descriptive evidence, with potential questions and interpretations encircled in margins, underlined, or put in parentheses. Other evidence was obtained through observation instruments, documents, teachers' journals, students' work, and other items as discussed in the section about the collection of evidence. What was on bulletin boards? How did the teacher reprimand a child? Where did students work? What did they do when they completed their assignments? What went on during the day? What can we document that children had an opportunity to learn, and what did they appear to learn?

Interpretation

Interpretation answers the question, "What does this all mean?" As humans, we constantly construct meaning about what we see. A student sighs in class. Is she or he bored? Sharing an inside joke about another student who sighs a lot? Trying to get rid of the hiccups? Identifying wistfully with something the teacher just said? The possibilities are many. Another example of constructing meaning is our response to the news. We try to make meaning of the national and international events we hear about in the news media. What does the situation in the Middle East mean for us in the United States? What does the federal budget imply about the President's view of how to deal with poverty?

This construction of meaning is an active process; meanings are not part of our immediately given environments. Rather, we have to make that meaning. We read our environments and compare bits from them to our prior experience, to what we know of the world, in order to understand what we have just undergone. This construction of meaning renders our world understandable and is a product of a transaction between a phenomenon and ourselves. Because we live in a particular culture, we have undergone similar experiences; thus, we are able to share most of the meanings that we construct. Three types of interpretation are patterning, interpreting social meaning, and relating phenomena to external consideration.

Patterning. Patterns reveal the interdependence of different pieces of the whole being studied. When patterning, we weave our observations into a fabric of interrelated facts.

Observations may lead a researcher to develop several sorts of patterns. One pattern concerns the apparent rules and customs for doing things. Some of these can be reported by the students and teachers, such as the daily schedule or not having recess at Pine Springs School. Their influence on what happens may not be evident to teachers, though.

Teachers and students may not be aware of certain patterns, but rather act upon them because of what Edward Sapir (1963) called the "unconscious patterning of behavior." In Sapir's and Ruth Benedict's (1934) views, an outsider to a culture is able to perceive such patterns. These patterns of behavior arise out of the ways in which the culture is oriented as a whole. Insiders, living from day to day within a culture, are less able to perceive these orientations. For example, an outsider might notice that our culture is highly goal-oriented. We rarely go out and meander along on a drive or a walk; we usually have an end in view. When our sons and daughters start college, our friends ask us what they want to be when they grow up; our friends appear to assume our children choose a college based on that goal. Much research about the "hidden curriculum" concerns unconscious patterns in classrooms. For example, unconsciously, many teachers, through the textbooks they use and their own statements and actions, present sexist and racist views to children. Without being aware of it, they may also teach children such things as being punctual, obedient to authority, and doing their own work. Since school and society as a whole are oriented to behave according to certain values, teachers' behavior has been unconsciously patterned (along with everyone else's), and they inadvertently maintain and teach attitudes supportive of the dominant culture through the hidden curriculum. Such attitudes can be negative or positive. One sort of patterning, then, involves the rules and customs for doing things in a classroom. Some rules and customs are known consciously by participants while others aren't.

Patterns may also present causal relationships. For example, when Mrs. Fleming admonished Mr. Jameson's children in front of him for their not acting "like *her* second graders," this might have caused Mr. Jameson to become more authoritarian for a while to prevent embarrassment and to secure his position if he hoped to continue teaching at Pine Springs School.

The construction of patterns gives discrete actions coherence, form, and meaning. Actions do not remain isolated. Patterns allow us to see certain features of a setting in a new light, to call these features into question, and to examine them. Without patterning, a jumble of disorganized details would be collected and presented to readers, which does not seem very helpful if we hope to understand a phenomenon such as class size and its relationship to instruction.

Social meanings. Many behaviors must be interpreted in terms of their social meaning to be understood. Gilbert Ryle (cited in Geertz, 1973: p. 6) has referred to the interpretation of social meaning as "thick description." For example, what does Miss Anderson's behavior mean when she snaps her fingers at Roger, then quickly points her thumb toward the ceiling? Is she calling on Roger? Is she signaling Roger to pay attention? To look at the ceiling? To sit up straight? Many possibilities exist, but over a long period of observing and talking with children and students, we found that Miss Anderson had several such signals to control children. This one signalled Roger to sit up and pay attention.

Social meanings of this kind are interpreted according to the meanings insiders ascribe to acts. However, particularly regarding unconsciously patterned behavior, insiders' meanings may be incorrect, or insiders may not even perceive what is happening. This is where the outsider–observer can help to discern phenomena and interpret them in ways insiders would not because they are unaware of those phenomena. For example, one white teacher posted no pictures of blacks in her room during the year, although approximately 65% of her class was black. She certainly was not an evil, overtly racist teacher. Unaware of the hidden curriculum of her bulletin boards, she may have been teaching children at least as much through what did *not* appear on the boards as through what did. This is an example of interpreting a pattern of which insiders may not be aware. Indeed, it is crucial for outsiders to a particular setting to interpret what they observe, for only after one can dredge up and perceive such actions can one wonder whether they are appropriate, worthwhile, and beneficial.

External considerations. In a third type of interpretation, the researcher relates phenomena about a classroom to external considerations such as theoretical principles from education and the social sciences, current trends, and historical events. For example, we might derive greater meaning from the description of a particular classroom scene when it is related to theory of behavior modification or to Dewey's theory of experience. This might permit us to understand how actions are in accord with those theories or in what ways they do not exemplify the theories.

Three types of interpretation, then, include patterning, considering the social meaning of events, and relating events to external considerations. Interpretations reveal both the phenomena described and the researcher, for it is through the researcher's frames of reference that phenomena are interpreted. A researcher views an event or phenomena and in order to make meaning of it, relates it to similar past experiences and to what he or she knows about schooling. Thus, the interpretation emanates from the researcher's experience with the event. As a result, interpretive work is both subjective and objective, for it reveals both the subject (the researcher) and the object (the phenomenon).

Interpretations can be judged by readers through at least four criteria. For one, the reader can wonder whether the interpretation fits what else he or she knows about schooling, human behavior, institutions, or whatever is considered in the interpretation. Does it relate to one's own experiences and to what one has read about schools? Second, the reader can ask whether evidence presented in a study is sufficient to warrant the interpretation. Interpretations are corroborated by citing many separate pieces of evidence. Is enough material presented to substantiate the interpretation? Third, the reader can wonder whether the line of reasoning behind the interpretation is faulty or sound. And, finally, the reader can consider the significance of the interpretation in facilitating an understanding of the phenomena under study. A relatively trivial interpretation may be easily corroborated, but it may do little conceptually to provide a rich understanding.

The Virginia and California studies call for active readership, use of the four criteria in assessing interpretations, and the readers' asking whether the settings and participants are similar enough to their own to warrant generalizing from these studies to their own classrooms. (See McCutcheon, 1981, for further discussion.)

Appraisal

In the Virginia studies, not only description and interpretation are employed, but explicit appraisal as well. Descriptions and interpretations form the subject matter of appraisal.

Two questions commonly asked by critics are "Was it worth doing?" and "Was it done well?" When considering whether a lesson was worth teaching, a behavior worth exhibiting, a statement worth saying, a critic considers several issues related to general concerns about children, society, and the living of the "good life." Judgments vary because of the descriptions and interpretations that evoked them; watching science experiments in an open classroom might evoke a different appraisal from that evoked if we were watching a spelling bee in a more traditional classroom. Judgments also vary because they are evoked by the researcher's frame of reference; what one researcher finds interesting or of value may not be interesting or cherished by another.

When considering whether the lesson was well taught, or whether the behavior or statement was well expressed, we consider its artfulness, its approximation of "ideal" practice, given the situation, the setting, and the participants.

In assessing appraisals, again the reader has several criteria to use. For one, the reader can ask about the fairness of the criticism, given what the teacher attempted, and given the situation. Second, the reader can wonder whether the appraisal raises a significant, important issue. And, third, the reader can decide if the researcher's line of reasoning is clear enough to be followed.

For both interpretations and appraisals, it is important to note that readers do not necessarily have to agree with the researcher *in toto*. Rather, a reader may agree up to a point, then disagree. Therefore, an entire study does not necessarily have to be discounted because of partial disagreements between the reader and the researcher. Rather, parts can be accepted while other parts can be disputed.

Processes of the research, then, include description, interpretation, and appraisal. Issues related to doing research are discussed in Chapter 14.

SUMMARY

Methods used in conducting this research have several characteristics. We selected approaches that seemed to have the potential to enable us to depict the nature and kinds of changes evident in classrooms when the number of students was reduced in addition to enabling us to quantify the amount of change in certain instances. We also collected information regarding what remained the same.

To collect evidence, we used many methods, including observation, analysis of teachers' journals and students' work, testing, interviews and discussions. A method was selected if it appeared to have the potential for answering our research questions.

Another aspect of the project was our attempt to keep the studies in both sites parallel—to study roughly the same questions and issues in roughly the same ways. An important feature of the study is that teachers were involved in varied ways in the project. Two were more active than the others, but in general teachers collected information, discussed the project, posed questions, and reacted to first drafts of the studies.

Part II

Virginia

As discussed in the methodology chapter (Chapter 2), in the autumn of 1978, Pine Springs School, in a rural area of Virginia, was chosen as one site for research on class size. In Chapter 3, general features of the school are discussed: Who goes to school there? Who teaches the children? What kinds of phenomena within the setting help account for some of the practices we can observe there?

In Chapters 4, 5, and 6, the individual classrooms are discussed. From the beginning of the school year in August until the end of the December holidays, two second-grade classrooms existed at Pine Springs School, with two teachers and 39 children. In second grade, then, before class size was reduced, classes contained only 19 and 20 children. This may already seem to be a small class size, although the teachers' perceptions that there was a high number of problem children made the class sizes feel larger. Indeed, the principal was faced with whether to provide for one class of 39 or two smaller classes. Thirty-two students is the maximum number permitted in second grade by state law, but the Board of Education hoped to hire an aide and have the larger class. Mrs. Fleming opposed this due to first-grade teachers' perceptions that many difficult children were in the group when they were first graders. The number appears to be small, then, but the difficult nature of working with some of these students must also be considered here. In early January, class size was reduced to 13 in each classroom, below the figure Glass and Smith's meta-analysis has indicated significantly affects student achievement. (See Chapter 1.) As of the 1981–82 school year, the school closed due to declining enrollments in the county.

In the following three chapters, the individual classrooms are described and interpreted. Chapter 7 summarizes our major generalizations about instruction in these classrooms and how class size may have influenced what transpired in second grade at the Pine Springs School.

3

Pine Springs School

THE SETTING

As we drive through the gently rolling hills of rural Virginia toward Pine Springs School, we pass through woods and a few fields. In the distance, hazy bluish mountains form a backdrop for our drive. Hiding in the woods is a trailer park. Several large farmhouses silently monitor their mostly fallow acreage. A few nearby brick houses appear to have recently escaped from a suburban subdivision. For the most part, though, our drive takes us through open fields and large stands of pine trees. We see few people and no factories. Also absent are community facilities such as swimming pools or recreation centers. Playgrounds adjacent to elementary schools contain climbing apparatus; near the middle school and high school are playing fields for softball, baseball, football, and basketball. Public libraries are small; a few drive-in movie theaters sit in deforested areas, reminders of bygone days. Not in evidence, though, are sports arenas or auditoriums that might attract sporting or cultural events. Abundant are quiet woods and streams.

The small, brick school, built in 1941, sits back from the road, looking into dark woods and over gentle fields. One long, high-ceilinged hall joins all the rooms. Halfway down the hall sits Mr. Hodges, the custodian, who seems always ready to converse quietly for a short time about the fish in the aquarium on the table to his left. Just behind him, the kindergarten is housed in the erstwhile auditorium; a boys' room is at one end of the hall, while the girls' room is at the other end. Standing in the middle of the hall, we can see the door to virtually every room in the school; only the room for learning-disabled children is out of view, because it is located downstairs. No room is unused. The building contains a small bookroom, a health office, the principal's office, and seven high-ceilinged classrooms with large windows permitting a view of woods, a large playing field, playground equipment, or the not-too-busy, two-lane state road in front of the school. Little playground equipment is available; only a jungle gym and some swings inhabit the large grassy playing field.

Who attends this school? Who teaches these children?

CHILDREN AND ADULTS AT PINE SPRINGS SCHOOL

On any given day during the school year, we find in attendance about 180 kindergarten through fourth-grade children and 10 or 11 teachers:

kindergarten—two teachers

first grade—one teacher

second grade—two (later, three) teachers

third grade—one teacher

fourth grade—two teachers

remedial reading—one teacher

learning disabilities—one teacher

Due to "mainstreaming," Ms. Lindley, the learning disabilities teacher, collects children who are learning-disabled from homerooms at scheduled times. This is also true for Mrs. Wilson, the reading teacher, who works with approximately 50 children and is substantially funded through Title I. Two aides, Mrs. Burkett, and Mrs. Evans, shared by all teachers, meet groups or assist in rooms. The school, then, is fairly small.

The student population is 65% black, 35% white. No Oriental or Hispanic children attend Pine Springs School. In the 1978–79 school year, 93 of 176 children received free lunch, and in the 1979–80 school year, 83 of 163 children. These figures imply that many of the families receive welfare money through Aide to Dependent Children. A few parents work at the small knitting and clothing factories nearby, and still fewer drive 60 miles each way to jobs at a frozen food factory in an adjacent county. Fifteen of the children's parents are teachers in the public schools or at a nearby private boarding school. No student is from a family that one would label "affluent." Both agriculture and logging have declined in the last 10 years, and no industry is located in the county other than the two small textile-related plants. In recent years, a vermiculite plant and a state prison have been proposed for the county, but according to residents, affluent people from another area of the county blocked both potential ventures, fearing a loss of the county's tranquil beauty. In addition to the lack of places of employment, the area lacks public transportation. The absence of places of employment coupled with no public transportation to the closest city contribute to high welfare rolls. While we have a lovely, serene view of rural Virginia on our drive to the school, then, we are also faced with evidence of rural poverty, with little opportunity to change the financial picture.

Most families who send children to Pine Springs School have lived in the area for several generations. Apparently, families do not see migration to areas with greater opportunities for employment as an option to escape poverty, or they are unwilling or unable to migrate. Among second graders, for example, Robert moved from New York during kindergarten, and Gina from Tennessee in the same year. Just before the start of the school year, Steve moved into the area when he was taken as a foster child by a family who had hopes of adopting him and his two siblings. During the year only one child moved; in May, Gina and her family returned to Tennessee. The stability of the population character-izes the school as does low absenteeism.

In Virginia, school districts are referred to as "divisions." Seven years ago, the county-wide school division voluntarily integrated. Many white par-ents of the second graders currently at Pine Springs attended Pine Springs School themselves, although most of the black second graders' parents attended Riv-erview School along with all blacks in the county. Riverview School has now become the middle school, also housing the program for gifted students. Six children from Pine Springs School currently attend the gifted program for half a day a week, where they study language arts and the creative arts for the most part.

Approximately half of the children in the school live with both parents and siblings. One fourth live in homes with an extended family (a mother and her sister and children or a mother and the grandmother), or share the home with another single-parent family. Another fourth of the children live in single-par-ent homes.

Ninety-five percent of the children in the school ride the bus for a trip averaging 25 minutes one-way. Fifteen children ride two buses for 45 minutes, changing buses at Riverview School. In winter, during snow or ice storms and in spring during floods, difficulties associated with maintaining some roads and bridges force the schools to close.

The principal, Mrs. Fleming, has a motherly concern for her children and staff. Her maternal presence is apparent in the halls, the classrooms and her office, as she chats with the children or admonishes them:

George, I've been hearing some good things about you from Miss Anderson.

Roy, have you settled down some this afternoon? Are you acting like one of my second graders? You have to settle down to learn, you know.

Mattie, that's such a pretty picture you brought me today! I've put it up on the wall. Come and see it. (Hug)

In Mrs. Fleming's view, the advantage of a small school is that "You get to know the children." She knows everyone's name, their relationships to others in the school, and seems to know something about most of the children's lives. She believes children need emotional security, and that the children living in single-parent or extended-family homes are more in need of touching and con-versation than those from nuclear-family homes. As she roams the hall, she solicits a hug, or receives a kiss, a tidbit of news, or a picture from the chil-dren. She believes in the power of education to influence children's lives, how-ever, so she keeps an eye on the daily fare children receive in classrooms, on notes and reports going home to parents, and on test scores, as we will see when school-wide policies are discussed.

Mrs. Fleming visits classrooms frequently. She also has a keen interest in establishing good communication with parents through teachers' contacting them. Mrs. Fleming herself makes many home visits, trying to help parents see the need for the school and the home to work together. When she first began, Mrs. Fleming relates that she went to the Stony Point neighborhood, a poorer part of the school's area, and felt residents did not trust her. Recently, though, due to such continued visits, she has felt less suspicion on the part of the Stony Point community.

Mrs. Fleming's concern for good relations with the community, and that the home and school work together to educate children has interested many parents in volunteering to assist in classrooms. She arranges for transportation, if needed. Several parents are steady, dependable volunteers, such as Mrs. Hill, whose daughter, Clara, is in second grade. Mrs. Hill assists in second grade, but also is an employee in the school kitchen, and is present each day to lend a hand as a parent volunteer, usually helping children with assigned seatwork. Other parents are less dependable, and as they find other interests and responsibilities or a rare part-time job, they leave their volunteer work at Pine Springs School.

Mrs. Fleming believes she can run the school, get to know the community, and manage the day-to-day administrative details, but says she does not know as well how to be supportive or what to suggest to teachers. Yet, she feels she has no one to turn to for help with such difficulties.

Until the December holidays, Mrs. Hopkins and Miss Anderson were the two second-grade teachers at Pine Springs School. One class had 19 children in it, and the other, 20. In January, Mr. Jameson joined the faculty, reducing class size in second grade to 13 for each teacher. All three second-grade teachers are white, and all are in their mid-twenties to early thirties. What are the backgrounds of these teachers?

Miss Anderson taught upper grades for four years and several summers in a reading camp, but this is her first year as a second-grade teacher. She grew up in the Pine Springs area; in fact, her parents still reside in the community and Miss Anderson has an apartment nearby. She has since left teaching and wants to change her career, although she is uncertain about a future career. While she says she enjoys children, she confesses to being "tired of the hassles of teaching."

This is Mrs. Hopkins' second year of teaching, having taught second grade here last year as well as this year. She is married to a high school teacher, and they live in the nearest city, a 50-minute drive. Having grown up in Virginia, she graduated from a state university teacher education program two years ago. Mrs. Hopkins continues to teach second grade in the area. With the closing of Pine Springs School, she transferred to another elementary school.

Mrs. Fleming, Miss Anderson, and Mrs. Hopkins have all resided in Virginia for virtually their entire lives. They attended Virginia's public schools and colleges.

Mr. Jameson is new to the area, having relocated earlier this year from Michigan, where he taught third and sixth grades in the suburbs and later in a blue-collar neighborhood, beginning in 1970. He was enthusiastic about teaching there, and moved to Virginia somewhat reluctantly, due to Michigan's winters. In his view, his Michigan colleagues were professional and dynamic and the children were eager to learn. He owns a small farm in the county where he lives with his wife and daughter. Mr. Jameson has recently left teaching to pursue his interest in carpentry; in addition, he is running for county treasurer. He is a member of the volunteer fire company, and his old, unique red-and-white truck was a ''hit'' with many second graders. Mrs. Fleming hired Mr. Jameson because her faculty contained no men, and she believed it to be important, particularly for boys from single-parent families, to have an adult male role model.

Mr. Jameson, then, unlike Mrs. Fleming, Miss Anderson, and Mrs. Hopkins, has resided in the Pine Springs area only a short time. His case is interesting in revealing how an outsider might conceive of schooling differently, and what the effects of those conceptions on his practice might be.

SCHOOL-WIDE POLICIES

The Schedule

Daily schedules.   While some buses arrive at 8:00, all children arrive before 8:35. Between 8:00 and 8:35, one teacher at each grade level supervises arrivals in one of the classrooms, where children generally do dittoed worksheets or boardwork assigned by their homeroom teacher. At 8:35, they move to their homerooms. Unless something out of the ordinary happens, the centrally devised schedule for second grade is followed daily.

Before class size is reduced, second-grade classes adhere to the following schedule:

8:35–9:30	language arts
9:05–9:15	bathroom break
9:30–10:20	mathematics
10:20–11:40	reading
11:40–12:00	bathroom break
12:00–12:30	lunch
12:30–1:00	rest
1:00–1:30	social studies
1:30–2:00	physical education
2:00–2:30	language arts
2:35	load buses

This schedule was devised by Mrs. Fleming and the two second-grade teachers at the beginning of the year. As can be noted, science was not scheduled. After the class size is reduced, Mrs. Fleming and the three second-grade teachers again formulate the schedule. The new schedule is:

8:35–9:30	language arts
9:05–9:15	bathroom break
9:30–10:20	mathematics (homogeneously grouped)
10:20–11:40	reading (homogeneously grouped)
11:40–12:00	bathroom break, get ready for lunch
12:00–12:30	lunch
12:30–1:00 1:00–1:30 }	science, language arts or guidance
1:30–2:00	physical education
2:00–2:30	science, language arts or guidance
2:35	load buses

Science is added to the curriculum with the arrival of Mr. Jameson, largely because of his interest in it. During science, language arts, and guidance, the three groups circulate among the three teachers for half-hour lessons. Each specializes in teaching one of the three subjects.

A traveling music teacher has a somewhat erratic schedule. She meets each class for two weeks in a row, then doesn't return for six weeks; teachers seem unaware of her schedule. On Tuesday afternoon, from 12:30 until 1:30, second graders go to the library, and an aide or Mrs. Fleming supervises seatwork to allow teachers to have planning time in common. Mrs. Fleming initiated this idea to promote communication among the teachers and to permit time for discussions with the researchers. On Friday afternoons, the classes have art, although they continue to have physical education at 1:30. This schedule is followed almost without exception. Perhaps one reason is the faculty bulletin for January 15, 1979, stating, "Class schedules—Principal must know of changes. Changes must be approved and have a rationale."

As can be noted, times to use the boys' and girls' room are centrally scheduled, as they are all grade levels, and no recesses are provided in the morning, afternoon, or during the lunch period for any grade level. In the third-grade teacher's view, the children might be "too uncontrollable on such a big field and hard to settle down when they come back inside." The kindergarten teacher said, "The children might get sick." A third teacher said, "It's always been like this as long as I can remember."

Changes in the daily schedule. Four times a year, the daily schedule changes considerably. It changes for two or three days in autumn and spring when nationally normed tests are administered. During this time, children take tests during the morning, but follow the regular schedule after lunch.

Late November brings another change: getting ready for the Christmas pageant. Because Mrs. Wilson (the reading teacher) directs pageants, she is unable to meet her groups for three weeks. The usual running of the school is otherwise altered for kindergarteners when they move to the reading room, as their regular classroom reverts to its former status as auditorium. The second-grade routine is interrupted when Mrs. Wilson calls for certain children or all second graders to come to practice for the pageant. As the holidays approach, practice becomes more frequent, almost frantic, consuming the whole day during the final week. "Christmas in America" is planned by teachers. Children sing about cowboy/cowgirl Christmases, Christmas in the city, Christmas on the farm, and so forth. Many parents and community members attend the pageant, and the pageant may further relations with the community, although it changes the regular schedule considerably for more than three weeks.

Again in late April, another event occurs which alters the regular schedule: getting ready for May Day, celebrated the third weekend in May. Ceremonies celebrating May Day have a long tradition in rural Virginia, particularly in the Pine Springs area. The faculty generally chooses the theme each year, and then teachers at each grade level plan how their children are to participate. For five weeks, the schedule changes slightly, but for the final three weeks, it changes substantially. Not only is Mrs. Wilson not meeting reading groups, but Miss Anderson is drafted to play the piano accompaniment for each group. Children learn songs of spring and are cajoled and threatened to stand in the appropriate place, to sing the correct notes and words, and not to fool around on stage so they won't embarrass everyone. Our second graders enter as flowers "asleep under the ground," and sing about each of the seasons. They seem rather unattentive, perhaps because they have rehearsed it so often, but when springtime arrives, they pop up out of the ground. All leave the auditorium after the one-and-a-half hour production, led by the fourth grade, singing their way to the Maypole. Around the Maypole they dance, interweaving brightly colored crepe-paper ribbons. Then the families have picnics, play games, view children's artwork displayed in the halls, and buy baked goods. Like the Christmas pageant, the May Day ceremony is well attended, and may also bring about improved or renewed relations with the community. With the lack of community recreational or cultural occasions (like high school football games) these events provide the entire community the opportunity to socialize with one another.

Textbook Adoption and Use

In Virginia, school divisions adopt only one text for each subject matter area, and in order to use state money, they must adopt it from a state-developed list. In this school division, series published by the following companies were adopted:

Spelling: McGraw-Hill (copyright, 1975)
Reading: Houghton Mifflin (copyright, 1976)
Mathematics: Holt, Rinehart & Winston (copyright, 1978)

These texts are virtually the only ones available, other than those stacked in the bookroom with copyrights of 1968 or older. Supplementary materials are also scant. The reading program is accompanied by a system of assessment tests with the intent of measuring proficiency in reading skills. It is a division-wide policy that these tests must be used, so, in effect, teachers must also use the texts. In a sense, Houghton Mifflin *is* the reading program; Holt, Rinehart, Winston *is* the mathematics program; and McGraw-Hill *is* the spelling program at Pine Springs School.

Promotion Policy

In addition to the factors mentioned, another factor affecting instruction is the promotion policy. This is particularly true of reading. For each grade level, at the beginning of the year the central office administrators issue a policy stating the books a child must complete in order to be promoted to the next grade. Second graders must complete *Sunburst* in order to be promoted to the third grade.

Emphasis on Order

Mrs. Fleming desires a smoothly running, orderly school. Her provision of a school-wide schedule (with bathroom breaks, but no recess) may be attributed to this, and faculty notices provide further evidence of it.

September 25 notices
    Water fountain privileges—devise ways to allow, but not to hinder class

January 15 notices
    Hall movement, bathroom use, logistical consideration for least disturbance

Items on faculty meeting agendas indicate discussions of similar matters during at least half of the meetings. This is not surprising, for many principals probably desire an orderly and controlled atmosphere in their schools in hopes of establishing an environment conducive to learning. At Pine Springs School, concern about discipline receives attention, not only in meetings and through faculty notices, but also on Mrs. Fleming's walks through the halls. Many of her discussions with students and her admonitions to them focus on behavior rather than on learning or other matters. This may transmit messages to teachers as well as to students about what is important in her view.

In the following chapters about the second-grade classrooms at Pine Springs School, we will examine the influence of practices and policies on instruction and on what children are given an opportunity to learn and to do, and their relation to class size. Such practices and policies undoubtedly influence what teachers believe they are able to plan and their views about what school is to be like for their students. The practices and policies remain in effect throughout the year as part of the school context, and it is in that context that the second-grade teachers—Miss Anderson, Mrs. Hopkins and, later, Mr. Jameson—conceive of what to do in their classrooms. The effect of contextual practices and policies is to set the conditions under which change may occur. Through policy, social pressure or established practice, teachers are likely to view certain beliefs as untenable or not to be acted upon, and certain actions as not appropriate in a particular school. Other beliefs about teaching are viewed as acceptable. In each classroom, we shall examine how certain policies may limit or support what teachers believe they are able to do.

What is the nature of each of these classrooms? In what ways do they change over the year? How do they not change? What are some possible explanations for changes or lack of changes? How do these relate to class size? In the following chapters, the second-grade classrooms at Pine Springs School are disclosed. First, we consider Miss Anderson's classroom. Then we turn to Mrs. Hopkins' room, and finally to Mr. Jameson's. A summary synthesizes, interprets, and critiques what we observed about the three classrooms and the school.

4

Miss Anderson's Classroom

As is true of many older school buildings, a sense of high-ceilinged spaciousness fills the classroom, sometimes creating a hum of echoes as Miss Anderson
and her 19 second graders carry on the day's activities. Tall, wide-sashed windows make up most of one wall and allow wandering glances to view the
serene, subtle changes of seasons in this rural setting. Yet spaciousness and
serenity characterize only part of the scene.

As we peer into this classroom before the class-size change, we see tiny
wooden desks filling most of the floor space, almost in at-attention order as
they face the teacher standing in front. Three tables, a few chairs, and a move-
able chalkboard complete the room arrangement—except for one small table
with a portable carrel isolated in the far back corner. Steve, recently identified
as having brain damage, remains here most of the day. Various posters decorating the classroom walls convey a number of "do this" messages:

Make the most of what you do.

Listen.

Paint large.

Raise your hand.

In contrast, one poster communicates a more personal slogan,

I am glad that I am me.

Do these messages provide any hints about the character of this classroom?
We wonder as our gaze wanders to teacher-drawn cartoon figures, commer-
cially made alphabet cards, boardwork assignments covering three chalkboards,
and a "good workers" chart. The products of two Friday afternoon art lessons
provide solitary examples of children's work.

Understanding life in this classroom, however, requires more than a visual
tour of the physical environment. In the following scene of one day's beginning, early in the year, we get a glimpse of the interactions between Miss
Anderson and her students.

The familiar slide-tap noises of chalk connecting with chalkboard echo in the room as Miss Anderson busily puts up the first assignment of the day. A few early-arriving children straggle in, followed soon by a crowd just dismissed by the teacher on bus duty. Lance and Jerome play catch with a thick, black, primary-size pencil, tossing it back and forth over two rows of desks. Gina jingles a purseful of change and taunts Della to guess her wealth; and Sidney, scowling fiercely, stomps over to his desk over by the far table. Miss Anderson notices the increasing noise level and turns,

Gina, get your coat off and sit down *now*. Lance, Jerome, get to work.

On and off until the assignment is on the board, Miss Anderson stops writing to prod a student, ask a question, or give directions,

Clifford, do you know what you're supposed to be doing? Then *do it*.

Was Louis on the bus?

Who needs something from the store? [The school sells a few supplies]. Roger, will you take up the money, please?

OK, Mrs. Wilson's [the reading teacher] group may line up.

She pauses briefly when two teachers walk in to get some hot water for coffee. While they chat, the children do boardwork, although Gina and Sandra find time to exchange glances and whispers, and Lance seems more intent on reorganizing the papers in his notebook than on doing boardwork. Jerome tosses a tiny eraser bit over to Sidney, causing a not-too-gentle reprimand from Miss Anderson,

Jerome, are you helping me? If you're not going to work I can send you home. Now settle down, *now*.

Do these features of the physical environment and the interactions between Miss Anderson and her students typify life in this classroom? In what ways, if any, do aspects of this setting relate to class-size effects? We begin by considering several issues—room organization, the day's beginning, the nature of instructional activities and techniques, and interactions—as they occur before the class-size change. Miss Anderson's views and practices of teaching and hopes for changes when working with a smaller number of students highlight the discussion.

MISS ANDERSON'S CLASSROOM: THE "LARGER-CLASS" VIEW

The Physical Environment

As described above, rows and columns of desks occupy most of the classroom space. The few tables scattered around the room have by-invitation-only status;

assigned desks are the rule here. The poster messages further reflect an emphasis on order.

In some ways, the features of the physical environment might relate to class size—Miss Anderson shares one of her feelings about teaching,

> The thing that bothers me the most is the amount of time I spend with discipline. Getting them to just sit down and listen and stay on tasks.

Perhaps, then, she believes it's easier to get a large group to "sit down and listen" when you assign them to desks rather than allow them to scatter around the room. With a smaller number of students, Miss Anderson may feel the press of the crowd less and, as a result, may feel more comfortable with a less formal room arrangement. Furthermore, Miss Anderson hopes that reduced class size will allow time for more varied activities. She envisions "breaking out my weather unit or one on dinosaurs." Possibly this interest will result in allocating certain sections of the room for special projects.

Within this environment, Miss Anderson carries on the day's activities with her 19 students. In reviewing the opening scene, we perceive a number of routines as the day begins.

The Day's Beginning

The stacks of papers, books, and forms on Miss Anderson's desk indicate one type of activity occupying much of her early morning time—clerical tasks. Each day, for example, Miss Anderson checks attendance, collecting absence and tardy slips which must be turned in with her monthly register. Also, each day Miss Anderson—or a designated child—collects money for supplies. On Fridays, this activity takes a little longer as children line up to pay 15 cents for an afternoon ice-cream treat. The following examples, taken from faculty memos, exemplify the varied nature of these clerical tasks:

1. New Student Records—Teacher responsibility—Pursue and pursue and pursue.
2. Parent–Teacher Conferences—Special invitations; All should be complete by end of American Education Week. Write up resumes immediately—special forms—use carbon to make duplicates.
3. Parent–Teacher Conference Calendar: Turn your Appointment forms in to the office so that a Master Calendar can be made. Keep sending back forms until you get a letter saying the parent absolutely cannot come for a conference.
4. Immunization Reports due October 1. All your Health Records should be complete.
5. Substitute-Teacher-Pak Checklist—Please have these paks ready to check. [The list of suggestions for inclusion in the Pak numbers twenty—from name tags for each child to statements of classroom policies and routines.]

During the first hour, then, we find the students quietly completing board-work and spelling assignments, usually of the "write-five-sentences about—" variety, while Miss Anderson finishes any number of clerical tasks vying for her attention. With a smaller number of students (thus reducing the record keeping), perhaps the fewer demands in this phase of teaching will result in changes during this hour of the day. For example, Miss Anderson might find more time available for activities other than boardwork or she might be more inclined to allow students to assume some responsibility for collecting money and taking the roll. In fact, she even suggests, "I have a couple of kids who could probably do some of the work."

The early morning routine soon flows in to the more academically related portion of the day. Next we examine instructional patterns that typically occur in this setting, and we reflect on their relationship to class size.

Instructional Activities and Techniques

The following scenes portray some of the characteristic features of activities with the larger class, focusing on how Miss Anderson directs lessons and manages groups and student behavior.

Directing a math lesson. Miss Anderson teaches two math groups, one of low achievers and one of average achievers. She notices her students chattering noisily in a zig-zag line outside the door.

> You people, that's *no way* to get a good-worker point.[1] Get in your assigned seats.

Children tumble into the room, the bustle increasing the noise level until Miss Anderson's sharp reprimand echoes over all,

> All right, if you take *my time,* there'll be no time to trade in points. *George, Sandra.* Get in your seats *now.*

Miss Anderson begins giving directions,

> Do pages 187 and 188 in your workbooks. Everyone do this first and raise your hand to have your work checked. Then go back and do any pages not finished, then 189, then boardwork.

A few listen to this recitation; others shuffle through notebooks, flip through workbooks, whisper to a friend, or just sit. Two or three, perhaps used to the routine, begin to write.

Directing a reading lesson. The sounds of occasional giggles and scraping desks punctuate the rising hum of voices as everyone gets settled for reading class. Miss Anderson, managing four reading groups, unsmilingly surveys the

---

1. Next to each student's name written on a good-workers chart, Miss Anderson records checkmarks for good behavior. Once a week these are redeemed for good-worker prizes.

scene, frequently arching an eyebrow in disapproval. Speaking over the noise, she demands,

> I need *everyone* quiet. Sidney, you're not listening.

As the rustling subsides, Miss Anderson directs the lesson.

> Let's review our phonics.

In a sing-song rhythm, the class chants the sounds; several seem to participate with appropriate lip movements but barely whispering a response. After a quick review of diphthongs, Miss Anderson directs the rest of the lesson,

> For your boardwork, mark the vowels [in 20 words], use five words in a sentence and five words in a question. Group 2, you read with Mrs. Conley [a parent volunteer]. Group 3, I'll call you up for your assessment tests. OK, let's get to work. Janie Mae, you're in the wrong seat.

For the rest of the period Miss Anderson scans the classroom while administering tests to Group 3, stopping often for quick reprimands.

Managing groups and behavior. Frequent interruptions of lessons occur as Miss Anderson finds it necessary to control student behavior. Examples similar to the following typify this aspect of instruction.

> Miss Anderson: "Why is it I hear voices?
> Roger do you have something to do?"

> Roger: "I'm not talking."

> Miss Anderson: "Well, who is it? Sandra, don't turn around; I might think it's you."

> Miss Anderson: "Those people who have to take their spelling test *again,* come up to this table. If you don't have to take it, *be quiet.* Sidney, if you aren't going to work, you don't need to be here."

> While giving out spelling words, Miss Anderson surveys the room, calling out, "Emmet, please work," "Lance, you take a time out; put your head down," "Janie Mae, check your voice box," "Jerome, I want that desk turned around the way I told you; you're not helping me."

These examples reveal several attributes of instruction and suggest possible areas of change when Miss Anderson's class-size is reduced. For instance, Miss Anderson seems to perceive transitions between lessons as too noisy and responds by directing students quickly to their assigned work. With fewer students, transition may occur more smoothly and, perhaps, Miss Anderson may allow more time for discussion, questions, or other motivational activities.

In the following sections, we elaborate these examples of instruction by considering types of lessons and use of materials, aspects of organization, and evaluation of student work.

Types of lessons and use of material. Boardwork assignments . . . workbook pages . . . assessment tests . . . once a week round-robin reading . . . boardwork assignments . . . workbook pages . . . the cycle continues throughout the week. Miss Anderson relies on boardwork during three portions of the day—the first activity in the morning, and for reading and math lessons. She states that students need to be able to copy and shares another purpose, "I always give them more than I know they can finish so they'll always have *something* they're supposed to be doing." Little variation occurs in these assignments; in fact, during two months' observation before the class-size change, the following exercises typified each day:

Homeroom: Write 5 sentences about ———.

Reading: Mark V's [vowels in 20 words].
    Use 5 words in a sentence.
    Use 5 words in a question.
    Use 5 words in a story.
Math: 20 problems $\langle \ \rangle =$
   $(6 + 7) \ (15 - 3)$

According to Miss Anderson, the children need a great deal of repetition in order to learn.

In addition to boardwork, reading and math lessons generally include several assignments in workbooks. Frequently, the sequence of pages spans more than one concept; for instance, in one math lesson, students finish computation problems on regrouping, then turn to problems about telling time.

Taking assessment tests and reading orally once a week with a volunteer complete the typical reading lessons. The county-wide adopted series, published by Houghton Mifflin, includes an extensive testing component, and since Miss Anderson administers these tests, she delegates to a parent volunteer the responsibility of directing students' oral reading. An excerpt from one such session follows. In this story, Ira looks forward to spending the night with his friend, Reggie, until he wonders—should he take along his teddybear Tah Tah?

The small group of five sit in a semicircle facing Mrs. Conley. In turn, each reads a short passage, sometimes hesitating over an unknown word.

Earl: "Reggie was asleep. Just like that he had . . ."

Mrs. Conley: "What's that word?"

Earl: "Fallen . . . he had fallen asleep. 'Reggie,' I said, 'You have to tell the end of the ghost story!' "

Mrs. Conley: "OK next."

George: "But Reggie just held his teddy bear tight and went on sleeping. And after that—there wasn't anything to do after that. 'Good night,' I said to Tah Tah. And I went to sleep too."

Mrs. Conley: "OK, on the next page, next."

Louis (beginning the next story): "What will you be? What do you want to be when you grow up?"

The oral reading continues, without discussion of the story read or preparation for the story begun. Not evident in this lesson are opportunities for the children to discuss their own feelings about being embarrassed or concerned about a friend's opinion, or to share any personal anecdotes about a favorite toy or stuffed animal. With reduced class size, perhaps testing time will be less, and Miss Anderson can devote more attention to providing a context for the reading and the follow-up discussions; as a result, students' views of what "reading" actually means may broaden.

Having examined several lessons in this classroom, we might wonder about Miss Anderson's planning process. She explains,

> I plan over the weekend for a week at a time. I take all my manuals home, although I don't get all my ideas from them. I use my own ideas for morning boardwork and for math boardwork. For math boardwork, I use whatever I think they need. We do go straight through the math workbooks.
>
> For reading I use a combination of things—my phonics program and the reading series.

And, Miss Anderson offers additional thoughts about instruction in her classroom through these journal entries, each reflecting views about math and reading before the change in class size.

> October 30–November 17: Math
> –two groups going at one time
> –each group doing boardwork every day
> –usually getting through with only one workbook page
> –group 1 (low) doing a lot of basic math drill work
> –no time for games for fun
> –individual help from Mrs. Conley [a parent aide]

> October 30–November 17: Reading
> –four groups of reading
> –not able to meet with each group daily
> –less time for oral reading—mostly left to volunteers who unfortunately do "round robin"
> –no choral reading done
> –never finish all expected lesson plans

As the above scenes, comments, and notes illustrate, reading and math instruction in the larger class includes mainly paper-and-pencil activities. There is no evidence of creative enrichment activities or a variety of instructional approaches; instead, emphasis appears to be based on order and routine. Certainly Miss Anderson's assignment of "more work than they can finish" supports such a conclusion. Activities allowing or requiring students to move around the room or contributing to an increased noise level may cause Miss Anderson to feel as if she's losing control, so she avoids them. With fewer students, she may worry less about this, and so try more "risky" activities.

The characteristics of reading and math instruction seem to extend to other areas of the curriculum. The patterned artwork displayed around the room, for example, suggests a lack of expressive lessons, and afternoon Physical Education habitually means few alternatives from calisthenics, and a teacher-directed game, a routine Mrs. Fleming requires, according to Miss Anderson.

Furthermore, little variety exists in materials used; textbooks and workbooks predominate. Miss Anderson rarely introduces her second graders to multimedia equipment or expressive and recreational materials. Miss Anderson speculates about changes in a smaller class,

> I think I'll be more willing to try things, to experiment. I can see a lot more fun things—maybe using my games a lot more. Now, with so many kids, you're bound to have, 'I got cheated on this,' or 'So and so didn't do this right!'

Organization of groups and time. As Miss Anderson's notes indicate, she teaches two math groups and four reading groups, although she points out the difficulty of "seeing" each group each day. In response, therefore, she organizes a sequence of activities for each group and relies on help from a parent or teacher aide. For instance, after a few minutes of introducing a math skill or concept, Miss Anderson directs each group's attention to the appropriate workbook assignments and the location of boardwork on one of two blackboard sections. Then, both the teacher and aide spent the rest of math time circulating, stopping occasionally to help with a problem ("The short hand tells you what?"), to point out a mistake ("Check this answer again"), or to reprimand an errant child ("Roy, if you can't be quiet, you can leave the second grade because you're not acting like a second grader.").

A similar routine occurs during reading class—a brief lesson for the whole class followed by small-group assignments in workbooks or by testing and oral reading. However, no differentiation occurs in boardwork; the emphasis on phonics appears to cut across grouping patterns. Additionally, less teacher mobility occurs during reading time. Miss Anderson remains at one table to oversee assessment testing, thus limiting careful supervision of seatwork.

Since grouping occurs only for math and reading, Miss Anderson organizes the rest of the day for large-group instruction, requiring the same work and pace for each child. Miss Anderson includes changes in the organizational features of her instruction as she envisions teaching a smaller class.

> It is easier if you've got a smaller group; you can get around to everybody.
> I hope to have time for individual needs.

Evaluation of student work. In a classroom with such apparent emphasis on written assignments, we might expect to find a large number of evaluative comments on student work. However, in looking through workbooks and a sample of checked papers, we find little support for our expectations. Instead, red or blue ink $\sqrt{}$'s and X's cover each page, only occasionally accompanied by teacher responses such as, "Do over," OK," "Super," "Good," or "See me." Furthermore, although she checks workbooks frequently, Miss Anderson returns boardwork papers only in time to accompany the progress reports or report cards sent home every four to five weeks.

Our observational data from the larger class indicate children in Miss Anderson's math class spend, on the average, five percent of their time waiting for help; in reading class, they wait eight percent of the time. Furthermore, children spend five and one-half percent of the time in math and seven percent in reading in "down" time, doing nothing, although Miss Anderson reports they can always find something to read. Possibly, instead of lost moments, effective evaluation could occur. Perhaps with fewer students in the class, we will find a greater amount of time devoted to evaluation, especially to teacher–student discussions of progress or problems.

Summary of instructional activities and techniques. Miss Anderson responds to the question, "What is important to teach?"

> Number one; to teach them or instill in them a feeling of self-worth, because I don't think they have a feeling they're worth anything . . . Also, a sense of responsibility, being responsible for yourself and your actions . . . I think they better learn those things before they can settle down and learn the academics.

As we have seen, though, evidence before the change in class size appears to contradict these instructional goals. For instance, in examining how Miss Anderson plans and implements her curriculum, we find few opportunities for students to accept responsibility by making any decisions regarding activities, use of materials, or allocation of time. Miss Anderson directs the scene, deciding what is to be done, how the class session and students are to proceed, and what use will be made of classroom space. The organization of the rooms and the illustrations of lessons combine to reflect these characteristics. Moreover, although she has occasional personal talks with a child, the nature of many verbal sanctions used to control behavior before and during instruction seems to contradict her concern for instilling "feelings of self-worth."

In examining patterns of instructional activities and techniques in the larger class, we find an emphasis on "basic skills" attainment in the reading assessment tests and in the extensive assignment of computation problems in math; the encouragement of rote memory and factual recall, especially in the phonics program; a scarcity of opportunities throughout the day for discussion, problem solving, or enrichment; and a limited range of activities following an almost unchanging routine of boardwork, workbooks, and testing throughout the week. Miss Anderson reports hoped-for changes in some of these areas when the class size changes.

Interactions

Teacher–student interactions. As Miss Anderson describes a recent encounter with Jim, we can glimpse some of the qualities of interaction.

> Jim yelled at me the other day. He was out of his seat doing something. I said, 'Jim, sit down,' and he yelled back, 'I'm *getting* a pencil.'

I brought him over to my desk, and I stood up, and I looked down—you know, in this very 'I'm bigger than you are' type thing—and using all the body language I could muster, I said, 'Who is the adult?' and 'Who is the child?' He told me. I said, 'You *never ever* yell at adults,' and he agreed. He knew he was wrong.

Although this didn't take place in front of the class, the desire for control and authority, evident in this passage, seems to pervade much of the way Miss Anderson relates with her students, and may have to do with her perception of the press of numbers in the larger class. Frequently she asks, "Are you helping me?" or threatens, "I can send you home." Even directions sometimes contain a note of demand, "Franklin, get off my chalkboard and stand up." Only occasionally do we find evidence of the concern conveyed in the following scene.

Miss Anderson, softly, gently, arms around George's waist, holding him close: "George, you're one of my kids. When I say *my* kids, I mean it. My kids are very special to me. I really care about you all. And sometimes I'm hardest on the kids most special to me. I'm going to try really hard to make you a good student because you can be. But I can't do it all alone; I need help. I need you to help me. I care, George, I really do."

Positive comments such as these take place privately, usually during class change, contrasting with the more public type of interactions.

Recording types of teacher-talk further clarifies interactions in the class setting. In analyzing Miss Anderson's comments during a 20-minute reading lesson, we find the following percentages for each category:

1. Gives directions—academic procedure — 10%
2. Gives directions—management — 11%
3. Criticizes, justifies authority, demands attention — 28%
4. Other teacher-talk—academic — 33%
5. Other teacher-talk—affective — 1%
6. Confusion — 5%
7. Pseudo-silence (Some noise due to movement, to classroom at work) — 9%
8. Student talk — 3%

According to this evidence, then, a little over one-fourth of Miss Anderson's remarks focus on criticisms or maintaining authority. A similar pattern continues throughout many lessons. Possibly, her experience in teaching older students causes her to try to enforce unrealistic standards for these younger students. Interestingly, Miss Anderson's perceptions of her interactions with students differ from observable behavior; for instance, she characterizes her teaching self with some of the following traits:

• Every so often, you must be a child yourself—laugh, be silly.
• Lots of touching—firm, soft, 'I'm here.'

- Look for the good.
- Point out the good.
- Soft-spokenness more than loudness.

When speculating about changes through teaching a smaller number of students, Miss Anderson focuses more on this personalized, relaxed aspect of teaching than any other. She hopes

- to be able to know each child better
- to do less disciplining
- to have more patience and feel less frustrated

Student–student interactions.   As described previously, students in the larger class seem to have few opportunities for interacting with one another. When they arrive in the morning, they're expected to settle down quickly and to begin the boardwork assignments, and, as revealed in the illustrations of lessons, little discussion occurs during instruction. Although some children may win the privilege of occasionally working at a table, starting to talk there usually brings a quick reprimand and a trip back to a desk. Even on the playground, school policies requiring certain types of activities limit the time available for children to talk informally with one another or to share important parts of their lives with a friend.

Certainly this doesn't mean student–student interactions never take place; although the risk of a scolding is ever-present, whispered, furtive exchanges occur often, and many children find excuses for classroom "errands" near a friend. Evidence from coded observations in the larger class indicates that, during math, students are academically engaged 63 percent of the time. During reading, they are academically engaged 61 percent of the time. Perhaps during a part of the remaining time in these classes, students turn from their work to seek out and connect with one another.

Interruptions.   With a reduced class size, the teacher would have to supervise the activities of fewer children, and might be able to anticipate questions or recognize potential problems more readily. This might reduce the number of in-class interruptions and scenes such as the following:

> Miss Anderson: "Steve get rid of that gum . . . OK Group 1 up here at the table. Sarah Ann, please sit down."

> Children scurry to find their places, chattering noisily until Miss Anderson commands: *"Emmet . . . Nelson, you sit here."*

> Nelson: "Why do I have to sit here?"

> Miss Anderson: "Because I said so . . . I expect Group 1 to be quiet while they're working. Can you do that? Emmet? Let me see what a good job you can do."

Turning to Group 2, Miss Anderson stands in front, holding a cardboard clock and asking telling-time questions ("How many minutes in an hour? Is this the before or after part of the clock?"). Soon, though, Nelson's restlessness catches her attention; she stops, stalks across the room, snaps her finger, and demands, *"Nelson, work."*

Interruptions in the larger class seem to occur, then, as the teacher supervises students' activities and behavior and responds to students' questions. Additional interruptions, unrelated to class size, occur from sources external to the classroom—from colleagues stopping by to chat, from memos the principal sends, or, as the following scene illustrates, from a "helpful" teacher aide.

Miss Anderson teaches one group while a smaller group works at a nearby table.

Miss Anderson, holding up a clock: "OK—these numbers tell you what?" (Choral response, "The hour.") "And these lines tell you the _____?" ("Minutes.")

Mrs. Burkett, an aide, enters. When Sidney calls out to her, Mrs. Burkett responds loudly while walking across the front of the room, "You better be quiet."

Mrs. Burkett goes to the table, asks Evelyn why she is crying. Finding out, she yells over to Sidney, "Did you hit Evelyn?"

Sidney: "Yeah, she was cheatin'."

Mrs. Burkett: "How many times have I told you not to hit someone?"

Miss Anderson pauses during this exchange, then continues the lesson about telling time.

Summary of "Larger-Class" View

Having examined a number of classroom scenes, instructional activities, and teacher–student interactions, what do we now know about the "larger-class" view of Miss Anderson's classroom? What changes does Miss Anderson hope for and envision when teaching a smaller number of students?

In the larger class we find evidence of a highly structured, controlled curriculum. The daily schedule, types of lessons, use of materials, organization of groups and time, even the room arrangement and wall posters combine to reinforce this assessment. Moreover, Miss Anderson interacts with her students most often in an authoritarian, often strident manner, spending almost as much time criticizing and demanding attention as she does teaching.

When speculating about instruction in a smaller class, Miss Anderson projects a number of changes: less need for disciplining, greater attention to individual needs, and more opportunities for varied activities. In the next section, we examine the smaller-class view of Miss Anderson's classroom, considering possible explanations for changes that did and did not occur.

MISS ANDERSON'S CLASSROOM: THE "SMALLER-CLASS" VIEW

The Physical Environment

"Think!" admonishes the six-feet-tall, winking pink panther, painted on red construction paper, watching over the 13 second graders from a front-of-the-room vantage point. Glancing around the room, we find little variation in poster messages; like the pink panther, most still convey some reminder of appropriate behavior, such as "Stick to the main point." And, shifting our view from wall to floor space, we detect how the room organization further reflects this limited change. Although fewer little people occupy them, the same rows-and-columns configuration of desks exists; the only noticeable move has been the teacher's desk from the side to front of the classroom. Neither do we find evidence of special-interest centers or indications of ongoing class projects.

Although Miss Anderson hasn't altered the physical environment of her classroom in any noticeable way, she finds advantages in having a smaller number of students "living" there. "There's more space. Everyone can breathe." She also believes greater control over student behavior is possible,

> If I walk around, I can keep on going with my lesson and not interrupt everybody by yelling at one. I can walk over and just take the paper they're drawing on out of their hands, or put the pencil down, or touch them on the shoulder, or something.

Has altering the room organization been a priority for Miss Anderson or has a need for control, suggested in the above statement, been one factor reinforcing limited changes? Does an explanation reside in the room itself? In other words, do the built-in bookcases and more-than-usual number of doors restrict the feasible ways of shaping the classroom? Or do the features of the physical environment suggest a larger issue, hinting at few changes in Miss Anderson's curriculum? Keeping these possibilities in mind, we examine how the day begins in this smaller class.

The Day's Beginning

Stacks of materials cover Miss Anderson's desk—student papers, a lesson-plan book, the monthly register, referral forms, report cards, and a teacher's manual. Half-hidden behind these stacks, Miss Anderson checks roll and collects supply-store money, then turns to a referral form about Steve. In her view, the number of clerical responsibilities is increasing continuously, but having fewer students helps provide additional time for such tasks.

> I can get more of my school paperwork done during times the kids are doing something else because I'm not having to monitor them as closely.

What types of activities are students engaged in as Miss Anderson completes her clerical tasks? Do we find the alternatives to boardwork we speculated about and the increased student responsibility she hoped to try? A quick glance at the chalkboard provides a clue:

Use each word in a sentence: mind, fight, might, wind, blend.

Even with a smaller number of students, a morning routine similar to that before the change in class size—boardwork and spelling book assignments—occurs during the first hour of the day. In addition to enjoying fewer interruptions of her own work during this time, Miss Anderson justifies the routine on the basis of her view of students' needs.

The kids expect a routine of coming in and doing that sort of boardwork. If you came in one morning and all of a sudden changed, I don't think they'd know what to do. They need that order. Maybe it's that particular age or the type children that we have, but they need a structure, to know we're going to do this, this, and this. It just throws them for a loop if we don't.

Certainly the management and functioning of any group necessitates structure, organization, and order; however, this may be accomplished in a number of ways. For example, other ways of starting the day could still provide time for clerical responsibilities and, in the process, provide students with more enriching learning opportunities. Children could assume responsibility for many of these tasks and might feel more involved in their classroom as a result. Additionally, such responsibility could foster independence or provide opportunities for problem solving (figuring out classmates' change from buying a pencil may be quite a challenge for a second grader!) Also, a variety of other early morning activities such as students working in pairs, small groups, or at learning centers could replace or supplement boardwork and still fulfill Miss Anderson's desire for a quiet morning routine. And, with fewer students, implementing such changes might be more possible.

The evidence suggests that class size has had little effect in this setting on how the day begins. This lack of change may be due to several factors—Miss Anderson's interest in having uninterrupted time for her own work, her belief in students' need for routine, or her lack of awareness of (or inability to implement) alternatives to boardwork. In the next section, we examine the instructional activities and techniques characteristic in the smaller class.

Instructional Activities and Techniques

Again we consider the features of instruction portrayed as Miss Anderson directs lessons and controls groups and behavior. Examples of math and reading lessons in the smaller class are followed by an example of an addition to the curriculum, guidance lessons.

Directing a math lesson.   Miss Anderson begins a review of points, lines, and line segments but soon becomes irritated by students' whispering and restlessness.

Miss Anderson: "All right, I want everything out of your hands. Desks flat. We can't get a lot done when you're noisy. Shall I go on?"

Randolph: "No."

Miss Anderson: "Randolph, if I don't go on, we don't finish the book, and that means staying in second grade."

In the quickly descending hush, Miss Anderson again explains line segments, then says: "On page 220 in your workbook, they ask you to draw a line between two points." After explaining the directions for the next two pages, she cautions, "The directions say to color the right answer. I don't have enough crayons, so I say put an X instead."

For the rest of the class session, the children complete the workbook pages, then start on their boardwork. Miss Anderson and a parent aide circulate, stopping to answer questions or check answers.

Directing a reading lesson. As the reading class files through the door, Miss Anderson occasionally directs a child ("Louis, get in the right seat") but generally seems pleased with the smoothness of this "getting-settled" time. A new column of Crayola—red√'s squiggles down the Good Workers Chart as Miss Anderson records them and remarks,

I hope at the end of today we have time to trade in some of these points . . . OK, I need everybody listening. We're going to work first on some things we're having trouble with. To listen, you have nothing in your hands, eyes on the person speaking and your mouth not moving.

After a quick review of vowel digraphs, Miss Anderson reviews the boardwork: "Mark the vowels, use 10 words in a story, and draw a picture about the story . . . Questions? . . . OK Groups 3 and 4 to Mrs. Hopkins."

Before starting their boardwork, however, the children remaining with Miss Anderson discuss a story in their basal reader. Miss Anderson sits on a chair in front of the room, teacher's manual open on her lap. Books slap desks, and pages shuffle as children around the room flip to the right story. Miss Anderson reviews briefly the story "Moon Mouse," then asks, "How do you mark the *oo* in moon?"

From the back row, Sandra calls out, "Other vowel sound." Several children do not look up but continue to look through the story.

Miss Anderson: "Yes, go on and read pages 90 and 91 silently."

Silence pervades for a few minutes until Miss Anderson begins again, "Find me the sentence that tells what it was like that night."

Janie Mae and George each volunteer to read a sentence. Most don't raise their hands. William, sitting far in the back, continues reading.

Miss Anderson continues: "Find a word that's in the family of *ight* words."

Keith, Lance and Rhonda call out: "Light."

Miss Anderson: "Yes. *Gh* is what?"

Scattered responses from a few: "Silent."

(The rest of the lesson follows the same pattern. "Read these pages silently . . . ; Find me the sentence that tells ———; Who can find a word with a ——— sound?")

In concluding the story Miss Anderson asks: "When do mice go out to look for food?"

Louis: "At night."

Miss Anderson: "Do they need the light of the moon?"

Most respond, "Yes," although by now some have closed their books; some have gone on to look at another story; Fred just sits, and Billy casually doodles on his notebook cover.

Miss Anderson: "George, is the moon really made of cheese?"

George: "No."

Miss Anderson gives directions for the boardwork, then starts giving assessment tests to two students at a time. For the rest of the period, she gives the tests, monitors the rest of the class ("Lance, you're doing a nice job." "Janie Mae, leave if you can't stop talking." "William, if you don't get to work you can do this during P.E."), stops to receive some forms the L.D. teacher brings in, and sends Rhonda to the speech therapist.

A couple of changes seem readily apparent in these illustrations. With fewer students, Miss Anderson seems pleased that transitions between lessons occur more smoothly and, in response, takes a few moments for praise and encouragement. Also, as the reading lesson indicates, she is now more involved in discussions with students about their stories. Other changes haven't occurred; in elaborating the latter more fully in the next section, we consider possible explanations.

With an additional teacher, the second-grade curriculum has been expanded. The next example indicates how Miss Anderson directs a guidance-program activity focusing on exploring children's opinions and feelings.

Directing a guidance program lesson. The lesson begins with Miss Anderson directing two boys pantomiming the building of a treehouse. "I don't see any sawing going on. That's a good door. Oh, do they need a window? Are you done? Good. Looks good to me. Now that the treehouse is done, we can all sit in it—there's a nice breeze going. You boys did such a nice job. Now I want to read a story to you. Are you all ready? Yes, it looks like you're all ready."

In a soft, animated voice, Miss Anderson reads the story of Max, a boy who built a treehouse but forgot his friends weren't exactly the same as he; one was shorter, one was heavier, and one couldn't see as well.

Two interruptions occur. Miss Anderson speaks quietly to Roy: "If you don't want to listen, you may leave." And, a child knocks softly on the door, reminding Miss Anderson to send a few of her students to the special reading teacher.

After listening to the story, the children pantomime different scenes—pretending they're small as they try to get up to the first rung of the ladder. Miss Anderson encourages discussion: "How do you suppose Mary felt when she was too small to get up to the treehouse? . . . Get your eyes all squinty so you can see how you can only see a little bit . . . How do you know Max liked his three friends?"

> Gina: "Cause he invited them up."
>
> Miss Anderson: "Would it be any fun if we were all the same?"
>
> Della: "No, but what about twins?"
>
> Miss Anderson: "Yes, but they're not *exactly* alike."
>
> Valerie: "I know—they don't think alike!"
>
> Miss Anderson: "Right!"

The relaxed atmosphere evident in this scene often contrasts with other portions of the day. This may be due to the program itself, which Miss Anderson reveals she follows verbatim, or perhaps Miss Anderson believes that such informality isn't appropriate during "academic" lessons or that "real" learning doesn't take place that way. Furthermore, parents and the administration don't exert pressure to complete these materials, as they do in reading and math. This scene, then, may illustrate how Miss Anderson's teaching is affected by external pressures and her perceptions of that pressure. The following examples, taken from three "academic" lessons, typify how Miss Anderson's instruction still includes strict control over student behavior.

Managing Groups and Student Behavior

Miss Anderson, teaching about telling time: "The long hand tells you the minutes; the short hand tells you hours. Sidney get in your seat."

Roy gets up to throw away a paper wad.

> Miss Anderson: "Get in your seat. Roy, look at me. Are you helping me? No. You're interrupting my class. Look at me. Do you want to go to the office? Then get in your seat right now."

Miss Anderson circulates, helping individuals with their math workbook pages. Frequently she stops, pointing an accusing finger at a talker or squirmer elsewhere in the room: "Lance, are you going to have to work in the hall today?" "Janie Mae, get in your desk the right way."

While sitting at one table giving reading assessment tests to two children at a time, Miss Anderson scans the room often, monitoring where children are and what they are doing: "Vernon, leave if you can't stop talking." "Valerie if you don't get to work, you can do this instead of going outside." "Rhonda, you're being nice and quiet."

In considering the features of Miss Anderson's instruction in the smaller class, we again examine the types of lessons and uses of materials, aspects of organization, and evaluation of student work. The focus is mainly on changes apparently related to class size.

Types of lessons and uses of materials. As we found in looking at the early morning activities, boardwork remains an integral part of math and reading instruction. Little variation exists in the type of boardwork assignments in this smaller class; the cycle of computation problems in math and phonics work in reading continues without interruption or alteration. Neither do we find changes in assessment testing or workbook assignments. Miss Anderson offers one explanation,

> Mrs. Fleming expects us to follow carefully the adopted reading and math programs.

And, leaving math and reading for a moment to examine the art and P.E. areas of the curriculum, we find little evidence there either of changes due to teaching a smaller number of students. The same playground routine and patterned art lessons characterize instruction.

Except for the time factor, Miss Anderson doesn't acknowledge significant changes in how she plans as a result of teaching a smaller number of students.

> It takes me about an hour and a half to plan for a week. Now that I have fewer groups, I stay pretty much on schedule.

In examining features not evident in Miss Anderson's planning and curriculum, we can speculate about possible reasons for their absence. For instance, Miss Anderson plans subject-by-subject; little indication exists of attempts to integrate subject areas. We might assume this feature of her planning can be attributed to a structured schedule imposed by the administration; however, Miss Anderson acknowledges she and the other second-grade teachers retain responsibility for organizing their day, except for the school-wide scheduled time for reading and math. Furthermore, we discern little variety in her plans, especially in reading and math, lunch, bathroom breaks, and P.E. Although fewer students might seem to provide a chance to attempt new kinds of activities, Miss Anderson perhaps has a limited awareness of the range and types of creative, alternative ideas she might implement that would be appropriate for second graders, regardless of how many she teaches. In addition, she may be unaware of available resources she could utilize for new ideas.

What instructional changes in activities and use of materials, then, are apparent in the smaller class? Miss Anderson shares her view of changes in math and reading in these entries from her journal.

January 22–February 9: Math
  –one group (middle)
  –getting done an average of two pages a day in workbook
  –more individual help

–able to check papers in class now
–immediate reinforcement
–everyone has more room to work
–play math games in class
–able to spend time each day reviewing skills

January 22–February 9: Reading
–using games
–more variety of activities
–meaningful reading stories—silent reading, questions, phonics incorporated. I
have time to do reading.
–more assessments being done
–using volunteers to better advantage
–by regrouping have reduced class size—now send small groups to other teachers.

Evidence based on several months of observation contradicts some of Miss Anderson's perceptions, most especially her view of varied activities and use of games. However, a distinct change as mentioned earlier is the greater responsibility Miss Anderson assumes for directing students' oral reading and discussion. She attributes this to class-size effects.

> With the larger number of kids I had, there wasn't anything I could do about oral reading. I had to get through the assessment tests. If I wanted the kids to get in any oral reading, using the aide was the only way. With the smaller class, we'll spend half an hour going over the first half of the story for comprehension and looking at the pictures and a little bit of everything. Then the next day they can finish the story by themselves.

While we might hope for more challenging and enriching discussions than those typically occurring during Miss Anderson's lessons, we can be grateful for the change from the round-robin reading taking place previously. The aide, Mrs. Conley, now helps individuals with sight vocabulary.

Another change in instructional activities attributed to reduced class size involves the addition of subjects to the curriculum, as we've seen. Having a third second-grade teacher seems to have provided the opportunity for incorporating science, language arts, and guidance activities in the school day. Miss Anderson uses a program entitled DUSO (Developing Understanding of Self and Others) when teaching lessons such as the one illustrated.

As the example indicates, the types of activities occurring during this portion of the day differ dramatically from those characteristic of other subject areas. Children role-play, pantomime, listen as Miss Anderson tells stories with the DUSO puppets, and share their opinions and feelings.

Also, with fewer students in the class, activities differ during the more informal times of the day. Waiting for lunch, for instance, used to be a time for monitoring bathroom trips and hand washing. Now, this getting-ready time doesn't take so long, and Miss Anderson often devotes a few minutes to reading Shel Silverstein's imaginative poems from *Where the Sidewalk Ends*. The children push chairs close, and soon their infectious giggles echo in the room.

As we reflect about the types of lessons and use of materials in the smaller class, several factors seem to be apparent. For example, in spite of the change in class size, we find little change in boardwork assignments, use of workbooks and assessment tests, or activities for physical education or art. Miss Anderson attributes this to the principal's control over the schedule, interest in maintaining the established reading and math programs, and desire for limited free play on the playground. Paper-and-pencil activities, then, continue to dominate the curriculum, reinforced by an emphasis on textbook and workbook usage.

Changes we can discern appear to occur during transitions, reading and DUSO classes, and the brief, informal times of the day. With fewer students Miss Anderson finds more time to direct students in their basal readers, to incorporate guidance lessons, and to allow a small number of just-for-fun events.

Organization of groups and time. The change in class size has reduced the number of groups Miss Anderson teaches each day. In math, for instance, she has only one group; Mr. Jameson now teaches several of Miss Anderson's former math students. In reading, also, one group remains after the initial phonics drill when two small groups leave to work with other adults. In her view, "It's easier to be organized. I spend less time giving directions and answering questions. This change, then, seems to have decreased transition time; with fewer directions necessary regarding assignments and work space, the lesson gets underway more rapidly. With fewer groups Miss Anderson discovers, "I can give more individual instruction time."

Reducing the number of groups and students would seem to provide an opportunity for change, for attempting different ways of developing a context for a lesson or of incorporating students' interests or of conducting class discussions. Instead, we find Miss Anderson utilizes the same routine of engaging students in the smaller class; that is, demanding attention, providing a quick review or explanation, and, occasionally reminding of grades or tests. The organization of groups and time, then, remains mostly the same instead of the sub-grouping or individualization one might expect with fewer students.

Several reasons may account for limited changes in the organization of instruction in Miss Anderson's classroom. Perhaps, in spite of class size, Miss Anderson lacks the skills necessary for altering established instructional patterns, or she doesn't see a need for changing her style, or she may be unaware of the possibilities for changes or of resources for ideas. Also, Miss Anderson may have developed specific habits of teaching and these, regardless of student numbers, may transfer to new situations. A further explanation may be Miss Anderson's need for control, evident in other situations, influencing what she feels comfortable about attempting. Consequently, the possibilities related to class size seem to be dependent on a variety of other factors.

Evaluation of student work. For Miss Anderson, having fewer students means she has the time to check papers during class, thus providing almost immediate assessment. She usually accomplishes this by circulating as the children bend over their workbook pages, rewarding correct answers with a full-page checkmark. Children making errors receive reminders to "check this one," or "redo these.'' With the smaller number of students, she can spend more time talking with each, sometimes as much as four or five minutes. In the larger class, these encounters were much briefer, usually one minute or so. The following exchange took place between Miss Anderson and Franklin during a spelling lesson:

> Miss Anderson: "What is the beginning of *blind,* Franklin? A consonant . . ."
>
> Franklin: "Cluster."
>
> Miss Anderson: "Good, Franklin. And what is that consonant cluster?"
>
> Franklin: "CVC?"
>
> Miss Anderson: "No, at the beginning of the word *blind,* what consonant cluster do you hear?"
>
> Franklin: "I know, it's *i.*"
>
> Miss Anderson: "Is *i* a consonant?"
>
> Franklin: "No—oh yeah, it's *bl.*"
>
> Miss Anderson: "Good, *bl* is the consonant cluster."

In the area of evaluation, then, class size has affected the time factor most of all. Before the class was reduced, we found students in "Wait" or "Down" time between five and eight percent of their instructional time. After the change in class size, we find these percentages reduced to zero. Also, we find the percentage of contact with the teacher during math seatwork increasing from zero to 13 percent.

Changes in the kinds of written teacher comments, though, are not apparent. An examination of reading and math workbooks and boardwork papers reveals comments similar to those we found when Miss Anderson had to evaluate the work of more students: "Fix," "Good," "Do Over," "Super," "Mark V's first." Neither do we find Miss Anderson incorporating alternative ways of gathering evidence useful for determining students' progress, such as keeping anecdotal records or providing opportunities for students' self-evaluation. Instead, the emphasis seems to be on correct answers and achievement on assessment tests.

Summary of instructional activities and techniques.   What instructional changes do we find in the smaller class? What instructional features remain the same?

Having fewer students seems to have facilitated a number of variations in instruction. For example, Miss Anderson is now more involved in reading instruction by directing students through their basal readers and providing opportunities for discussion of the stories. Also, in the smaller class, Miss Anderson is able to direct her students through the materials at a faster pace, to evaluate their work more quickly, and to spend more time offering individual help. The fact that Miss Anderson not only has fewer students but also has fewer groups to manage appears to have contributed to these changes.

Additionally, the class-size change has provided an opportunity for expanding the curriculum. We find new subjects such as science, language arts, and guidance as well as briefer, more spur-of-the-moment lessons such as poetry reading during informal times of the day.

Other aspects of instruction, however, seem to have remained the same regardless of class size. For instance, we have little evidence of changes in the types of activities; boardwork, workbooks, tests—in other words, paper-and-pencil assignments—continue to dominate the curriculum. We don't find indications of ongoing student or class projects, enrichment activities, learning centers, peer teaching, creative drama, and so forth, even though having fewer students might seem to provide the chance to try out some ideas that might be difficult to manage in a larger class. Although the kinds of activities are limited, the assignments are generally extensive, combining to create a sense of never-ending work. Even when students do finish, they're often faced with more of the same, as the following exchange reveals:

> Janie Mae (glancing at the math boardwork): "Miss Anderson, I finished that yesterday."
>
> Miss Anderson: "It will be good practice to do it again."

Additionally, Miss Anderson seems to employ the same repertoire of routines in planning, "engaging" the students, and evaluating. We don't find motivation based on student interests, nor occasional shared responsibility for planning, nor alternative evaluation techniques—changes some might suggest as more possible in a smaller class. The final summary includes possible factors affecting change and lack of change.

Interactions

Teacher–student interactions.   Miss Anderson hoped mostly for improved interactions with her students when speculating about changes in a smaller class. The following statements reveal her perception that these improvements have indeed been realized.

> I know the kids better. I have the time to pull them to the side and say, 'Did you have breakfast this morning?' You can do that with a small group, and you can't do it very well with a large group.
>
> My counseling times have become more frequent. I have more time to spend with Sidney talking about both positive and negative aspects of his behavior.
>
> I have talked with Jim about dealing with days when everything goes wrong for him—how to accept them and move on.
>
> At times I've pulled Janie Mae aside simply to touch and talk with her in hopes of helping her open up.

Certainly, these statements appear to reflect a significant advantage of teaching a smaller number of students. The increased time for personal interactions and the teacher's perception of improved relationships have the potential for creating a more relaxed, more positive environment. We find, for example, more occasions when Miss Anderson smiles and relaxes with her students. These changes probably contribute most to Miss Anderson's feeling, "There's more of *me* left at the end of the day."

However, while these changes point out an important aspect of smaller-class instruction, in this particular setting the attempt to control pervades much of the interaction between Miss Anderson and her students, and, as previous examples illustrate, this attempt often interferes with a lesson. Although Miss Anderson states that she endorses a behavior modification approach to discipline, and on occasion provides prizes for "good worker points," she most often relies on verbal sanctions and threats as disciplinary measures. Or, sometimes she utilizes a trip to the principal's office to shape behavior. Comments such as the following occur frequently, "Are you helping me?" "If you can't be quiet you may leave." "Do you want to be sent home? I don't think your grandmother would be happy to see you."

In addition to pointing out administrative pressure, Miss Anderson believes part of the discipline problem resides in the type of students in this classroom. In her view, "Most of the kinds come from low-income, low socioeconomic families. For some reason they just go-go-go!" We can speculate about other contributing factors, however.

We might begin by considering some of the routine student assignments, such as the typical boardwork, workbook pages, and assessment tests. With little variation in the assignments, with rare opportunities for interacting with their friends, and with few occasions for activity and movement, students' restlessness, talking, and other "misbehavior" becomes more easily understandable. Also, the nature of the work may have little meaning for the students. Franklin's confusion about consonant blends suggests this may be true. The work, because of its similarity, routine, and repetition, may be boring to the students.

The school schedule might also contribute to discipline problems; for instance, no provision is made for morning recess, so for several hours these children have no break except to go to the restroom. Even lunch is eaten in the classroom where the children are expected to remain in their desks and talk quietly.

Miss Anderson's concern for order and for maintaining a managed room supports Adams' and Biddle's (1970) findings regarding teachers' classroom behavior:

> The spectre of loss of control continues to haunt teachers to the extent that they are unwilling to create informal pupil activity situations where "insurrection" might rear its ugly head. (p. 45)

Apparently, several teachers believe informal pupil activity creates a greater potential for a loss of the teacher's control. And this concern may prevail regardless of the number of students in the classroom.

We also have evidence of teacher–student interactions revealed in the following percentage of teacher-talk, recorded during a 20-minute reading lesson:

1. Gives directions—academic procedures   5%
2. Gives directions—management   7%
3. Criticizes, justifies authority, demands attention   20%
4. Other teacher-talk—academic   31%
5. Other teacher-talk—affective   1%
6. Confusion   1%
7. Pseudo-silence   16%
8. Student-talk   19%

Compared to the percentage recorded in the larger class, we find less time taken up with giving directions and more evidence of student talk. Also, Miss Anderson's critical remarks are fewer; nevertheless, they still constitute one-fifth of her comments.

Miss Anderson frequently asks a misbehaving child, "Are you behaving like a second grader? If you can't behave like a second grader, you can go sit in the first grade for a while." Perhaps part of the problem in this setting concerns Miss Anderson's limited or inaccurate perception of the characteristics and needs of children of this age. Surely opportunities for developing verbal facility, for encouraging active involvement with a variety of materials, for fostering problem-solving skills, and for facilitating social development would be appropriate. Miss Anderson's experience teaching fourth graders may be creating some unrealistic expectations on her part for these second graders.

As the guidance lesson indicates, Miss Anderson appears to have the potential for an animated, positive way of interacting with students. She may find she can accomplish this manner more effectively with the upper-elementary children she prefers to teach. In addition, she may benefit greatly from suggestions from other teachers' successful instructional ideas and classroom management strategies for children similar to her own. As long as she perceives herself as primarily positive, though, she may not see the need for change.

Student–student interactions.   In examining the types of activities, use of classroom space, and daily routine, we still find rather limited opportunities for students to interact with one another. The children have few assignments involving group work, and they have no reading corner or interest center for more informal encounters.

A few changes, however, can be discerned. With Miss Anderson leading discussions in reading class, students can share their ideas, and, as we've seen, the DUSO activities and some of the spur-of-the-moment activities often provide opportunities for students to talk. Perhaps these changes account for students spending less time finding ways to whisper or "visit" with one another. According to evidence from the coded observation instrument data, students in the smaller class spend more time "academically engaged," 65 percent of the time in math and 79 percent of the time in reading. This compares to data from the larger class which indicated students were "academically engaged" 63 percent of the time during math and 61 percent of the time during reading.

Interruptions

In Miss Anderson's view, class size has an influence on the number of interruptions occurring throughout the school day: With smaller groups you have a better chance of keeping explosive kids apart from each other; consequently, there's less disruptive behavior to contend with.

Furthermore, with fewer groups to manage, fewer student questions or problems vie for her attention. Nevertheless, this is a classroom where a great number of interruptions still take place, as the following scene depicts.

Miss Anderson and her homeroom students read through the day's spelling lesson.

Miss Anderson: "OK. If we want to change a word ending in *y* to show more than one, what do we do? Gina?"

Gina: "Change *y* to *ies.*"

Miss Anderson: "Right. So baby becomes _____?"

Unison response: "Babies."

Miss Anderson notices Steve, working alone in the back corner, leaning out of his desk: "Steve, are you finished with your work?" (Steve shakes his head no.) "Well, get to work then. Sit down in your chair right."

Jerome gets out of his desk, sort of jogs around the front of the room. It is now almost time for class change. Miss Anderson sits Jerome on her lap, talking to him but also watching the class.

Miss Anderson: "If you get out of your seat once more, Jerome, when you're not supposed to, you'll go sit in the first grade. If you don't shape up, you're not going on to third grade. (Steve, you go on to Ms. Lindley's room now.) Jerome, you can do this work. (Mrs. Hopkins group for math.) Can you do a better job? (Jim, get up here in line. Mr. Jameson's group line up.) Now do you think you can do a better job? (Jerome nods yes.) Well, try to do so. Telling me is the easy part."

Pauses during lessons and discussions, then, continue to occur as the teacher manages the children's movement to other parts of the school and closely supervises behavior. Certainly many of these pauses are to be expected during a school day. Kounin (1970), for instance, discusses how necessary it is for teachers to develop a sense of "withitness" in order to contend with the many, often simultaneous, classroom events.

However, in some ways Miss Anderson may be contributing to the number of interruptions. For instance, she retains control over students' access to the pencil sharpener, use of supplementary materials, and excursions to the restroom and water fountain. Because she must approve each activity, students must ask permission, creating more in-class interruptions.

Through establishing alternative classroom routines and management techniques, students could be given responsibility for making a number of decisions as members of the setting, such as recognizing the correct time for moving to another class and for keeping appointments with specialists or deciding the appropriate occasions for sharpening a pencil. Not only might students benefit from these opportunities for making choices, but Miss Anderson also might profit from having more time to devote to instructional activities. Furthermore, reducing the number of in-class interruptions may permit greater continuity during lessons, thus increasing the possibility for students to glean more from the experience.

With a smaller number of students, implementing such changes might be more feasible. What could account, then, for the few changes evident in this classroom? Perhaps Miss Anderson believes changes of this type are inappropriate, or she may be unaware of a range of possible alternatives. Her interest in maintaining control may override any concern about contending with interruptions.

Other, more external intrusions such as memos from the office, unexpected visits from parents, requests from colleagues, and special programs also interrupt but have little to do with class size. The following interruption, created by a teacher aide in this smaller class, mirrors the one we viewed previously in the larger class.

> Miss Anderson: "OK today we want to review what we know about points, lines, and line segments. What is a line segment?"

> The door suddenly opens. Randolph slowly moves toward his desk, followed to the door by Mrs. Evans, an aide.

> Mrs. Evans, loudly: "He's late because he's misbehaved. I didn't know whether to bring him back to class or not. It's bad enough he disturbed one class without disturbing another. You remember what I told you, Randolph."

> Miss Anderson: "Well, if he can't behave I don't know whether I want him here."

> Mrs. Evans leaves; Miss Anderson continues with the math lesson.

Summary of Smaller-Class View

Having examined a number of features of Miss Anderson's classroom, what changes appear to relate to class-size effects? What possible influences may account for changes not apparent in this setting?

Certain changes have not taken place. We find little evidence, for example, of significant difference in types of activities, the physical environment, classroom routines of organization and management, or methods of evaluation. Mandated competency testing, required textbook series, and administrative priorities and policies have been suggested as possible factors contributing to limited change. Gradual changes with support might be a possibility for Miss Anderson.

Perhaps a key factor in this study, though, is Miss Anderson's perceptions of significant changes in the smaller class. For instance, she finds greater calmness in her life as a teacher, "There's more of *me* left at the end of the day." Consequently, she believes she enjoys her students more, spends a greater amount of time chatting with them privately and thus gets to know them better. In her view, a smaller number of students enables her to provide more individual help and to incorporate some of the "potentially disruptive" activities she would be hesitant to try with a larger group.

In addition to Miss Anderson's attitudinal changes, we find other differences occuring with the reduction of class size. For instance, Miss Anderson assumes a more involved role during reading instruction; new topics expand the curriculum; informal teacher–student interactions occur with greater frequency, and students wait less time for evaluation of their work. According to Miss Anderson, these changes have been feasible because of having fewer students.

5

Mrs. Hopkins' Classroom

At 8:10, another fall school day starts as Mrs. Hopkins rushes into the classroom and, in one almost continuous movement, reaches out to flip on the overhead light, shrugs off and hangs up her coat, and finds a place to set down an armload of graded papers. During the next hour she seems to be occupied constantly with morning preparations of putting up boardwork, making hurried trips throughout the school to the office and supply areas, and readying the room for a day's activities. By 8:20, early-arriving students begin to enter, usually asking for a moment of Mrs. Hopkins' attention.

Larry: "Look at my finger, Mrs. Hopkins. It got smashed in the car door."

Mrs. Hopkins: "That really looks sore. Have you done anything for it?"

Larry: "No, but I might have to go to the doctor."

Students continue to straggle in until all are present by 8:40. Myriad sounds pervade the room. The constant squeak–bang, squeak–bang of the coat-closet door opening and closing as children store their belongings for the day, and the grinding of each handle-turn of the pencil sharpener underscore childish giggles, chatter, and jostling until everyone settles down for boardwork.

Valerie hands Mrs. Hopkins a note from home, Roy needs to borrow a pencil, and the third-grade teacher comes in with a question about filling out monthly registers. These events occur while Mrs. Hopkins takes roll, collects money for pencils and erasers, glances over the day's lesson plans, sends four students to the special reading teacher, and answers student questions about the boardwork. And then the first-grade teacher enters:

May I make an announcement? Some people have lost library books; maybe you can help find them. One is *Charlie Brown's All-Stars*. Thank you.

And so the day begins, but what happens during the time spent in Mrs. Hopkins' classroom? Can we trace any of the characteristics of this setting to the effects of class size? We begin first by examining carefully the features of Mrs. Hopkins' room during the first half of the year when 20 children were on her roll. Although this may not seem to be a large class, many children had problems, and the principal kept this in mind when deciding class sizes.

MRS. HOPKINS' CLASSROOM: THE "LARGER-CLASS" VIEW

With a larger number of students, what does the room "look" like? What features seem to typify instruction? What kinds of interactions take place between teacher and students and among students? In what ways does class size appear to affect what occurs here? These questions guide our study.

The Physical Environment

Crayon-colored ghosts swaying on a clothesline in one corner quickly catch our attention when we first enter Mrs. Hopkins' second grade. On closer look, we find a remarkable similarity among these "spirits," each cut from the same pattern with accordian-folded, construction-paper strips for arms.

Glancing to one side of the room, we find a decorated bulletin board, divided into three sections, extending along one wall. At one end, identical brown turkeys count off the days of the month on the teacher-made calendar. In the center, a "Helping Hands" chart reminds everyone of classroom chores. And small, colorful rectangles cover the remaining space, each illustrating a child's response to the caption, "We are thankful for . . ." Large windows fill the wall on the other side of the room, providing a vista of pines, oaks, and maples in this rural setting.

Desks and tables occupy most of the floor space; the teacher's desk in back seems to watch over the rows of children's desks stretching toward the front. In one back corner, tiny chairs hug a round table equipped with listening station and earphones in anticipation of the day's reading class. And in the front, stacks of workbooks and dittoed worksheets on two oblong tables identify the meeting area for reading and math groups.

Further examination reveals a number of features not evident in this classroom, features that could be present in an environment for second graders. For example, nothing indicates the students' current interests—books or other material on a special topic, "discoveries" brought from home, or ongoing projects. Except for a bookcase/reading center set off in one corner, no area of the room seems to be set aside for children to work together informally.

Perhaps class size has had an effect on Mrs. Hopkins' rather formal organization of the room; having responsibility for fewer students, then, may motivate her to create the more casual environment she seems to value. In the following journal entry, Mrs. Hopkins envisions her ideal classroom.

> First I would take out most of the desks in the classroom and purchase a large rug. Many activities would take place sitting in a circle on the rug. Then I would purchase oodles of educational centers and games, which I would locate throughout the room. I would have an easel and finger-paint table set up so it could be used every day during the children's free time.

Perhaps some of these changes will occur in the smaller class. With fewer children, Mrs. Hopkins may be able to incorporate opportunities for more informal interactions implied by the "circle on the rug" comment, and to utilize some of the activities she seems to view as ideal.

Examining the physical environment provides clues, but can only hint at what occurs in the setting. In the next section, we see how the day begins for Mrs. Hopkins and her second graders before the change in class size.

The Day's Beginning

Many teachers may relate to the tasks Mrs. Hopkins confronts during the first part of the school day; it's a time seemingly created for record keeping. Roll must be taken, absences recorded, notes from home checked, supply-store money tallied; sometimes a number of other-than-daily tasks increase the list—collecting report cards, sending memos home to parents, or writing referral forms.

In order to accomplish this work, a teacher has a number of options, such as delegating responsibility for some tasks to children or an aide, completing only essential tasks in the morning and leaving others for parts of the day when time permits, or providing activities for the children not requiring the teacher's close supervision and involvement. These activities, for example, might include project work, learning centers, recreational reading, and so forth. What do we find here?

Mrs. Hopkins assigns boardwork activities for her students. As she explains, "I have so much to do in the morning, I need something quiet for them to work on." Each day an assignment similar to the following greets the children:

Name   Date

Ship   Fish   Shop   Brush   Shed

1. I have a ——— for a pet.
2. Put your bike in the ———.
3. We took a ride on a big ———.
4. I like to ——— in the city.
5. I need to ——— my hair.

In conversation, Mrs. Hopkins reveals her hope of being able to reorganize this early-morning time when she has fewer students, allowing them to be involved in more creative activities. In this setting, then, class size seems to influence the kinds of early-morning learning opportunities the teacher believes she can provide; as a result, children begin every school day with the same routine of written work. In the next section we consider how instruction typically occurs and speculate about what changes might take place in a smaller class.

Instructional Activities and Techniques

The following examples portray how Mrs. Hopkins directs reading and math lessons and manages instructional groups and children's behavior in the larger class.

Directing a Math Lesson

Twenty children scatter to different parts of the room at the start of the math period, six to the back table where Mrs. Hopkins waits impatiently and 14 to their desks.

Mrs. Hopkins frowns as she surveys the scene and raises her voice for emphasis: "*OK*, get in your seats; it's time for math. Earl, everyone turn around. Valerie, Gladys.''

Turning to the six grabbing for their math booklets and flipping pages, Mrs. Hopkins directs: "Open your booklet to the first page. Listen because I'm going over about five pages. Kirk, are you listening? On page 1, count the number in the picture and circle the number. Do the same thing on pages 2, 3, 4, 5, 6 and 7. It's all the same. Count the number in the picture and circle the number. Quiet back here now.''

Mrs. Hopkins has been with this group for less than two minutes. Moving to the 14 in front, she directs them to page 201 in their workbook. For the next eight minutes, children take turns reading directions and a couple of problems about graphs. Soon they're told, "Do the rest on your own. Raise your hand if you have a question.'' For a while, quiet descends as the children begin to work, and Mrs. Hopkins moves from desk to desk to monitor their work.

Directing a Reading Lesson

Two yellow-chalked sections of the board announce the reading work for two groups, requiring students to copy sentences and fill the right word in the blank; in the other section, students are to unscramble the listed words to make a sentence.

Glancing around the room, we find some following the directions, but we also find Nelson reading a magazine and Cynthia connecting dots and coloring a ditto. "I've finished my work,'' she explains. The 80 minute reading class has only been underway for 10 minutes.

Mrs. Hopkins sits with seven squirming children at the front table, directing them through a ditto of *ide* words with such questions as, "What's the word? What's the sound?'' A few minutes later she sends them to their seats with directions for completing an assessment test, "For pages 4–9, read the sentence and circle the picture that goes with it. Look on page 10; read that story at least two or three times. On page 11, you have five questions; circle the answer. The last page is page 12. In each box they tell you to find something. When you find it, put a circle around it.''

Confusion reigns for a few minutes as groups switch. Five children now join Mrs. Hopkins. Nelson still flips through his magazine, and Cynthia continues to color.

During the rest of the period, Mrs. Hopkins continues with reading activities. Some children take assessment tests about homographs, and others respond with short answers to the comprehension questions Mrs. Hopkins reads from the teacher's manual open in front of her.

Toward the end of the period, seven have joined Cynthia in coloring dittos, four work with Mrs. Hopkins, and five concentrate on finishing their assignments.

Managing Groups and Behavior

> One reading group works on phonics dittos and boardwork while Mrs. Hopkins and the other group read, "My Dog is a Plumber," a poem about aspiring to be what you want to be. Mrs. Hopkins asks, "What could you be when you grow up?" but before Clair can answer, Mrs. Hopkins notices three students wandering around the room. "All right, I don't want to see all these people up. Some are trying to see the board."

> The children take turns reading the poem, but soon five in the other group finish their work and whisper softly to one another or get up to explore. Again, Mrs. Hopkins notices, "If you have finished, find something, but *do not* get up every five seconds." With hardly a pause, she turns back to ask, "What does the dog do that makes you think he's a boy?"

In these examples, we can find illustrations of the kinds of lessons Mrs. Hopkins provides, the use she makes of instructional materials, and the ways she organizes groups within her classroom. In the following sections, we consider these and other features of instruction in the larger class.

Types of lessons and use of materials. Observation reveals that students in this second grade spend a major portion of their time engaged in activities involving boardwork assignments, workbook pages, and assessment testing, and Mrs. Hopkins relies on dittos for many lessons.

The kind of activity beginning the day is mirrored in lessons occurring throughout the day, in math, in reading, in spelling, and so on. When the children move out of the classroom for physical education, they experience activities remarkably similar to those in class. For the first 10 minutes, Mrs. Hopkins leads everyone in calisthenics; following this, children race to the end of the playground and back, then join a teacher-directed game. Free play, when allowed, takes the last five minutes.

Even in art lessons, we find little diversity. The typical activity, illustrated in the ghosts and "We are thankful" pictures decorating the room, requires children to follow a specific set of directions for using a limited number of materials, usually a pattern, crayons, scissors, glue, and a few items for decoration. Often a "model" is displayed to guide the children in their creative efforts.

Class size may relate to the features we find here. With a large number of students, Mrs. Hopkins may perceive a marked necessity for controlling and directing what occurs and may accomplish this by requiring the same or similar activities of everyone. Her comments seem to indicate that she values greater diversity than she implements, and class size may be one reason for the discrepancy.

In addition to class size, however, there may be other explanations for Mrs. Hopkins' instructional decisions. For instance, she believes she must follow the adopted textbook series for much of the academic program, especially in reading. In her view, Mrs. Fleming, the principal, emphasizes this subject and expects little deviation from the materials. Knowing that every teacher in the school conducts reading during the same 80 minutes of the day and that the promotion policy is based in large part on the level children reach in the reading program can subtly convey the importance of adhering closely to the established routine and program.

An examination of the reading series, however, reveals suggestions for enrichment activities designed to extend the skills and concepts introduced. Perhaps the absence of these activities relates to the number of children in the class. Classroom management, Mrs. Hopkins acknowledges, becomes difficult when the teacher has several groups to organize and watch over. Some students are difficult to control; they don't seem to "know that they're not the only ones in the class," in Mrs. Hopkins' view. Perhaps the relatively large number of students with special problems, then, reinforces her to choose the expected and quieter routine of activities. Or perhaps she lacks awareness of ways or skills necessary to incorporate other activities and still manage the classroom effectively.

Several factors, therefore, may be influencing the decisions about the types of lessons Mrs. Hopkins provides—class size, her perceptions of the principal's expectations, her desire for control, and her awareness of possible alternatives she might attempt. Perhaps with fewer students she will explore new ideas and feel less pressure for control. Certainly she hopes for change:

> I want to prepare individual learning packets for each child. The packets would contain sheets on the child's strengths and weaknesses. It would also contain activities in which the child is particularly interested. I also want to set up an independent reading program.

Organization of groups and time. According to Mrs. Hopkins, each day follows this schedule:

8:30– 9:30 boardwork, roll, money collection, bathroom break, opening exercises
9:30–10:20 math
10:20–11:40 reading
11:40–12:00 wash up
12:00–12:30 lunch
12:30– 1:00 quiet time
1:00– 1:30 spelling, art, or special work
1:30– 2:00 physical education
2:00– 2:30 story and clean up
2:30   first bus

This schedule reveals, in outline form, the allocation of time in this classroom. We can see, for example, how reading dominates, as it does throughout the school. In addition to the obvious emphasis on reading and math in the schedule, however, it appears that large portions of the day are spent washing hands, straightening the room, or resting. During quiet time, we observe children finishing their morning work or reading silently; it's not a time when children turn to instructional games, puppets, art materials, or other types of creative activities.

So the schedule, combined with observation, provides us with evidence of how the organization of time appears to influence what is and is not provided in the curriculum. Perhaps this organization has developed as an efficient way for Mrs. Hopkins to manage her large class. With fewer children in each class, and a third teacher, changes may result in how the school day is "carved up."

Mrs. Hopkins also organizes the time within her classroom. For most of the day, she teaches the class as one large group, introducing the lesson and assigning follow-up work. In spelling, for instance:

Mrs. Hopkins: "Look at number 1 at the bottom of page 36. What is picture A, Robert?"

Robert: "Black."

Mrs. Hopkins: "Yes, Spell *black.*"

Robert: "B–l–a–c–k"

Mrs. Hopkins writes this on the board, asking over her shoulder: "So how do you spell the k sound?"

Robert: "ck"

This question–response pattern occurs for each number: "What is the picture? How do you spell it? How do you spell the *k* sound?"

After each picture has been discussed, Mrs. Hopkins gives these directions: "OK, I'm going to give you paper. I want you to do what we've just gone over. Start on page 36 with number 1; do page 37 also."

Mrs. Hopkins teaches two groups in reading and math, and finds managing them to be difficult, as we've seen in the lessons previously illustrated.

I am just kind of torn between the two groups. I just wish I could give every kid the same amount of time. I really get frustrated. I can help the one kid, and over here there's five or six just about to die because I don't get over to help them.

Possibly class size has an effect on the number of groups in the room as well as the number of children. The addition of a third teacher may alter the organization of groups in this setting. Consequently, we may find Mrs. Hopkins feeling less frustrated and, perhaps, attempting new ways of organizing her instruction.

Evaluation of student work. By Friday afternoon, the designated box for completed boardwork and spelling assignments overflows with green-lined, primary-size papers. Over the weekend, Mrs. Hopkins checks through this work, dispensing comments such as, "Practice," "Be neater," or "Nice." Occasionally she draws a smile face or frown face on the papers to convey the message. On Monday, these papers are not returned but are filed in students' folders, ready to be sent home with workbooks and report cards each nine weeks or midway through the report period when progress reports go home.

Mrs. Hopkins sometimes finds time to check workbooks before or after school or as she circulates during children's time for seatwork. In her view, it's difficult to reach everyone in the available time. Data from the coded observation instrument supports this view. Children in the larger class wait for the teacher an average of 12.5 percent of the time in math and four percent in reading. They spend 25.5 percent of their time in "down time" in math and three and a half percent in reading. With fewer students, Mrs. Hopkins may find it possible to expand her ways of collecting information to make evaluations, such as keeping notes on each child, and she may find more time for discussions with students in order to help them develop skills in self-evaluation.

Summary of instructional activities and techniques. In examining lessons in this classroom, we find children spending the majority of their instructional time engaged in paper-and-pencil activities. For example, Mrs. Hopkins appears to respond to the demands of clerical tasks by assigning early-morning boardwork activities; however, this type of activity also extends throughout the day.

Small-group work in reading and math generally follows a pattern of a brief, introductory discussion followed by workbook assignments, assessment testing, or dittos. We find scant evidence of creative enrichment activities provided for the children, of the use of manipulatives or multimedia materials, or of varied approaches to the presentation or extension of concepts or skills.

How might the types of activities and materials' usage we find here relate to class size? With a larger number of students and groups to manage, perhaps Mrs. Hopkins (and other teachers) respond by planning an extensive amount of seatwork in order to create a fairly quiet setting where working with groups is more possible. Also, having more children may increase the pressure Mrs. Hopkins feels regarding their promotion; consequently, she may concentrate more instructional time on skills to be tested later than on enrichment activities. A smaller class, then, may result in changes in the kinds of activities and the use of materials.

Interactions

Teacher–student interactions. As described previously, lessons in this setting rarely include opportunities for discussion; for instance, even when small reading groups meet to talk about a story, the conversations most often focus on brief answers to the list of comprehension questions from the teacher's guide. A concern for "basic skill" development seems to override any view of the potential advantages of incorporating time for children to express and explore feelings, ideas, or reactions. Mrs. Hopkins acknowledges this as an occasional conflict: "It's hard sometimes when you want to let them talk when they seem to want to—like in reading—but you also have to get on with the lesson." "Getting on with the lesson" for Mrs. Hopkins appears to mean doing what's in the teacher's guide.

The more personal interactions between Mrs. Hopkins and her students seem to take place during the less academic times of the day, before and after school, or while getting ready for lunch. Even then, however, Mrs. Hopkins doesn't believe she can devote a great deal of her attention to nonacademic activities: "A lot of the kids seem to have a need to talk in the morning about what's going on at home, but that's just when I'm so busy trying to get the day started."

The following percentages describe categories of teacher-talk during a 20-minute math lesson, providing us with evidence of interactions in the larger class and a basis for comparison when the class size changes.

1. Gives directions—academic procedure	8%
2. Gives directions—management	5%
3. Criticizes, justifies authority, demands attention	12%
4. Other teacher-talk—academic	43%
5. Other teacher-talk—affective	0%
6. Confusion	4%
7. Silence	19%
8. Student-talk	9%

This evidence indicates the dominance of the teacher in classroom interactions. With a reduced number of clerical demands and fewer children vying for attention in a smaller class, Mrs. Hopkins may find she can incorporate more varied opportunities for interacting with her students.

Student–student interactions. As revealed in examining the physical environment and the types of lessons in Mrs. Hopkins' room, we discern few opportunities for these second graders to interact with their peers. Instruction tends to be either teacher-directed or quiet seatwork. As mentioned in the overview, these children have no recess in the morning, further limiting time for visiting with one another. Perhaps this is why the children take advantage of the time during class changes and risk Mrs. Hopkins' frequent, stern reprimand, "I'm tired of all this noise out here. You know how to behave in the hall. Now line up and *be quiet.*" In the smaller class, then, we might find changes in teacher–student interactions and in opportunities for interaction among students.

Interruptions

Interruptions throughout the school day seem to occur both within the class and from sources external to the classroom setting. For example, other adults in the school comprise one major source, as they enter the classroom on a variety of errands. Some of these interruptions may be due, in part, to the schedule. A teacher knowing recess would occur at 10:00 might wait to ask a question or discuss an idea. Without this option, teachers may visit a colleague more often. The following examples represent only a fraction of the number of interruptions occurring during several weeks of observation.

> The fourth-grade teacher comes in to ask Mrs. Hopkins to switch lunch periods with her for today. Mrs. Hopkins agrees. Seven minutes later, Miss Anderson enters, concerned about how the switch affects the afternoon schedule.

> The first-grade teacher comes in to ask if any of the children have seen a purse one of her children has lost.

> A parent aide, working in the school today, stops by to chat while Mrs. Hopkins sees that the children get ready for lunch.

In addition to interruptions from colleagues and other adults, faculty memos and bulletins constitute another major source of external interruptions. Since this school doesn't have an intercom for general announcements, often the teachers must read a memo immediately, initial it, and send it on. The following is a typical example:

> For Your Attention:

> At any time when it is necessary for you to answer the telephone, please write the message on the pink form (sample attached) which you will find on the secretary's desk.

> Sign and send on right away.

Mrs. Hopkins views interruptions as a key problem in her life as a teacher: "All the memos really get to be a problem. Some days there are so many, and they always seem to come at the busiest times—then you have to take your attention away from the group."

Interruptions arise from situations within the class, too, as we've seen in a number of classroom scenes. Most often these interruptions seem to occur when children in one group finish or have questions while Mrs. Hopkins works with another group.

Class size may be one factor contributing to the problem of interruptions. More children certainly could mean more unexpected visits from parents or more notes sent to children from the office. As previously mentioned, reducing the class size may facilitate more effective classroom management.

Summary of "Larger-Class" View

What features seem to characterize the "larger-class" view of this setting? How might they relate to class-size effects? The evidence suggests that Mrs. Hopkins has established a number of instructional routines in her second grade, possibly in response to dealing with many students and groups. For example, clerical tasks, more extensive in a larger class, demand much of her early-morning attention; consequently, she assigns boardwork each day to free her own time.

We have seen how the instructional format usually proceeds with a routine mode of presentation—introductory explanation and directions followed by quiet seatwork. Perhaps Mrs. Hopkins believes this allows for easier classroom management.

Observation indicates that children in this setting engage mostly in paper-and-pencil activities throughout the day. We find little evidence in this environment of manipulative materials, instructional games, puppets, art materials or other resources some consider appropriate for second graders. As we considered previously, Mrs. Hopkins may be making some decisions in response to dealing with a larger number of students. However, other factors (administrator expectations, mandated programs, the teacher's awareness of alternatives, and so forth) may also have an influence.

Except for hoping to develop individual learning packets, Mrs. Hopkins had little vision of possible changes when working with fewer students, "I'll just have to feel my way. I don't know what it might be like." In the next section, we examine instruction in the smaller class, focusing on what has and has not changed and possible reasons why.

MRS. HOPKINS' CLASSROOM: THE "SMALLER-CLASS" VIEW

In considering the effects of class size on instruction in Mrs. Hopkins' classroom, we again examine features characteristic of this setting as revealed in the physical environment, the day's beginning, instructional activities and techniques, and so forth. Throughout our smaller-class view, we will explore possible explanations of the changes we do and do not find.

The Physical Environment

A door covered with crimson and pink anthropomorphic Valentine hearts greets us as we approach the classroom, each heart a reflection of the others, identical in shape with glued-on eyes, nose, and mouth and accordian-folded strips for arms and legs. A metamorphosis of Halloween spirits, perhaps?

We enter the room to discover a remarkable sameness in the physical environment in spite of the fact fewer children now "live" here throughout the day. Tables still enclose the floor space in front and back with children's desks in rows and columns filling the middle of the room. The number of desks is the same as in the larger class. The only noticeable switch has been Mrs. Hopkins' desk from the back to window-side of the classroom. Glancing at the bulletin boards, we find hearts instead of turkeys marking off the days on the classroom calendar, and the "Helping Hands" chart still serves as a reminder of classroom chores. What might account for the few changes visible in this setting, especially for a teacher who envisions her ideal classroom decorated with rugs and cozy cushions instead of desks and tables?

Although Mrs. Hopkins teaches fewer students throughout the day, she still, on certain occasions, has a classroom overflowing with children. On Wednesdays, for instance, Mrs. Hopkins takes her turn for lunch duty, monitoring nearly 40 second graders who crowd into the room with their lunch trays. Similarly, she watches over the same number of children during bus duty on Thursday mornings and afternoons. These continuing responsibilities and the need for seating capacity may be reasons Mrs. Hopkins retains the same number of desks in the room.

But what about some of the changes that might be possible as a result of having fewer children during the instructional portions of the day? Although learning centers and space and materials for individual and group activities might have been more possible in the smaller class, such changes are not apparent. Mrs. Hopkins offers one explanation by indicating a lack of awareness of materials available in the school for her use:

> Last year the learning disabilities and reading resource teachers made a list of all the materials they had, but we haven't gotten any list like that this year. And then new materials come in I don't know about.

However, many teachers develop some of their own materials or use what is already available in new and creative ways. For example, teachers write contracts for students, pacing their work through textbooks, workbooks, and other materials. Apparently, Mrs. Hopkins has not explored these possibilities; perhaps she lacks the required skills or doesn't view such changes as necessary in her classroom. Perhaps, also, the routines established in the beginning of the year have patterned her behavior with these children. Consequently, the physical environment reflects few changes as a result of class size. Maybe we will find greater evidence of effects in the day's beginning and during instructional activities.

The Day's Beginning

Rode, note, scold, rose, smoke, rope and accompanying fill-in-the-blank sentences constitute today's boardwork assignment, the same as almost any day earlier in the year. Despite the class-size change, morning is still a time when Mrs. Hopkins checks roll, collects money, prepares dittos, checks materials, and readies the room for the day.

Mrs. Hopkins' response to the problem of creating time for clerical and other work, however, represents only one of several options. She could, for example, delegate a number of these tasks to students, thus increasing their involvement in and responsibility for running the classroom. For instance, many of the children could assume responsibility for collecting money for supplies and ice cream, for taking roll, for checking the condition and availability of materials, and for many of the classroom's housekeeping chores. Although it may take more time initially to teach children these tasks and to establish their sense of responsibility, this may be more possible with fewer students, and the long-term effect may be to provide Mrs. Hopkins with a greater amount of time for more student-oriented activities or for the "talking time" she says she values.

Furthermore, desiring a "quiet" time for students does not necessarily imply boardwork activities as the teacher's only choice. Mrs. Hopkins' home-room is heterogeneously grouped, yet she requires the same boardwork activities of each student. The morning could begin with students working in pairs, small groups, or at learning centers and still, if properly organized, remain a time of independent, quiet activities. In this situation, then, alternative responses to the demands of clerical tasks could reduce the number vying for Mrs. Hopkins' attention and could provide more enriching learning opportunities for her students.

Moreover, Mrs. Hopkins may be contributing to this problem of having so much to do. For instance, the boardwork activities she assigns add to the number of papers she must grade, as do the dittos she uses as supplementary work.

While a reduction in class size presumably has presented the opportunity for adopting new early-morning routines for both the children and Mrs. Hopkins, we find each day beginning in much the same fashion as before. Although Mrs. Hopkins hoped to provide more creative activities during this time, and was given many suggestions during our meetings, such activities do not appear to have been incorporated. Perhaps this teacher needs more intensive help, guidance, and support in order to facilitate change. Or perhaps she doesn't really desire change. Maybe she feels it's easier to continue the way she has in the past.

Instructional Activities and Techniques

The following scenes show how Mrs. Hopkins typically directs lessons and manages instructional groups and student behavior in the smaller class. These portrayals provide a basis for discussing the types of lessons and materials' usage, the organization of groups and time, and the evaluation of student work, they also provide a basis for comparing the findings to earlier observations in the larger class.

Directing a Math Lesson

Mrs. Hopkins passes out a ditto and says: "We're going to go over the first page together. This is something a little different. William, read this. The rest of you listen."

William reads the word problem.

Keith: "Can I get my sweater? I'm cold." After receiving an "ok" nod from Mrs. Hopkins, he walks to the closet in the back of the room, gets the sweater, and returns to his desk.

Mrs. Hopkins: "How do we find the answer to the problem William read? Jim?"

Jim: "Put down 335 and 338 and add them."

Mrs. Hopkins: "Yes, let's solve it."

After going over two more problems with the group, Mrs. Hopkins hands out a ditto and begins moving around the room, answering questions and offering help when needed.

Directing a Reading Lesson

Mrs. Hopkins readies the room for reading, setting up the listening station in the back, and stacking workbooks and dittos on the front table, where five children wait restlessly. Seven boys rush through the door, laughing and shoving as they enter.

Mrs. Hopkins: "OK, you all sit up here in the desks, and you three go over to the listening station." She hands a ditto to the ones doing seatwork.

Mrs. Hopkins sits down at the front table. Just as she begins, "Today we want to review these two sounds," Randolph, obviously confused, shouts from the listening station, "Mrs. Hopkins, they went on to number two."

Clarence, too, calls out: "It's too loud, Mrs. Hopkins."

Mrs. Hopkins gets up, goes to the back of the room, checks the volume setting on the tape recorder, makes sure everyone's on the right page, and returns to her reading group.

Again she starts, but a soft knock on the door draws her attention and, also, she notices Cynthia leaving her desk to wander the room. On her way to see who's at the door, Mrs. Hopkins reminds Cynthia, "There's too much going on for you to be up walking around." During the next minute, Mrs. Hopkins reads and responds to a memo and, once more, returns to the by-now-noisy reading group, this time with a command, "All right. I'm not going to have so much noise in here. Ronald, turn back around."

The group at the listening station finishes, and an insistent Randolph yells, "Teacher, we're at the end of the tape."

Mrs. Hopkins, with an audible sigh, leaves the group at the front to go turn over the tape. Glancing over her shoulder, she watches three boys talking instead of working and says: "Roy, Ronald, and Sidney, no one can work here while you're talking."

Back with her reading group, Mrs. Hopkins continues once again, "Let's go over these *fr* words."

Managing Groups and Student Behavior

Even teaching only one group in the room during math doesn't eliminate the activity of monitoring behavior. While giving individual help, Mrs. Hopkins scans the room often, stopping to say: "Carl, get back in your desk. Louis, are you finished? Allen, if you're going to help Clarence, you'll have to be quieter. *All right*. I don't appreciate all this noise. I can't believe how rude some of you all are."

Mrs. Hopkins (to one reading group): ''OK, today we want to talk about words with these sounds, *ad* and *dr*. Who can tell us an *ad* word?''

Kirk (in another group doing boardwork) walks up to Mrs. Hopkins: ''Mrs. Hopkins, what's that third word?''Mrs. Hopkins turns around, glances at the board, reads the word, and turns back to the group.

Franklin moves up to the reading group next, asking, ''Mrs. Hopkins, can I sharpen my pencil?''

Mrs. Hopkins steps, checks the pencil point, and responds: ''You have other pencils there; use one of those.''

Kirk returns, needing help with another word; soon he's joined by two classmates who need help, too, and by Nelson who wants permission to leave for the restroom.

Mrs. Hopkins tries to ignore them: ''Shh, I want to hear Cynthia read this sentence.''

Types of lessons and use of materials.   These scenes indicate few changes in the types of lessons provided, at least in reading and math. Mrs. Hopkins follows, almost verbatim at times, the wording in the teacher's guide open in front of her. Although she teaches fewer students, Mrs. Hopkins continues to rely on the adopted textbook series or program, utilizing available supplementary workbooks, dittos, and assessment tests; she appears to use these materials in much the same manner as before.

Again we might consider the activities not apparent in Mrs. Hopkins' teaching. We don't observe, for example, much variety in her preparations; textbooks, dittos, and written assignments predominate. We see no evidence of planning for learning centers, incorporating ongoing classroom projects, setting up special-interest areas, or developing the individualized learning packets she mentioned earlier.

What reasons might account for what we *don't* see in this setting? Mrs. Hopkins may lack certain knowledge and skills she needs to do these things, although some were suggested to her. She had limited opportunities for visiting other teachers to see alternatives, a problem in a small, rather isolated school. Furthermore, Mrs. Hopkins believes she is required to follow the adopted textbook series for reading and math. When asked about choices for students who may need an instructional style different from these stories, she responds, ''I could only use something else in addition to the series, not instead of.'' Moreover, she believes the principal wants teachers to follow closely the instructional format of the series, utilizing accompanying dittos and assessment tests. Remembering the promotion policy, we can understand how such influences may affect Mrs. Hopkins' choices. However, Mrs. Hopkins acknowledges little administrative control over aspects of her curriculum other than reading or math. Perhaps, then, her limited choices also stem from a lack of creative ideas of her own and little awareness of resources she might use for new ideas. We have some indication of this possibility when we observe how Mrs. Hopkins uses the Peabody Language Development Kit, one of the additions to the curriculum made possible by having a third second-grade teacher.

After reading the story, "The Boy and the North Wind," Mrs. Hopkins asks the following short-answer questions:

> Why did the boy go to the North wind?
> What happened to the flour?
> What did the North wind give the boy?
> What happened to the cloth?
> What happened when he got home?

Children take turns answering, reminded frequently by Mrs. Hopkins, "Raise your hand if you know the answer; we can't get anything done if you keep talking." Contrast how Mrs. Hopkins implemented this lesson with the suggested directions from the kit:

> Ask the children to recall the story of "The Boy and the North Wind." Choose different children to play the different parts and let them dramatize the story. Repeat this activity with different children, if time permits and interest is sustained.

Certainly the opportunity exists for a creative approach to developing children's verbal facility—only 11 children are involved in the lesson; the manual suggests an activity, and this is an area of the curriculum not as susceptible to administrative control. Perhaps not knowing how to envision and direct this more creative lesson causes Mrs. Hopkins to rely on the format of the more structured lessons she's familiar with. Also, if she's concerned about control, she may view structured lessons as easier to control than more creative lessons.

Organization of groups and time. Organizational changes in scheduling and grouping can be attributed to having fewer students in each class and to the addition of the third teacher. For instance, new lessons expand the curriculum, replacing the previous rest time. Also, Mrs. Hopkins has responsibility for only one math group now instead of the two taught earlier in the year.

Certain changes, however, have not occurred. The morning still does not include any time scheduled for recess, and the time allotment established for math and reading remains as before. Administrative policies appear to influence these areas greatly.

Within Mrs. Hopkins' classroom, therefore, we find a smaller number of groups as well as fewer students in the setting. Has this affected instruction?

Mrs. Hopkins teaches the highest math group of 12 students and comments early in March, "This group is almost finished with the book, but I'm not allowed to start them on the third-grade book."

With a smaller number of students, we might think finishing the text would afford Mrs. Hopkins the opportunity for organizing a number of subgroups and developing individual and small-group activities. We recall her earlier hope of developing individual packets when she had responsibility for fewer children. Furthermore, we made available to her a boxful of supplementary materials and suggested activities appropriate for her students. Instead of incorporating new materials and approaches, Mrs. Hopkins relied on boardwork and dittos to extend instruction from the text. She might also have changed to another area of study. For example, the second-grade book constitutes, for this school, second-grade mathematics. Once finished with that content, maybe they could have turned to social studies or library skills.

We find similar events occurring in reading class. Although the possibility would seem to exist for regrouping and providing a varied routine of activities, we find little evidence of such changes.

Consequently, class size, in this instance, appears to affect broad organizational decisions such as "How can we divide the four reading groups among three teachers?" or "Who will teach the high math group?" Within Mrs. Hopkins' classrooms, though, class size appears to have little effect on the organization of groups. We observe mostly large-group instruction with few opportunities throughout the day for students to work within other organizational patterns—alone, in pairs, or in small groups.

Evaluation of student work. According to Mrs. Hopkins, "A smaller class gives the teacher more time to deal with individuals and their individual needs." The evidence indicates Mrs. Hopkins does spend more time with each student as she circulates and checks students' progress. In the smaller class, for instance, students' percentages of "wait" and "down time" reduce to zero for reading. A zero percentage is also recorded for "down time" in math, although "wait time" rises slightly from 12.5 to 14 percent. Also, the percentage of student contact with the teacher increases from zero to three percent in math and five to 11 percent in reading. These findings support Mrs. Hopkins' perception of having more opportunities to evaluate student work and target in on potential problems. Occasionally she discovers a pattern of difficulty and responds swiftly with an additional explanation.

Evaluative comments written on student work tend to be the same as those used previously, checkmarks and smile or frown faces sometimes accompanied with a note of "Do Over," "Nice," or "Messy." And, Mrs. Hopkins doesn't appear to incorporate new evaluation techniques in the smaller class—techniques such as conferences with students in order to encourage self-evaluating, or keeping narrative accounts of students' progress in areas other than academics, such as socialization skills.

Summary of instructional activities and techniques. Class size appears to affect certain features of instruction in this second grade. For instance, with fewer students Mrs. Hopkins is able to evaluate students' work more carefully, assessing problems and responding with further explanation and clarification. Furthermore, in the smaller class, she has responsibility for only one math group, providing greater opportunity for concentration on meeting their instructional needs. Mrs. Hopkins reorganizes the extreme amount of time previously spent resting and cleaning up by expanding the curriculum with language arts activities.

In examining the typical kinds of activities, we find most remain similar to those in the larger class. Mrs. Hopkins continues to engage students with a brief introduction and directions rather than appealing to student interests or providing connections with children's out-of-school experiences. Paper-and-pencil activities dominate the curriculum, most often involving workbooks, textbook, and dittoed materials. In addition to class size, effects on the types of instructional activities and techniques characteristic of this setting seem to result from sources such as administrative policies, the teacher's interpretation of those policies, and the teacher's awareness of appropriate instructional activities and ways of implementing them.

Interactions

Teacher–student interactions. According to Mrs. Hopkins, "One of the *biggest* problems for me is having to deal with so much that's happening at the same time." Even with fewer children in the room, the press of time and various demands, it seems, contributes to conflicts as Mrs. Hopkins tries to listen to the children but also tries to maintain the flow of a lesson or the day's events. So Jim's story about a favorite pet is interrupted in reading class by directions for the phonics ditto, and Valerie's concern about her sore arm occupies only a moment of Mrs. Hopkins' attention before she turns to direct the other homeroom students, "OK, let's settle down and get to work now."

In examining percentages of teacher-talk, however, during another 20-minute math lesson, we find some changes in the small class.

	Smaller Class	Larger Class
1. Gives directions—academic procedure	2%	(8%)
2. Gives directions—management	12%	(5%)
3. Criticizes, justifies authority, demands attention	23%	(12%)
4. Other teacher-talk—academic	9%	(43%)
5. Other teacher-talk—affective	0%	(0%)
6. Confusion	10%	(4%)
7. Silence	21%	(19%)
8. Student-talk	23%	(9%)

Perhaps the most apparent change is reflected in the reduction of "teacher-talk—academic" and the increase in student-talk. This evidence suggests that having fewer students and only one group has provided greater opportunity for students to interact with the teacher.

Furthermore, for reading class, data from the coded observation instrument indicates that the percentage of group time during which a child has an individual turn to respond increases from three and a half percent to 17 percent in the smaller class. These findings point out the influence class size can have on opportunities for teacher–student interactions.

Student–student interactions. With few changes in instructional activities, we also find few changes in opportunities for students to interact with one another. During most of their instructional time, they work in teacher-directed groups or alone on seatwork. According to Mrs. Hopkins, "Some children tend to take advantage of the situation when given enrichment activities."

We still observe children inventing errands in order to "visit" a friend in the room; however, with fewer children, we discover fewer occurrences of this type. Observation data indicates children remain academically engaged 82 percent of the time in math (an increase of over 30 percent) and 62 percent of the time in reading (a 14 percent increase). Some might hope, though, for that increased engagement also to include time for the children to develop socialization skills through interacting with their peers.

Interruptions

Much of what occurs in the course of Mrs. Hopkins' day at school involves unexpected events originating from a variety of sources. Certainly, some of these events are unavoidable; this feature of the school setting simply reflects a characteristic of life in general, the inability to control or foresee all possibilities.

So, when Jerome leans out of his desk and gets quite sick during a language arts lesson, Mrs. Hopkins, although unprepared, responds almost instinctively. Picking Jerome up and rushing him from the room, she sends Della for the custodian and directs the rest of the class, "You all stay quiet now." And, when a sudden snowfall causes early school dismissal, Mrs. Hopkins stops the lesson, allowing the children to watch out the window, "oohing" and "aahing" as the snow gets deeper.

In other instances, however, Mrs. Hopkins believes administrative policies create some of the unforeseen problems she contends with. As we see in the following scene, the principal's concern for contact between school and students' homes, for instance, permits an unscheduled parent–teacher conference during class time. This visit results in the secretary, the principal, and the parent entering the classroom and distracting children's attention from their work.

Mrs. Hopkins sits with her reading group at the front table. The school secretary enters to ask a question. During the two-minute conversation, Kirk and Samuel start giggling and pushing their books across the table; Nelson tips his chair far back against the blackboard.

Turning back to the group, Mrs. Hopkins says sternly: "OK, you all settle down. Nelson, one day you'll move back like that and fall and hit your head."

Eight minutes later a parent comes to the door, then walks away. The secretary re-enters. Mrs. Hopkins responds then turns back to the group. "Everyone should be following along."

> Two minutes later the visitor returns and again walks away. Soon the principal steps through the doorway, glances around, and leaves. Mrs. Hopkins hasn't seen her, but Franklin has: "Hey, Mrs. Hopkins, Mrs. Fleming just came in."
>
> Mrs. Hopkins: "I wish you all would be quiet and pay attention."
>
> Ten minutes later the parent returns, expecting a conference. Mrs. Hopkins leaves; the class gets noisier until an aide walks in to watch them.

Class size, then, appears to have little effect on these external influences on instruction. As we've seen in other lessons, though, Mrs. Hopkins continues to contend with a great number of in-class interruptions in the smaller class, stopping to answer questions, to check on necessary pencil sharpening, and to turn over cassette tapes. We seem to have evidence here of how classroom management, regardless of class size, also relates to the existence of in-class interruptions. These occur most often when one group finishes an assignment before Mrs. Hopkins finishes working with another group. With few options within their control and with few supplementary activities available in the room, many of the students interrupt with questions. If these children had interesting supplementary activities to turn to when finished with an assignment and understood their responsibilities, fewer interruptions might take place. Furthermore, such classroom management limits opportunities for children to develop a sense of responsibility and to practice effective decision-making skills, thus limiting what they can learn in the classroom setting. Developing these skills would seem to be more possible with fewer students. Perhaps Mrs. Hopkins doesn't know how to make such changes or, perhaps, she does not believe these changes are necessary or even appropriate.

Summary

In spite of reduced class size, certain changes have not occurred. For example, Mrs. Hopkins' instructional strategies and classroom management techniques remain similar to those utilized with the larger class. A number of factors have been suggested as possible explanations for changes not apparent in this setting: administrative policies and expectations, the teacher's interpretation of those policies and expectations, and the teacher's knowledge of and ability to implement appropriate changes.

Nevertheless, we find a number of changes in Mrs. Hopkins' room, apparently attributable to class-size effects. With fewer students and a third teacher, additional subjects expand the curriculum, providing a greater range of learning opportunities and a better utilization of time. Also, in the smaller class, Mrs. Hopkins is able to evaluate students' progress more carefully, and students have more time to interact with her. The evidence also indicates students remain academically engaged for a greater percentage of instructional time, thus enabling them to have increased access to the curriculum.

6

Mr. Jameson's Classroom

Until the December holidays, Mr. Jameson's classroom had been a bookroom. After class begins in the converted bookroom, the expelled books lean against one another, neglected in sagging cartons in the hall immediately outside his room.

Some evidence remains, though, of the room's former status. Painted wooden bookcases line parts of two walls; two small blackboards and a small bulletin board face each other on two walls, and large windows consume another entire wall, admitting sunlight on occasion and permitting a view of tree-tops behind the playground. When the sunlight is too bright, Mr. Jameson lowers the shades, casting a yellowish hue over all. The lack of a classroom clock to tick off the minutes of the day also attests to the former status of the room. It is about one-third the size of other classrooms in this building. We see no corners where students might work alone or spend a quiet moment with a book or a thought; furniture and children crowd into the small room. Mr. Jameson, unhappy with the provided one-piece, slant-topped desks, has raided the library of 13 small tables and chairs. Because the tables have flat tops, they can be clustered together and moved around to form work areas of various sizes. Some equipment from the erstwhile bookroom—a few old, tattered books, seven microscopes and assorted slides, and two stethoscopes—has escaped from the hall and now rests on nearby shelves. The tables huddle together; the sun streams in through unshaded windows.

What happens in this bookroom-turned-classroom? Can we trace some happenings to having only 13 students? Because Mr. Jameson is not a native of the area and is not as familiar with the school and its regulations, is he able to try things that do not occur to Miss Anderson and Mrs. Hopkins? In this chapter, let us consider Mr. Jameson's class through a typical day, subject by subject. Between January and school's end in early June, several changes occur as Mr. Jameson becomes familiar with the new setting and having only 13 students. These changes will be discussed subject by subject, and Mr. Jameson's reflections about the influence of class size will be reported. Through the chapter, attention will also be paid to his experiences as a newcomer to the area. Perhaps as an outsider, he conceives of schooling differently and sees potential changes not considered by the principal and other second-grade teachers, who have lived in the area for virtually their entire lives.

THE DAILY FARE

Homeroom

Between 8:35 and 9:30, children remain in their homerooms while teachers attend to details necessary for the running of the day, such as taking roll and lunch count while students work on spelling, phonics, boardwork, and other language lessons. Throughout the year, all use the second-grade spelling book, *Basic Goals in Spelling* (McGraw-Hill, 1975), and in January all work on the same page. By February and March, Mr. Jameson assigns different lessons to certain children. On one day in March, for instance, nine children put the 28 words from a review lesson into alphabetical order, three are on a different page, and another child is on yet a third. Mr. Jameson lets the one-page-a-day fare suffice for roughly two-thirds of the group. In this way, he permits more able learners to advance rapidly through the system-required text, but maintains most of the children in one instructional group. This form of individualization can be thought of as pacing. In other words, all students do the same work in the same way, but may have it assigned to them at different times. In this class, all children study the same words, even if they already know how to spell them and already know the spelling rules included in a week's lessons.

We might wonder whether other ways exist of structuring spelling lessons to provide for differences among students, taking into account what they already know and their learning styles. The textbook is the only instructional material available for Mr. Jameson's use, so this restricts his options significantly. Additionally, Mr. Jameson uses the time when children work on spelling to do the chores common to many elementary school teachers—checking on absences, counting people who want to buy lunch, and so on. Having students engaged in a task that is not confusing, almost routine, may facilitate his carrying out such chores. Again, though, we might wonder whether students could undertake some of these chores, or if the chores could be attended to in ways that might permit more educative activities. For example, children could check their names as they enter the room in the morning and note their responses to matters such as whether they want to buy lunch or potato chips. Or one student could check absences while another checked lunch count. This would free Mr. Jameson to deal with instructional matters. He believes the chores consume less time because of having only 13 students in his classroom. At any rate, during this time in the morning, Mr. Jameson monitors children working on assignments while he performs the many necessary managerial and clerical tasks required of him. He quickly finishes taking roll, collecting potato-chip money, and filling out a form pertaining to reading levels, then circulates, smilingly asking George, "How can you tell which of these "G" words to write first?" Or, assisting Clarence, who needs help:

Clarence: "What's this a picture of, Mr. Jameson?"

Mr. Jameson: (Looking at a picture of a big-city suspension bridge) "Well, it doesn't look like what you'd see out here, but it goes over a river."

Clarence: "Oh, I know. It's a bridge. I thought it was a tent!"

At times, then, Mr. Jameson is accessible to help students, and he circulates to spot difficulties. While he has a friendly demeanor, he is also firm. "Sit down," or "Let's get started," can be heard on almost any morning. A gentle buzz of discussion about assignments or last night's television shows forms a backdrop to the work. "Do you like pizza?" asks Randolph to his neighbor, while Mattie quietly and laboriously reads, "Write these words in ABC order."

By 9:00, finished with clerical tasks, Mr. Jameson walks around to check pages individually with students. Sometimes Mr. Jameson and a student correct an answer together, and on other occasions a child corrects answers after meeting with Mr. Jameson. At 9:05, the venture is interrupted when they line up for the centrally scheduled second-grade bathroom break; they return by 9:15, on most days. In conversation, Mr. Jameson points out the influence of class size on his individual work with students:

> Well, obviously I can help everyone sooner after they finish something. With only thirteen students, I have time to reteach some things to those who need it, and I can check everyone's work right after they do it. That's great.

By 9:15, many children have completed their assignments. One day in March, for example, 10 of 13 are finished by 9:15, and on another day in April, nine have their work completed. After getting out a book, they wander through its pages, exclaiming softly about a riddle or a picture. Or plugging stethoscopes into their ears, they listen to their hearts. Others work with number-fact flash cards. Some look through microscopes. As more finish, the noise level seems to increase. In January Mr. Jameson reports they have some difficulty knowing what to do when they finish. Perhaps this is due to the nature of their former classrooms, where more boardwork was assigned than they could possibly complete, so they had rare opportunities to decide about leftover time. By March, however, they are able to choose more easily, and Mr. Jameson adds a few items to the shelves such as the Walt Disney readers, bought for his daughter. Many children have found a favorite thing to do. Emmet and Randolph usually enjoy looking at microscope slides, and Mattie and Evelyn read Walt Disney riddles to one another or show each other flash cards.

Some of us might believe that it is important for students to have the opportunity to learn how to make choices and to pursue some matters of interest to them. Yet, how might Mr. Jameson's provision of free-time activities have been improved? For one, he might have helped students with the activities just as he did with their assigned work. In this way, students might perceive their selected activities to be important, worthwhile learning activities, on the same level with spelling. Second, discussions about activities such as what was seen through the microscope or proper uses of flash cards may have enhanced their value as a learning experience.

As we have seen in the other second-grade classrooms, the problem of what students should do when they finish work is handled quite differently. Virtually no one finishes all the work in the other two rooms, so no one can choose. Mr. Jameson's notion of helping children make choices and the need for pursuing their own interests presents some difficulties for three reasons. For one, children are not used to this because of their previous experiences where their time and tasks were managed for them. They haven't learned how to choose or control themselves with freer activities. Second, materials are limited. Many of the materials are old, but interesting, and others Mr. Jameson has purchased. Finally, the size of the room limits the options. A biology corner cannot be constructed, nor can a large collection of local rocks and books about them be started. Nothing noise-producing or space-consuming can be considered. Yet having only 13 students may have eased problems of overseeing the activities.

At 9:25, with spelling usually finished, checked and corrected, students put their materials away and line up to go to their homogeneously grouped mathematics classes. Mr. Jameson has the 13 in the lowest group, and Mrs. Burkett, an aide, works with four of them for part of the period.

Mathematics

In January, children tumble into the room somewhat noisily and amble slowly to seats; a few children seem to be testing Mr. Jameson's authority, as often happens when a new teacher enters the scene. "Sit down in a chair," he commands firmly, but quietly. Once in a while a child is banished to the hall for part of the period because in Mr. Jameson's view, "he wasn't doing *anyone* any good. He was bothering others and interfering with their learning, but also he wasn't learning anything himself." After 10 to 15 minutes in the hall, occasionally resulting in an assigned sentence to write 15–20 times, "be quiet in math class," the miscreant returns. As he gets to know children, Mr. Jameson separates some, the combination of whom leads to difficulties, but the smallness of the room limits this somewhat. After two weeks pass, children generally enter the room more quietly, and Mr. Jameson gets lessons underway more quickly, with less testing of authority. He believes this period of testing authority has been easier and shorter with a smaller class.

In mathematics, Mr. Jameson generally holds lessons at one of the small blackboards with the whole group. Not referring to the teacher's guide, he puts problems on the board for the group to discuss. Little theory of mathematics is discussed; rather, the class focuses on how to do problems. Following this, children generally work on a ditto or a workbook page, practicing what has been taught that day.

Like other classes, mathematics is not immune to interruption. One morning in March, for instance, a dental hygiene program arrives, unannounced and unanticipated at Mr. Jameson's door at 9:30, the beginning of mathematics class. Mr. Jameson announces, "If you get this, come on up. If you don't, sit down." A few children walk up and gargle with the fluoride treatment, spit back into their paper cups, wipe their mouths, and return to their seats with a minumum of confusion.

By 9:35, everyone has finished, and Mr. Jameson says in a businesslike way,

> Everybody, let's go to the back table. Close your books, we won't need them for a while. This morning, people, we're going to start some story problems. A story problem . . .

Mrs. Burkett, the aide, enters the room with Randolph, who is in a different mathematics class. She announces in a disgusted tone, "Randolph is coming back for his book. He *forgot* it!" Mr. Jameson and the class glance up for a brief moment at the intrusion. Randolph enters somewhat guiltily, silently retrieves the book, then exits. Patiently, Mr. Jameson continues,

> A story problem is just that—a story with a problem in it. What we have to do is take the words and turn them into numbers. Here's one:

On the board, Mr. Jameson prints:

> Sue has a dog. It had five puppies. How many dogs does she have now?

They continue together.

> Mr. Jameson: "How many dogs did she have at first?"
>
> Franklin: "One."
>
> Mr. Jameson: "How many puppies did it have?"
>
> Emmet: "Five."
>
> Mr. Jameson: "What are you going to do, add or subtract?"
>
> Ronald: "Add."
>
> Mr. Jameson: "The problems are easy, but figuring out how to do them is hard. Here are some more."

And he writes on the board:

> Emmet had two candies. He gave one to Clifford. How many does he have now?

Mrs. Burkett enters the room again, and Mr. Jameson sends four children with her for more individual attention, an everyday occurrence. For most of mathematics, then, only nine children are in Mr. Jameson's class. As Mrs. Burkett enters, attention is diverted momentarily, and then the pattern of locating the numbers in the problem and deciding whether to add or subtract continues, although reasons are not elicited for the choice of process to be used. Other problems follow:

There were 10 children in Mrs. Hopkins' room. Four went to Mrs. Wilson's room. How many were left?

There were six boys in class. Two were sleeping. How many were awake?

Mr. Jameson has concocted these last two problems himself; perhaps Mrs. Burkett's interruption has led to his inventing the problem about children going to Mrs. Wilson's room. After the children successfully solve them, he directs them to write story problems of their own on small papers he's cut. Later, they are to read their problems aloud, and the rest of the class will solve them, they are told. At 9:45, they begin writing story problems, some needing help with spelling. Once, Mr. Jameson approaches Clifford, holds his hand in a friendly way, and warns him in hushed tones, "Clifford, you have got to remember to work quietly."

Ten minutes later, Mr. Jameson says, "Okay, let's read them so other people can work on them. Kirk reads, "There were six boys and six babies. How many in all?" Cynthia goes to the board and writes, "$6 + 6 = 12$."

Emmet reads, "My mom had six dogs. Two went away. How many are left?" Ronald writes on the board, "$6 - 2 = 4$."

Franklin reads, "It is three boys in Mr. Jameson room." "Franklin," Mr. Jameson says, "we can make a problem out of that. Who can help Franklin, here?" Ronald says, "and three boys in Mrs. Hopkins' room. How many in all?" On the board Sarah Ann writes, "$3 + 3 = 6$."

Mike reads, "My dad had six trucks. He drove five away. How many are left?" Mattie writes, "$6 - 5 = 1$."

Within 10 minutes, each has a turn reading a problem and writing its solution. Mr. Jameson asks them to turn to page 93 in their books. "Emmet, would you tell us all about number one?" he asks.

Emmet reads the problem, all agree they know how to do it, and Mr. Jameson says, "Tonight, if you're not up to page 92, I want you to do it tonight." He also passes out a ditto, with story problems on it, that accompanies the math series. Until 10:15, the children work quickly on the 18 problems. A low hum pervades the room as they read quietly. Mr. Jameson circulates, helping them read certain words. Children read, count on their fingers and write answers busily.

This lesson has several characteristics in common with most mathematics lessons in Mr. Jameson's room. As on most days, he is interrupted three times from the outside. Interruptions during mathematics class usually occur between two and five times. In a classroom with fewer children, a teacher might have fewer such interruptions, merely because of fewer children to contact regarding forgotten items, special events, and so on. And the interruptions, such as the dental hygiene program, may be of shorter duration due to the involvement of fewer children in a smaller class than in a larger class.

The lesson itself has several important qualities. For example, Mr. Jameson talks informally about story problems on this day, as he had about telling time and two-place addition on other days. He interweaves examples from the children's experience when possible, in this case constructing story problems about Mrs. Hopkins' class and boys falling asleep in class. This quality and his sense of humor may render the examples more relevant and interesting. On other days, he asks questions such as,

> When do we get ready for lunch? What does the clock look like then?
>
> If your mom says to be home at 5:30, what does the clock look like?

Some examples are personal, rather than directed at the entire class, such as the story problem about candy involving Emmet and Clifford. With fewer children in the class, a teacher might be able to use everyone's name in an example more frequently than with a larger class.

Another quality typical of most lessons is Mr. Jameson's involving individuals in the lesson in several ways: they answer questions, read problems and respond to them, and work out problems on the board. Because it is a smaller class, in 10 minutes everyone has a turn reading at least one story problem to the class and working someone else's on the board. All but one child has another turn of some sort. Having turns involves children in a lesson, perhaps keeping students' engagement high, and it also permits the teacher the opportunity of diagnosing a difficulty a child is having. For example, Mattie does not understand two-place addition with regrouping on the day it is first introduced. At the board she writes:

$$\begin{array}{r} 32 \\ +29 \\ \hline 511 \end{array}$$

Mr. Jameson can see her error quickly during the instructional part of the lesson, diagnose reasons for the error, and reteach the process to Mattie before she begins her seatwork. Not only can he see each child's performance in two-place addition with regrouping, but he also has time to reteach when necessary. With more children in the classroom, it may not be possible to do this, nor might all children receive turns.

The number of children may influence this class in another way. Early in his experience in this school, Mr. Jameson had authority contests with a few children in mathematics class. Apparently the contest is over for the most part by mid-January (in just two weeks), allowing him to display his sense of humor and his informal way of talking with children. Having fewer children in the room may contribute to the ease of control over what transpires in the room, and may shorten the time of the initial contest. As Mr. Jameson wrote in his journal about the smaller class,

> I'm more relaxed. It's easier to talk with kids on a very informal basis. I may have my feet up on a chair, and we're all working, but it is informal. It's difficult to run a class on such a basis if it's larger. I can see what sorts of problems—personal and behavioral problems—kids are having and I can really talk to them about those

problems or try to head them off before they happen. You can see, with just 10 or 13 in a room, when a kid is going to have a problem, and you have time to help him.

It is not impossible to do this in a class with more students, although Mr. Jameson believed it to be more difficult with more students. This informal control permits Mr. Jameson to begin lessons quickly and to continue talking about instructional matters rather than about behavior. The informal style, his sense of ease with the children and the sense that he is in charge, but not in a heavy-handed authoritarian fashion, sets a tone in the room. This atmosphere permits him to teach more because he does not have to use disciplinary tactics frequently. In his view, these factors may be partly due to his having fewer students.

Another characteristic of this lesson is Mr. Jameson's dwelling upon the practical matter of how to get the answer to a problem rather than emphasizing theory or reasons for using particular mathematical processes. For example, when he asks whether to add or subtract in specific problems, children frequently say in a querying voice, "Add?" and then read his face and either change the answer or remain with the first one. They do not appear to understand conditions or clues in a problem leading to decide whether to add or to subtract. Indeed, the most frequent errors on the assignments are due to the choice of the wrong process. The second most frequent errors are due to inaccuracy with number facts. With only nine students in his class, at times, it seems that Mr. Jameson might be able to discuss matters such as reasons for adding or subtracting and develop some notions about the structure and theory of mathematics.

Mathematics, then, usually takes the form of a discussion about problems, frequently exemplified by events children might encounter. How to get answers is the focus of lessons rather than reasons for manipulating numbers in particular ways. Mr. Jameson uses one presentation style virtually exclusively. We might wonder about the children whose learning style does not correspond to this instructional style. Why does he not use manipulative objects to help students learn what subtraction or addition means? Why does he teach so little theory, turning instead to how to get an answer? Perhaps he believes it is more important to learn how to get the answer than it is to understand various properties and laws or the structure of mathematics.

At 10:25, Mr. Jameson says, "Okay, people, let's put things away and get ready to go to reading."

Reading

Children spill from their orderly line in the hall into the room, chatting quietly with friends. By mid-January, all know where to sit. One group, working below grade level, sits by the windows and blackboard; another working at grade level is near the middle of the room. In late March, Mr. Jameson forms a third group comprised of two, and later three students doing well in their below grade-level text, workbook, and assessment tests accompanying the series. The move is partly motivated by Mr. Jameson's realization that unless the children complete the book in which they are working, they will not move to third grade, according to a school-system policy, as discussed in Chapter 3.

As in mathematics, several children leave the room to work with a specialist part way through the period. At the beginning of the period, Mr. Jameson has 12 children in three groups, but after 45 minutes, seven go to see Mrs. Wilson, the reading specialist, leaving only five children in the *Tapestry* group in the room. On Fridays, however, Mrs. Wilson tests children and completes reports rather than meeting with groups, so Mr. Jameson meets with all 12 for the entire period.

At the beginning of reading class one day in April, Mr. Jameson passed out two assessment tests accompanying *Tapestry* to five children. Jim, Mike, Adeline, Evelyn, and Clara put words into alphabetical order, as directed on the test. Meanwhile, Mr. Jameson erases the mathematics work, then lists several questions on the board for the *Cloverleaf* group. While he does, Mattie works on a mathematics page and Emmet reads the names of books in the series, listed in the teacher's guide, open on the table in front of him. He and Gina talk quietly:

Emmet: "My cousin's in *this* book" (pointing to *Keystone*).

Gina: "Good, that means he's going to pass."

Emmet, Gina, and Robert, the three in the group who recently have been moved to a higher book in hopes of passing second grade, leaf through their book or workbook, waiting for Mr. Jameson to return to them from his work with the *Cloverleaf* group. Mr. Jameson cannot put questions or work on the board for them to do, as board space is severely limited and needed for the preceding mathematics lesson. But with only three in the group, might he write them a note with directions on it? Could he give them assessment tests?

Mr. Jameson finishes writing the questions for *Cloverleaf*:

1. What kind of street would "a very doggie" street be?
2. Why was the noise on Henry's street so terrible?
3. Why didn't Henry want Miss Miller to ask him about Alfred?
4. Can you think of any dogs you would not want to walk by? Tell about it.

"Now listen up," he says, "Okay, *Cloverleaf*." The *Cloverleaf* group sits down as he whispers to Gina that he'll work with her in a little while. Mr. Jameson reads the questions aloud that appear on the board to be answered after reading the story. Sarah Ann passes out light green, primary lined-paper, and the children began to read the story quietly.

Mr. Jameson gives Emmet, Robert, and Gina two assessment tests to complete. The *Tapestry* group, finished with their assessment tests, begins to talk among themselves and Mr. Jameson says, "Quiet!" as he begins writing *Tap-*

estry's work on the board. Today, as the board instructs, *Tapestry* people are to:

Do workbook, 55–56
Read 153–165
Write a sentence using each of these words:
    annoy   loyal
    moist   warmth

The words to be used in sentences were discussed yesterday, and children may do tasks listed on the board in any order they choose. The lack of sufficient space on the blackboard appears to interfere with Mr. Jameson's spending time instructing groups. Again, he might have considered other ways to assign the group its tasks.

As he finishes putting up the directions, Emmet and Robert complete their assessment tests and begin building with small blocks; they continue as Mr. Jameson helps the *Cloverleaf* group understand what might be meant by "a very doggie street." They share some stories about doggie places and difficulties they've had with dogs.

Quickly, Mr. Jameson moves back to work with Emmet, Robert, and Gina. Adelina, absent yesterday, is working on the *Tapestry* boardwork immediately behind Mr. Jameson. She points to the word "annoy." He reads it to her, and she responds, "I know what it say, but what do it mean?" Mr. Jameson says, "We worked on it yesterday. If you don't know, I'll be over there in a minute. Do the best you can till then." Perhaps another student could be helping Adelina. However, she may be so accustomed to Miss Anderson's and Mrs. Hopkins' rules about not talking that she would not consider asking a classmate for assistance. Adelina returns to her seat and goes on with other work.

As Jim approaches Mr. Jameson, he says "No, I'm working with this group." Mr. Jameson later explains that he is trying to get Jim to be less dependent by forcing him to think for himself. Around the room, Mattie reads softly aloud, Sarah Ann writes answers to the questions on the board, Clifford whispers the story to himself, and Evelyn stands doing her workbook pages at Mr. Jameson's desk. Mr. Jameson and the threesome go over phonics rules related to the various sounds of "oo."

At 11:00, he gives two more assessment tests to Emmet, Gina, and Robert. They are to work on the tests and begin reading the next story afterwards. As he leaves them, he reminds them to work alone; they build bookwalls around their work spaces, blocking neighbors' views to secret their answers from one another. At 11:10, all three have begun reading the story. They appear intent as they huddle over books, pointing to words and reading.

Meanwhile, the *Cloverleaf* group and Mr. Jameson discuss the story they read:

Mr. Jameson: "Was Henry a chicken?"

Clifford: "He was crying."

Mr. Jameson: "How do you know?"
(Clifford points to a picture.)

Mr. Jameson: "No, that's sweat."

As in mathematics class, Mr. Jameson seems to be concerned more with helping children get right answers than helping them understand. In this exchange, for instance, having Clifford reread aloud particular passages might help him understand the point. The further point might be made that pictures accompanying the text sometimes have several interpretations, and it is therefore necessary to read in order to understand the appropriate interpretation.

Gina asks if she may write her name on the board; Jim asks why they had to reread a story they read yesterday. Mr. Jameson, trying to discuss the *Cloverleaf* story, says to Jim, "Just to be sure you know it." Robert's and Emmet's eyes begin to stray and the bookwalls they built earlier to hide their work come down as the assessment testing continues. At the time, Mr. Jameson is inaccessible for answering questions, yet pressure is on them to pass the tests necessary for moving to third grade.

Perhaps by now, Mr. Jameson is harried and impatient; he usually counsels students about reasons for assignments. The lack of blackboard space, not conceiving of ways to work with less board space, and the work with three groups simultaneously seems hectic; Mr. Jameson is in continual motion during reading, and he must be constantly thinking when he is with one group of what to do next with the other groups. Distractions like Adelina's, Gina's, and Jim's questions are brushed aside, almost as a pesty fly is when one is enjoying a day at the beach. Could students with problems solve them in ways that would not distract him from his teaching? For example, could students who need to see him write their names on a piece of paper and hand it to him so he could answer their questions at his convenience? Could they know they need to ask particular other students if they encounter a difficulty? Might a list be posted of "permitted things to do when finished with work?"

At 11:15 Mrs. Wilson, the reading teacher, arrives to collect the *Cloverleaf* group and Gina, Emmet, and Robert for special reading help. Mr. Jameson circulates among the remaining five until 11:20, quickly checking workbook pages individually and discussing errors. Jim has been absent several days earlier in the week, and Mr. Jameson discusses the pages he needs to complete, with Jim on his lap. Later, he gives Jim the assessment tests he has missed.

At 11:20, Mr. Jameson meets the *Tapestry* group again to discuss boardwork sentences. He helps Adelina with "annoy" by discussing the word with the group:

Mr. Jameson: "What does "annoy" mean? Adelina needs a little help from all of us."

Jim: "It means, like, to bug. If you bug someone, you annoy them."

Mr. Jameson: "When have you been annoyed?"

Adelina: "My sister—she annoy me."

Mr. Jameson: "How?"

Adelina: "She always bothering me, asking me stuff when I'm working and stuff."

They take turns reading the four sentences they were to write today, comparing meanings. When Jim reads, "Babies have moist diapers," the group chuckles knowingly.

At 11:40, Mr. Jameson reminds the children to put things away and to line up to return to their homerooms to get ready for lunch.

Reading class, with three groups, keeps Mr. Jameson in continual motion, physically and mentally. He generally writes directions or boardwork for three groups, passes out one or two assessment tests a day to each group, meets with each group at least twice to read aloud or to discuss a reading skill or completed work, answers questions when children are puzzled and checks assessment tests, workbooks, and boardwork. In addition, he monitors the activity of children in the groups not being given direct attention at the time to see if they are finished, too loud, having difficulty, or gainfully employed. Despite his constant motion, he confesses he usually gives one group less attention than he would like. Today it is Emmet's, Robert's, and Gina's group that receives less. Like mathematics class, reading suffers from its share of external interruptions. Aides and specialists enter to retrieve students, and memoranda circulate from the office to be signed by the teacher. One day, Mr. Jameson is to announce a summer swimming program being held at a nearby school. Another day, he is to ask the person who removed the Girl Scout cookies from the kitchen to return the cookies immediately or pay for them.

With fewer children in the room, his groups are fairly small, although he still has to plan for, instruct, monitor and check work for three groups. How does a smaller class size come into play, then? As Mr. Jameson says in a discussion:

> Several things can happen in a smaller class. Children can relate what's been happening at home and we've got time for it. We can deviate a bit from the story and incorporate it into a lesson, for example, in discussing a story. How do you do it if you have 10 in a group instead of three or four? I may be working with one group, but others listen in and join in sometimes.

Mr. Jameson's concern for the individual is revealed, but also, as in mathematics class, children receive a great deal of individual attention through Mr. Jameson's reteaching and correcting work, and they have frequent and sometimes lengthy turns. They also have their work checked on the same day they complete it. Mr. Jameson feels paperwork and checking are far less time consuming with fewer students. Promptly checking work may permit children to understand errors more easily while the work is fresh in their minds. These factors may facilitate learning. In addition, Mr. Jameson usually devotes time to instructional matters rather than matters related to discipline, permitting more material to be covered in a class session, or its coverage in greater depth. As discussed in the mathematics section, Mr. Jameson believes this to be related to class size. In his view:

A smaller class gives a teacher a chance to *teach,* to really work with a child. You're able to find out what the real problems are and tackle them right when he needs the help. I can go get materials or go back in the book to an earlier part, or find a different technique. It's a direct attack on the problem.

Mr. Jameson, then, believes a smaller group enables him to diagnose and remedy problems more quickly than a larger group would. He also says:

It gives you a chance to be human—you're another being there to help and guide. I look forward to reading groups each day because they're the smallest group I get to work with. I like being able to relax and be myself.

However, these classes are not without problems. Mr. Jameson's lack of sufficient blackboard space and the problem of how to help individuals with difficulties when he works with a different reading group are not resolved. His focus on locating the answer rather than understanding useful processes for finding the answer in mathematics and reading is also prevalent.

Lunch

Between 11:40 and 12:00, following the school-wide schedule, Mr. Jameson supervises children as they use lavatories, wash hands, and chat quietly. They get into line and receive their hot-lunch trays, then go to one of the larger second-grade classrooms where all 39 second graders are supervised by one of the three teachers.

On most days, students finish eating their lunches, then read a book or work on dittos or boardwork assigned by the homeroom teachers. Teachers are responsible for sending sufficient work along with students to keep them occupied during lunchtime.

On Groundhog Day, Mr. Jameson has lunch duty, and after the children finish their lunches, they take turns being the groundhog looking at its shadow while other children interview the groundhog. Perhaps due to the unique activity, Mr. Jameson relates, they get excited, and rather noisy. The principal enters and tells the children, "I cannot believe these are my second graders acting like this!"

Science

On three afternoons a week, Mr. Jameson teaches science to each of the three second-grade classes. One class meets him from 12:30 until 1:00, another from 1:00 until 1:30, and the third between 2:00 and 2:30. From 1:30 until 2:00, following the school-wide schedule, the children play organized games on the playground, weather permitting. Mr. Jameson's schedule for the afternoon, then, is:

12:30–1:00 Science to Class 1

1:00–1:30 Science to Class 2

1:30–2:00 Physical Education

2:00–2:30 Science to Class e

At 2:30, many children leave to catch their buses. On Tuesdays, from 12:30 until 1:30, all second graders go to the library, permitting common planning time for the three second-grade teachers, and Friday afternoon from 12:30 until 1:30 is art time.

Mr. Jameson has decided to teach science because he enjoys it; had he enjoyed social studies or creative writing, perhaps another subject would have entered the curriculum when he arrived on the scene, instead of science. Science units about microscope use, electricity, plants, fire science, and animals comprise most of the lessons between January and school's end.

Mr. Jameson's lessons generally follow the pattern of his having an informal discussion, then arranging for an activity of some sort. At a unit's end, he administers a teacher-made test about concepts discussed. For example, following the electricity unit the following three items are among the 10 on his test, read aloud to the group with key words or pictures on the board:

1. One of these is a magnet. Put down which one:

   a. | $- + - + - +$ | b. | $+ - -$ |
   | $- + + -$ |

2. Is the answer "Yes" or "No?" Will a magnet pick up aluminum and paper?
3. Which *two* of these do you need to make a battery? List two letters.
   a. two metals of the same kind
   b. two metals unalike
   c. water
   d. acid

Most items tested, then, are information-based rather than based on processes, as in mathematics and reading. The items involve material from the activities as well as from Mr. Jameson's discussions.

In May, Mr. Jameson introduces a lesson about microscopes. He chose the unit primarily because of the availability of seven microscopes and the children's interest in using them after they finish other assignments. The introductory discussion begins:

> Mr. Jameson: "Scientists use microscopes. We can't see everything. Some small things we can't see alone with just our eyes. The microscope is a very old instrument. The first one was built about 250 years ago. What can we see with a microscope?"
>
> Vernon: "How some things are made. Like a chicken."
>
> Mr. Jameson: "Part of a chicken, maybe."

After they discuss other small things they might be able to view through a microscope, Mr. Jameson distributes seven microscopes and seven manufactured slides of an embryo of a chicken. He instructs the children:

You'll have to adjust the mirror. Look down in it until you see the light flashing up. Then place the slide in.

Children work in pairs, moving closer to the window where more light reflects from the mirror, and try to focus the slide. A congested group of 13 second graders help one another and exclaim as they see in detail what appeared to be a spot on the slide only moments earlier. Mr. Jameson helps four pairs, and after 10 minutes, all meet success in seeing the slide. Other slides are viewed, slides of onion skins, paramecia and the like, although children rarely read the name of the slide they view. They seem excited by what they see, and perhaps intrigued to see other things or to practice their new-found competence in microscope use. They do not seem to care to know what they are viewing. As a result, the exploratory time is intense and shared with others, and Mr. Jameson's announcement, at 12:58 of "Okay, people, it's almost time to go" is met by groans. Hurriedly they replace the microscopes on the window sill and line up.

A new class enters as the previous one departs. Mr. Jameson teaches much of the same material to them, although the class goes more smoothly and he elaborates on certain ideas such as the staining of onion skins so their cells can be viewed. His instructions about using the microscope are more complete, and as a result, the children fumble less and all are successful more quickly. The level of involvement is again very high, and Mr. Jameson is able to assist everyone, to explain what is being viewed, and to suggest another slide to view.

This science lesson is like others in that discussion is followed by activity. As in Mr. Jameson's other science lessons, the second class goes more smoothly than the first. Mr. Jameson believes the second group is easier to work with, but he also understands that teaching the first class helped him know what to alter in order to facilitate instruction and activity in the second class. His third class does not always proceed as smoothly, perhaps because it comes at the day's end, when all are tired. Also, as in other lessons, Mr. Jameson does not explore or extend many concepts; rather, material is covered without much depth. Perhaps this may be due, in part, to Mr. Jameson's expectations of second graders, but it is also due to the amount of time allocated to science. By the time children travel to his room and sit down, only 25 minutes remain. Usually the discussion consumes five to 10 minutes, the activity 10 to 15, then the children clean up and return to their homerooms. As a result, little exploration or elaboration of concepts can occur during either the discussion or the activity.

With regard to class size, Mr. Jameson can weave more children's responses into the discussion and is able to supervise activities more closely in a smaller class than he might with a larger class. Sufficient materials are available to teach 13 students; with a larger class, Mr. Jameson would have to restructure the activity, have children wait longer, or choose a different topic. Supervising experiments with more students would be difficult, in his view, but not impossible. A larger block of time would be necessary, he believes.

THE CLASSROOM STYLE

Having gone through a fairly typical day for Mr. Jameson and the second graders he teaches, let us consider several different aspects of the situation as it relates to class size. What patterns can we construct to help explain Mr. Jameson's teaching, and what have they to do with class size?

Informality

In general, Mr. Jameson has a personal, informal style, although he tolerates no foolishness. He usually deals with mild misbehavior through private discussions. In extreme cases, a child is banished from the class, although this happens less frequently as the year progresses. In his words:

> It is very important to be sensitive to the emotions of students. I feel many problems that they have are shown by how they act. Sometimes a child may be reached by one day having a conversation with him to find out what the problem is about.

With a class of only 13 students, it is easier to have these conversations. For one thing, maintaining order among the other 12 seems easier. Also, a teacher with Mr. Jameson's attitude probably finds it easier to observe individual children and to arrange for conversations about problems. Getting to know individuals and helping them with their problems, then, seems to be facilitated by a smaller class. This may improve discipline in his classroom.

Mr. Jameson's informality is also evident in his presentations to groups or to the entire class. These presentations generally occur in the beginning of a period for mathematics and science, and are interspersed throughout the period as he visits various groups in reading. The informality is manifested through his weaving of children's anecdotes, comments, and names into discussions. Because of a smaller class, Mr. Jameson believes he is more able to "be himself," in his words, and to incorporate more children's examples or comments into the text of the daily goings-on. When these group lessons necessitate use of the blackboard, as for mathematics problems or science diagrams, Mr. Jameson generally stays near the board; when the board is not an integral part of the lesson, he roves around the room. This permits eye contact at close range, an exchange of smiles, or a pat on the head.

Because the class is informal, yet Mr. Jameson is business-like and tolerates no foolishness, a lot of work seems to get done. He has created an environment where work is expected and can be done. He has control over the class, gained through conversation, enabling him to cover subject matter rather than having to deal to a great extent with discipline. Lessons proceed smoothly, not being interrupted too frequently by disciplinary messages. During mathematics, one week in April, for instance, Mr. Jameson says five disciplinary statements, on the average, in the 50-minute period: (statements such as "Clifford, sit down!" "Della, ssh!" "Nelson, do you have to do those problems out loud?") Often, these are spoken quietly to individuals rather than aloud for all to hear. Because there are few interruptions for disciplinary statements, the flow of ideas can continue. Mr. Jameson does not have to start over again after interruptions to remind children what is being discussed. As a result, not only may continuity be increased, but also more material may be discussed, or it may be discussed more fully than if Mr. Jameson were interrupted constantly by discipline problems.

Clearly, whether classes are smaller or larger, control is important to maintain if learning is to occur. And the way in which the teacher gains and maintains this control is important, for it can disrupt lessons. Mr. Jameson's quiet, private comments to students may render disciplinary statements less visible, causing students less embarrassment, but also reducing the amount of attention derived from misbehaving. In larger classes, teachers might pass out "tickets" to offending students, symbolizing the need for more control. They might work out signals—a pointed finger, a warning glance. The point is to try to develop tactics to maintain discipline that do not interfere with the normal flow of instruction. Sometimes, such tactics disrupt lessons, as we have seen in Miss Anderson's and Mrs. Hopkins' rooms.

Individual Diagnosis and Assistance

During the group discussions and seatwork, Mr. Jameson listens and watches children to spot difficulties, to diagnose the reasons for the difficulties, and to assist the children in learning how to do things correctly. Work is checked quickly, usually in the presence of the child. Children are frequently told to rework incorrect answers. This assistance is also affected by class size, in Mr. Jameson's view, for with fewer children's work to check, he is able to spend more time with individuals needing help. Because of his control over the class, if a child does not understand something during the group presentation, Mr. Jameson can reteach it quickly at the time he sees the difficulty, rather than having to wait until the time for seatwork. Mr. Jameson believes this may be more difficult with a larger group.

This individual assistance has been influenced by Mr. Jameson's reliance on the school division's adopted materials. Reliance on these materials is expected by the administration. A lack of varied materials means that Mr. Jameson is able to vary the work only in the amount of time used to cover the materials; he varies this aspect with a few children in spelling and in one reading group. In Mr. Jameson's view, if a child is in a program obviously unsuited to him, the principal will permit use of another program, but it must be compatible with the adopted program. Thus, the county-wide adopted series in mathematics and reading strongly influence what he provides.

Other factors influencing Mr. Jameson's teaching are school-wide requests for information and external interruptions. Paperwork consumes 10 or more minutes daily of his homeroom period, preventing him from having time to interact with students through part of the period. Interruptions also influence his teaching by breaking the flow of what transpires, diverting attention for a moment and causing him to remind the class what was being done or discussed just prior to the interruptions. Mr. Jameson finds these two features of this school—requests and interruptions—to be frustrating. As mentioned in Chapter 3, school-wide celebrations such as the May Day ceremony also influence Mr. Jameson's class activities by reducing the amount of time he has with students.

As we have seen, then, Mr. Jameson has a personable, informal style, yet he tolerates no nonsense and expects to see children working. He generally has a group presentation where he explains a process or a concept, interweaving children's names or anecdotes to make the material appear more relevant and interesting. Rather than doing all the talking, he generally orchestrates this group lesson as a discussion, although he is the dominant figure. This informality is more easily achieved in a smaller class than with more students, in Mr. Jameson's view.

Mr. Jameson relies heavily on individual diagnosis and assistance, both easier with fewer students. In reflecting on the year, Mr. Jameson says in his journal:

> I would not have had the success I did had the class been bigger. I would have not been able to cover as much material or to go into it in depth as I did. It gave me a chance to expand my horizons. I was able to just *do* more. As far as I'm concerned, there's a definite advantage in that the children are able to have some learning, and also for myself that I'm having good teaching. It was obvious I was able to get around to them more and talk to them more, and this was important for the *way* I teach.

Mr. Jameson has a strong professional commitment to teaching. Why, then, has he left Pine Springs School to work as a carpenter in a large shopping center being constructed 40 miles away? His frustration with the situation at Pine Springs School is the major reason. However, it is also unlikely that Mrs. Fleming would have rehired him because of his undiplomatic, very vocal criticisms of the school. Mr. Jameson challenged many policies and practices of the school division and also those of Pine Springs School. He believed teachers should have an active role in decision making, as they had where he taught in Michigan, and was frustrated by policies he believed constrained his professionalism.

For example, he wanted to have more active lessons than he perceived he could. He believed the principal, Mrs. Fleming, wanted to see children at work in their seats. This belief was probably based upon Mrs. Fleming's entering his class several times to admonish children when they were chatting or out of their seats. She did this to the entire class, while he was teaching. Once, as already described, on Groundhog Day, children took turns interviewing one another. One child was the reporter, and one was the groundhog. Not engaging in such activities very often probably increased the children's enthusiasm for the activity, and they became very excited. Mrs. Fleming, at this point, admonished them. Such exchanges serve to inform a teacher new to the school about the unwritten, informal policies about what is and is not desired and what is and is not permissible. In other words, not all policies are written in a handbook for teachers, yet certain things are expected in certain schools. Teachers learn of them through a principal's and other teachers' statements and actions. Mr. Jameson curtailed certain activities, but was critical of the school, for he believed children needed some active lessons and that they learned through them.

He was also critical of several other policies and practices in the school. Since he was vocal but not particularly diplomatic in his criticism, Mrs. Fleming did not welcome the criticism, and became defensive and critical of Mr. Jameson.

The daily schedule, devised by the principal and the teachers at each grade level, included two scheduled bathroom breaks in the morning, but no recess all day. Children and teachers had half an hour for lunch, and remained in the classroom when they finished eating, doing and supervising work much like work done the rest of the day. Mr. Jameson believed both children and teachers needed recess in the morning and after lunch. In his view, the children needed to run off steam, chat with a friend, or spend a quiet moment relaxing with a dandelion, and teachers needed to run off dittos, write part of a lesson on the blackboard, get a cup of coffee, chat with friends, or be alone with their thoughts for a peaceful moment. However, no recess was established.

In winter and spring, children rehearsed for six weeks for pageants involving the entire school. While Mr. Jameson was not at school for the Christmas pageant, he was critical of both pageants for several reasons. For one, the children did not assist with their creation. Rather, the teachers chose a theme, decided upon songs, poems, and other parts the children were to learn, and cast the various roles for those parts. Second, he believed the pageants disrupted teaching for too great a period. Third, he believed the discipline tactics during rehearsals were too harsh. As a result, he was only peripherally involved in the production, assisting with sets and costumes. The pageants had a long history, and were events believed to bring the community together, so they were sure to endure.

Mr. Jameson was also critical of the promotion policy. To be promoted to third grade, a child had to have successfully completed the 2–1 reader, its workbook and assessment tests. This particular reader is seen by many teachers as being very difficult because of the number of decoding skills reviewed or taught for the first time. Mr. Jameson could not change this policy; it was a mandate of the school division. However, he was able to individualize three children's progress through it to enable them to be promoted. He felt he was able to do this because of the small class size; with more children, he would not have been able to plan the individualization nor spend as much time instructing the three children. He believed the time lost due to rehearsal for the pageants prevented at least one child from being promoted.

Finally, he was critical of the role of teachers' aides in the school. The aides disapproved of several of his teaching strategies in front of his class. For example, one day Mrs. Burkett said the children needed no more work about ones and 10s, but should memorize math facts. Aides also devised plans for teaching particular skills to small groups. He believed they were rude and unprofessional in their public disapproval and that they had been granted too much responsibility for their roles considering their somewhat limited knowledge of children and education.

Mr. Jameson's case is important, then, for he exhibits a style of teaching different from Miss Anderson's and Mrs. Hopkins', and we can see how class size was a factor in what transpired in his classroom. It is also important because it reveals some of the features of Pine Springs School that influenced what he was able to do. As an outsider to the school, these features were more evident to him. To be sure, not every school in the country is like Pine Springs, and not every teacher is like Mr. Jameson, but the influences of class size and setting on what teachers do is considerable everywhere. While the details may differ, the influences of these factors are present.

7

Class Size and Instruction at Pine Springs School: What Did and Did Not Change?

What can be said, then, about instruction in the second grades at Pine Springs School in relation to class size? This section analyzes changes in relation to three factors: (1) the context, (2) the skills and knowledge the teachers possessed, and (3) the teachers' beliefs and attitudes. These three factors appear to contribute to changes occurring or not occurring after reducing class size. Although they can be separated for purposes of discussion, in reality each relates to and is affected by the others. For example, we might consider why Pine Springs' second-grade teachers did not adapt to any great extent the text materials in order to suit the needs and interests of students, a change we might expect when teachers have only 13 students. One factor affecting this lack of adaptation is the textbook and promotion policy which, in effect, forces teachers to use the text. These policies can be thought of as part of the school context. Yet another factor contributing to teachers' not changing text materials might be that they had little skill or knowledge in adapting text materials or did not see it as their role to do so. These factors can be thought of as the skills and knowledge teachers possess in addition to their beliefs and attitudes. So in practice, these three factors are related. If we wanted major changes to occur, intervention would probably be necessary in one or more of these factors. In other words, changes would need to be made regarding the textbook policy, or teachers would need to augment their skills or broaden their perspectives on their role if we were to see major changes.

THE CONTEXT

Within the context, what features seem to affect instruction? In what ways are influences evident? As a result of these influences, what changes have and have not occurred?

School Size

At Pine Springs School, standing in the hall, one could see virtually every classroom door. This smallness enabled Mrs. Fleming, the principal, to visit classrooms frequently and read every report card and note going home to parents, and may have rendered classrooms and teachers highly visible and public to Mrs. Fleming. Through her comments to teachers, she may have communicated what she expected. For example, one day when Mr. Jameson's supervision of lunch was noisier than usual in her view, she entered and sternly said, "I can't believe these are my second graders!" Such actions may cause teachers to conform to the policies of the system and to the principal's views of what schooling should be like.

Additionally, with few teachers in the school, the chances might have been slight of finding a colleague with a kindred view of teaching or with skills to trade or share. As Miss Anderson and Mrs. Hopkins related, no discussion of the class-size study took place during any faculty meetings. While a few casual discussions occurred during lunch or before or after school, the two teachers involved throughout the study did not have the advantage of hearing colleagues' suggestions of ideas to try with fewer students. As a result, they were limited to their own ideas. They also did not have the opportunity to feel supported by colleagues in any attempts to change. Other than provision for common planning time, nothing was done to assist teachers in exploring options within the confines of policies or creative deviations from textbook suggestions. Teachers confessed a lack of knowledge of the supplementary resources available to them within the school. Many teachers believed they faced similar problems—discipline, interruptions, and children who weren't learning from the texts. But no common exploration of the problems occurred. Did teachers not see this as part of their role? Did they need a leader to facilitate this? Were any provisions made for opportunities to do so?

But the size of the school was also at work in the principal's knowing each child and knowing something about everyone's background—children and teachers alike. This familiarity had the potential for promoting a family-like environment where children's needs and interests could be taken into account, which seemed to occur as Mrs. Fleming strolled through halls and visited classrooms, talking personally with children about their lives and their schoolwork. Miss Anderson and Mrs. Hopkins, though, generally did not mirror this behavior. We recall Mrs. Hopkins' comment of needing to "get on with the lesson" and the conflict it created when children wanted to share a personal anecdote. For Miss Anderson, fewer students provided a chance for her to get to know more about their out-of-school lives, but we found little evidence of her weaving these insights into the instructional fabric. Both teachers knew a lot about their children, then, but rarely acted on the knowledge. Mr. Jameson, however, was more likely to interweave into discussions notions of potential interest to his children or examples from their daily lives, and also had time for a personal chat with a student if he saw a difficult situation arising or if a child appeared to be troubled.

Emphasis on Control

Also discussed in the chapter about Pine Springs School (Chapter 3) was Mrs. Fleming's emphasis on control, a concern reflected in both Miss Anderson's and Mrs. Hopkins' rooms. Fear of losing control may have led to their assigning more boardwork than children could hope to complete, to their regulating use of the pencil sharpener and toilets, and to their choices of instructional activities. Easily managed and directed activities may have been chosen more frequently, but those thought to be less easy to control may not have been. Thus, we found many easily managed paper-and-pencil activities but no potentially disruptive learning centers, special interest or project areas, or spaces in the room where children could work alone or with a friend. Furthermore, evidence from using the Modified Flanders observations (See Chapter 12) indicated a high percentage of the teachers' comments directed toward criticizing and maintaining authority, particularly before class size was reduced.

With a reduced class size, Miss Anderson was observed to smile more and to let her class draw closer as she read them poetry. She attempted this potentially disruptive activity when she had fewer children to manage. While both teachers felt that control problems diminished, our findings provide evidence of a reduction in critical, authoritarian teacher comments in Miss Anderson's classroom, but not in Mrs. Hopkins'.

Mr. Jameson practiced less authoritarian control than Miss Anderson and Mrs. Hopkins, by speaking to children privately about difficulties. Because his classroom was small, he had no spare corners to which he could send misbehaving students. He occasionally banished them to the hall, although this was rare. He believed discipline was easier with fewer children.

Partly because the teachers perceived less need for control, they felt they were able to cover more material with fewer students. For example, starting in January, our evidence indicates in-class interruptions occurred less often and for shorter durations. With fewer students to control, attention was diverted less often from the instructional activity for both teacher and students. According to our findings, students remained academically engaged for a greater percentage of instructional time and had more turns in the group (See Chapter 12.) With fewer students in a room, the number of discipline problems probably decreased merely because there were fewer possible troublemakers in the classroom. Proximity might also have accounted for part of this decrease in Miss Anderson's and Mrs. Hopkins' rooms. With more space between children, certain problems were less likely to occur.

When fewer discipline problems were present, then, teachers spent more time instructing. When the instruction was not interrupted intermittently, students might have gotten more involved in it, learning more. The relationship may indeed be reciprocal—involved students may have caused fewer discipline problems, permitting greater involvement; uninvolved students may have caused more discipline problems, permitting less involvement.

Emphasis on Texts and Influences of the Promotion Policy

As discussed earlier, teachers adhered closely to texts in mathematics and reading, even though they recognized difficulties associated with them. For instance, some basal reader stories seemed unrelated to the students' interests and backgrounds. All three teachers questioned the relevance of one story about a zoo, another about unicorns, and a third about urban children's problems in finding a place to play. Their second graders had never been to a zoo, and didn't know what unicorns were. Places to play were one abundant commodity in this county. For these reasons, the stories were deemed irrelevant. Because stories were independent of the skills presented in the reading program, the teachers might have used stories from other sources or skipped those stories. Or, they could have shown a film about zoos or big cities or read children stories about unicorns. But they didn't. Rather, they adhered to the text virtually verbatim. Texts were not adapted to accommodate the needs or interests peculiar to the Pine Springs children. Special programs were not developed. We saw little evidence of attention to rural flora and fauna, or assistance in coming to understand rural life. Sixty-five percent of the students were black, but this was not reflected in the curriculum. Rather, an adherence to nationally produced texts was the norm. This adherence allowed for little individualization; everyone did the same work, usually paper-and-pencil tasks, and covered the same material. Why was this adherence so evident? Reliance on the texts may have been due, in part, to the mandated use of assessment tests accompanying the reading series. As stated in Chapter 3, the tests were mandated by the division, which in effect mandated the use of the texts. Textbook usage may also have been due to the promotion policy, again determined by the division's central office. This policy was based on whether a child had finished a particular reader. In order for second graders to be promoted, they had to complete *Sunburst*. According to the publisher, Houghton Mifflin, this book is designated as the reader for the first half of second grade, and a Spache Readability Formula analysis of it shows its average readability to be at 2.38. Hence, children a half-year or more behind in second grade reading were retained. We could question whether being half a year behind in reading, as determined by a single reading text, is severe enough to retain a child. The table below reveals some interesting features of *Sunburst*.

Table 7.1 shows data from eight readability samples taken from *Sunburst*. While only eight pages were sampled to check the readability of *Sunburst*, this table raises some questions. The book was designed for use in the first half of second grade; however, if we look across line 5, we can see great variation and unevenness in readability on the eight sample pages. Sentence length (line 4) varies greatly, usually an indication of the difficulty of reading material.

TABLE 7.1   Application of the Spache Readability Formula Sample Estimates for Grades I–III
Sunburst .... Second (2–1) Grade Reader (Analysis by Christine Swager)

Page number	25	50	74	99	133	167	206	235
1. Total number of words	107	103	103	111	106	105	106	106
2. Number of sentences	8	16	10	8	7	10	13	8
3. Number of words not on revised word list	4	1	3	6	10	4	4	3
4. Average sentence length	13.38	6.43	10.3	13.8	15.14	10.50	8.15	13.25
5. Estimated grade level	2.60	1.52	2.15	2.83	3.31	2.26	1.97	2.50

Average of estimate   2.39

While the average indicates its appropriateness of this level, the extreme variation raises some questions.

Moreover, many teachers have noted that *Sunburst* contains a lengthy list of skills to be retaught or taught for the first time and mastered. While readability can be assessed to a certain extent through some instruments, the number and appropriateness of reading skills for various levels is open to question. Perhaps too many are included in *Sunburst* for many students. Based on the promotion policy and information about this reader, it should not be surprising that in several grades at Pine Springs School as much as one third of the class has been retained and that children have frequently repeated a grade more than once. More than one-fourth of the second graders (10 or 11 of 39) were retained. This policy caused Mr. Jameson to create a group of three children to enable them to complete *Sunburst,* and hence be promoted to third grade. Since Gina, a member of this group, moved, we do not know whether she was promoted.

The teachers relied on the same textbooks, then, throughout the year, continuing to emphasize the content in generally the same way. In reading, this meant a continued focus on learning phonics as the main goal, largely because the reading assessment tests emphasized phonics, as did worksheets and workbook pages. While phonics is one tool for learning to read, in this school it became synonymous with reading.

The policies regarding textbook use, testing, and promotion remained the same throughout the year, regardless of changes in class size, and thus influenced the options available for the teachers. The policies set the limits with regard to what could be changed. For instance, if Miss Anderson, Mrs. Hopkins, or Mr. Jameson had wanted to attempt a language-experience approach to reading instruction, the existing policies would have constrained them. If they implemented such an approach, their students might not have succeeded on the skills being tested; Houghton Mifflin's assessment tests were used for making promotion decisions. How could teachers tell if a child had completed *Sunburst?* In analyzing changes that did not occur, therefore, we must be cognizant of possible effects of existing policies in reinforcing the status quo.

Schedule

The schedule was jointly determined at the beginning of the year by Mrs. Fleming, Miss Anderson, and Mrs. Hopkins; with the arrival of Mr. Jameson, the afternoon portion was slightly modified through the addition of science, an interest of Mr. Jameson's. Because children changed classes for reading, mathematics, and the three afternoon subjects, teachers felt compelled to finish on time: letting children out early or late might interfere with other teachers' plans.

Furthermore, much of the daily schedule was part of the school-wide schedule, such as time established for lunch or reading and math or restroom break. The specialists in the school arranged their own schedules of when to see children needing help. Consequently, even though the second-grade teachers might have wanted to make certain decisions about allocating time differently, they were limited to a certain extent by the contextual influence of the school schedule.

Finally, with respect to scheduling, the day was arranged in such a way that all teachers and children were engaged in classroom activities all day. No breaks for recess were included, and children had dittos or boardwork to complete when they reported to rooms from their buses, after they finished eating lunch, and whenever they finished their work in Miss Anderson's and Mrs. Hopkins' rooms.

How might the exclusion of recess have affected what transpired at Pine Springs School? If children had no time to let off steam, to find a quiet place to look at something they wanted to examine such as a tree or a toadstool, to visit friends or to get acquainted with children they didn't know very well, such activities might have occurred during lessons. In the Pine Springs area, many children lived miles from one another, without scout troops and other after-school group activities. School was the only place where many children saw children other than brothers and sisters. With no recess, they may have attempted to find ways of "visiting" one another during class, behavior Miss Anderson and Mrs. Hopkins perceived as a discipline problem. This may have been particularly difficult for several second graders—for example, those who seemed to have a great deal of energy. Steve, for instance, was buckled into his chair and wore a safety helmet because of nervous problems that caused him to fall occasionally. A hyperactive child being taken off of Ritalin was given seven or more cups of coffee a day. A third child's arm was held occasionally during reading lessons to remind him to stop rocking his chair violently. All three children, and others, got into trouble a great deal. We might wonder whether a schedule allowing for some active play, or a classroom management system providing for some movement to and from the pencil sharpener or waste basket might have helped these children by letting them "run off steam" or move away from their work for a moment. For every one, the day went from 8:35 at the latest until at least 2:35 without substantial breaks.

Additionally, this schedule provided for no time when all teachers could get together to address common problems, to chat together as professional colleagues, or to offer or solicit advice or move away from their work for a moment. This lack of contact between colleagues relates to difficulties discussed in the section about school size, regarding the possibility of not having many colleagues who might share a particular teacher's views. It did not seem to be condoned socially to have serious professional discussions; teachers could have remained after school for such discussions, but did not.

Because the schedule did not alter after class size changed, it is another feature of the context that may have limited the options open to teachers.

Community Relations

Mrs. Fleming stressed continually the need for cooperation between the school and the home and often visited the families of Pine Springs' students. Teachers, too, sent frequent notes, made telephone calls, and, on occasion, made home visits regarding student behavior and progress. The principal's concern for good community relations led to several parents volunteering to assist in classrooms, at the annual book fair, and on other occasions.

However, certain results were not as positive and appeared to affect instruction. On occasion, for instance, teachers were asked to leave their classrooms with no prior warning to confer with a parent. Additionally, the Christmas and May Day programs, aimed in part at developing a closer relationship with the community, each altered the regular schedule for a period of three to five weeks. Undoubtedly, pageants and celebrations have the potential for being worthwhile experiences if they involve children in various ways, leading to multiple outcomes such as increased feelings of self confidence, learning how dramatic plays are produced, and sensitivity to singing on key. However, the pageants and celebrations at Pine Springs School disrupted the normal flow of events; interruptions of many instructional activities occurred throughout the rehearsal weeks, often unexpectedly, since the teachers were frequently unaware of when their classes were scheduled to rehearse. Several teachers, such as the reading teacher and Miss Anderson, were given extra duties and other teachers took over the responsibility of teaching remedial reading or Miss Anderson's class. Also, the time spent for rehearsals meant less time available for instruction. In Mr. Jameson's view, this had significant consequences for one child who had made good progress in the smaller class, but didn't have quite enough time to finish *Sunburst,* the reading book necessary for promotion, and so was retained in second grade.

Furthermore, while establishing close community relations meant that more parents volunteered to help at Pine Springs, we found evidence of aides interrupting classes and being given instructional responsibilities they were not adequately prepared to assume. These findings raise questions for us to consider if we are to suggest the use of aides or volunteers as a possible means of reducing class size. Again, these elements did not change and set new limits within which teachers could conceive of changes when class size was reduced.

Specialists

Children left the room during reading and mathematics to work with the reading teacher, the learning disabilities specialist, or an aide, and the appearance of the specialist at the door often interrupted the normal flow of events. One teacher announced her presence each day in an intrusive way, while others appeared less intrusively. The phenomenon of childen leaving forced teachers to decide whether what they missed was crucial enough to be taught individually upon return. Having fewer children in the room reduced the number of children leaving, and meant that the teacher had to spend less time being concerned about teaching students what they missed. Additionally, if teachers had to reteach what an individual or a few individuals missed, it may have been easier with a smaller number of children because teachers could monitor the rest of the class more easily. Perhaps such children did not become "lost in the crowd" in a smaller class.

Physical Facilities

The lack of an intercom system within the school resulted in notes being sent around to be read immediately and passed along. While intercom announcements would have had the same effect, this interrupted the flow of the day as well.

In addition, the absence of a lunchroom meant children had to eat in classrooms with all the children of their own grade level. No one went home for lunch, due to distance and the schedule's provision of only 30 minutes for lunch. Rooms were used for bus duty before and after school, times when the teacher had responsibility for looking after approximately 40 children. Even though fewer children "lived" in the classrooms throughout the day, then, the physical facilities still had to serve a number of functions before and after school and during lunch; this necessity was not affected by the class-size change. Perhaps this fact explains, in part, why much of the arrangement of seats and other aspects of the physical environment remained the same.

Miss Anderson and Mrs. Hopkins were provided with slant-topped, one-piece desks and a few tables. Moving the desks together to form clusters might have been unworkable, for the desks were of somewhat different heights, so a cluster would not have resulted in one flat working space. Also, children could not have retrieved materials as easily if desks were clustered. These might be additional reasons why we found the same rows-and-columns configuration throughout the year.

Mr. Jameson commandeered tables from the library for his classroom. When children first entered, they had difficulty adjusting to shared space. Initially, they dealt with it by placing physical boundaries around their individual space with rulers, pencils, and the like, rendering the space their own, as it had been in Miss Anderson's and Mrs. Hopkins' rooms. Later, they were observed to remove the boundary lines and even share materials, such as a highly prized eraser, a ruler, scissors, or a particular color of crayon. In Miss Anderson's and

Mrs. Hopkins' rooms, though, personal space was clearly defined by a child's desk, so using someone else's ruler, eraser, scissors, or crayon was seen as an intrusion on personal property rather than as sharing, and hence became a behavior problem.

Students

Pine Springs School was located in rural Virginia, and 65 percent of its students were black. Yet these two features of the children's backgrounds were not acknowledged in the curriculum in either the larger or smaller classes. Mrs. Fleming certainly had a great deal of knowledge of the people in the community, based on her having resided there for many years, her involvement in community affairs, and her visits to children's homes. She passed this knowledge on to teachers through anecdotes; despite this information, the materials were not adapted accordingly. Provisions were made for some individuals who were considered to be hyperactive, as discussed in the section about the schedule. Restrictions on movement may have exacerbated the situation for such children.

Summary of the School Context

Many aspects, then, relate to the context in which these teachers planned, taught, evaluated children, and engaged in other activities. The size of the school, the emphasis on control, the textbook and promotion policies, the schedule, community relations, specialists, the physical facilities, and characteristics of the children were some of these aspects. Changing the class size had a minimal effect on these contextual features; although the schedule was altered, for instance, the promotion policy remained in force as did the emphasis on textbooks. In several ways, we could discern how these contextual factors appeared to influence the possibilities for change in these second-grade classrooms. They dictated the conditions under which change could occur. Additionally, the small school lacked a support-system for teachers to help them conceive of alternatives or to solve problems collegially. They worked alone; the only person to challenge them or to generate a new option was the individual teacher himself or herself or possibly the principal.

SKILLS AND KNOWLEDGE

Miss Anderson and Mrs. Hopkins appeared to lack knowledge of various instructional strategies; rather, they relied on a similar format for most lessons. So, both before and after the class-size change, they most often gave brief introductions and directions for lessons rather than incorporating motivational discussions, demonstrations, or other activities. They did not provide opportunities for students to become involved in expressive activities or in small-group or individual projects. Possibly the teachers lacked the skills and knowledge necessary to create instructional approaches requiring new forms of classroom management. The sameness of the lessons might also have been related to the teachers' need for control and their belief that they had to use textbooks. Teacher's guides usually offer many suggestions for supplementary activities. When a teacher's guide or program suggested an alternative strategy, however, it was frequently not followed. For example, Mrs. Hopkins' use of the Peabody Language Kit did not incorporate the kit's suggestion of role playing. Perhaps she did not know how to involve children in role playing, or perhaps she was concerned about the lesson getting out of control. Introductory and follow-up lessons suggested in texts involving manipulative materials were not used. Mrs. Hopkins' mathematics group finished the text in April. At a meeting with the team, she copied many ideas for activities involving games, puzzles, and manipulative materials commonly found in math labs. Some of the materials were available at Pine Springs School, and others were borrowed from one of the researchers, as was a copy of Edith Biggs' and James R. MacLean's *Freedom to Learn,* a book concerning an active approach to learning mathematics. However, after having finished the text in April, Mrs. Hopkins' mathematics group used dittos and did boardwork, much as it had done earlier in the year.

We could ask questions about changes not found in Miss Anderson's classroom: Why didn't she teach her hoped-for unit on dinosaurs or incorporate the games and fun activities she thought would be possible with fewer students? Was she unaware of resources for ideas? Did she hesitate because she couldn't envision how to implement new types of activities? Did her concern for control overwhelm her desire for change? Had she already decided to leave teaching, and as a result did not desire to grow professionally?

The three teachers also appeared to lack knowledge about art. Through reading and mathematics texts and workbooks, children had access to certain principles in those subjects, but they did not have access to principles of art. In some art programs, teachers help children understand line, shape, texture, harmony, composition, and other elements fundamental to art. The children see those elements in artists' work and learn how to manipulate them expressively in their own work. In these classrooms, though, art was seen as making a product like the teacher's pattern, rather than as an expressive act and medium. This way of instructing art may have related to the teachers' training and to a lack of awareness of the arts in our culture at large.

Although we found teachers had more time to devote to evaluating students' work and assessing and responding to students' academic problems, the types of evaluation remained the same in Miss Anderson's and Mrs. Hopkins' rooms—check marks, smile or frown faces, and brief, written comments. Papers were not returned to children until just before report cards went home. Possibly the teachers lacked an awareness of how to keep anecdotal records, of how to gather evidence of students' progress or problems in several areas of development, or of how to conduct conferences focusing on helping students develop skills in self-evaluation. Perhaps the teachers were unaware of the importance of diagnosing children's difficulties by examining their dittos, workbook pages and other papers. Mr. Jameson checked work with individual students and remediated problems, usually soon after the children had completed assignments. He believed this was easier with a smaller class.

At work, then, with regard to teachers' skills and knowledge were an apparently limited knowledge of alternative instructional and evaluation strategies and a limited knowledge of art and other subject areas. Certainly our expectations for elementary school teachers are high, perhaps at times unrealistically so, since only a "renaissance person" could teach seven or eight subjects as well as we might hope. Nevertheless, the limitations revealed in the settings described indicate possible areas of skills and knowledge that need to be strengthened in teacher-education programs, or in teacher centers or in-service programs, to increase teachers' expertise in meeting the demands of elementary classrooms.

BELIEFS AND ATTITUDES

Miss Anderson and Mrs. Hopkins both stressed control. Perhaps by assigning more work than children could finish, they reflected a notion of "keep them busy, and they'll stay out of trouble." As we have seen, this concern about school appeared to influence choices of easily managed instructional activities and may explain, in part, why activities allowing for informal student–student interactions didn't increase significantly in the smaller class. With fewer children, the teachers' attitudes about teaching seemed to become more positive, perhaps because they found a psychological benefit in having a smaller number of students to control, and therefore they could be more relaxed. With less record keeping to do, they felt less harried. Mr. Jameson believed he won the "teacher-testing" battle very quickly.

Miss Anderson and Mrs. Hopkins did not appear to have a coherent set of beliefs about the purposes of school or how children learn with which to guide their decisions about practice. This may explain, in part, their limited vision of possible changes to attempt with a reduced class size, and may also have been a factor in their reliance on the text.

Mr. Jameson, on the other hand, believed schooling should be related to children's lives and that controlling children could be accomplished best through individual counseling or individual action, usually in private. Consequently, he wove children's names into discussions. When he asked them to relate a situation in a story to their own lives, several children reread the story, trying to locate the answer, perhaps indicating how used they were to seeking answers in the book. Mr. Jameson was quite critical of several school-wide policies and practices, such as the schedule (lacking time for any recess), the manner in which the Christmas and May Day ceremonies were designed and practiced, and some of the paperwork required by the school, because these were not compatible with his beliefs about how and what children should learn, the nature of an ideal educational environment, and teachers' professionalism. In fact, this incompatibility was the primary reason for Mr. Jameson's leaving teaching at the end of the year.

These factors—the context, the teachers' knowledge and skills, and the teachers' beliefs and attitudes—contribute toward shaping what transpires in a classroom. A particular classroom practice prevails when that practice is supported by the context and when the teacher possesses skills and a belief system sustaining the practice. For example, let's pretend a teacher believed in role playing as an instructive activity for children and knew how to implement it. He or she still may not have done so if he or she believed the principal would frown on it. Or, if that teacher had not known how to do role playing, but believed the principal would support it, he or she still might not have attempted it out of a feeling of inadequacy and fear of trying something new.

In reflecting about the findings of this study in Virginia, we can identify a number of reasons why reduced class size might account for increased student achievement.

Teachers believed they spent more time teaching than disciplining students in smaller classes. This permitted them to cover more material; in addition, students had fewer distractions that might have occurred from discipline problems. Students had more turns and were engaged in tasks more often in smaller classes than in large. Clearly, these were not matters teachers planned: they happened as a function of having fewer students. Reading was scheduled for one hour and 20 minutes before and after the reduction in class size. Because Miss Anderson and Mrs. Hopkins structured lessons in the same way before and after class size was reduced, they had the same amount of time for questions and for supervising seatwork. The odds were better that students would receive the teacher's attention in a smaller class. We can almost hear a child say, "The teacher talks to me more." "I can't hide; I have to be prepared." "I have more space." "I don't have to wait as long to ask a question." "I like being here more." "My teacher teaches me more."

But by and large, few changes occurred in instructional style or in the curriculum. As outlined, this is because nothing apart from class size changed. The context in which teachers planned still constrained or supported certain practices. Teachers had to use the reading textbooks, for instance. Teachers' beliefs and attitudes remained the same, coloring the choices they made. As the data chapter (Chapter 12) and the case studies demonstrate, many positive changes did occur. But while achievement was increased, perhaps we expect too much if we expect massive changes in classroom practice just from reducing class size.

Second Graders as Third Graders at Pine Springs School

During the 1978–79 school year, a second grader began the year in Miss Anderson's or Mrs. Hopkins' room with 18 or 19 classmates. In January, with the addition of Mr. Jameson's classroom class size was reduced from 19 or 20 to 13.

What happens to these children the following year? Ten or 11 are repeating second grade during the 1979–80 school year. The textbook policies remain in force, and no new textbook adoptions in reading and mathematics have been made. These subjects comprise the major portion of the day, and reading level still constitutes the primary basis for decisions regarding retention or promotion. The children who failed with the materials last year are using the same materials this year. We might wonder why children who failed with a series should use it a second time. It may not be suited to them, and they may be bored by reading exactly the same stories, doing exactly the same workbook pages and problems a second year in a row if they have to repeat a book. However, the textbook policy and adoption procedures mean only one series is available. A resourceful teacher might perceive options for using old texts or library books, but teachers are also compelled to use the assessment tests accompanying the series. They may not see other options as viable, they may also fail to see the options.

The rest of the class is in third grade. The three former second-grade classes are in one third-grade classroom with Miss Carne, who has a full-time aide, Mrs. Nesbitt, to assist with the 33 children. Six of these are repeating third grade. In the school division, 32 is the maximum allowed in one classroom at this level, but in Miss Carne's words:

> I guess they got around it, because one of the kids is being transferred to another school in October when he moves to his grandmother's house. But I'm not really sure if he is.

Having all of these children in the same room presents many difficulties, in Mrs. Fleming's and Miss Carne's views. For instance, many of the children live in the same neighborhood and ride the same bus, so they are in one another's company a great deal. Some live in the same house. Mrs. Fleming is concerned about this because she does not believe children see a reason for making new friends if they are in constant company with children they already know, thus limiting what they can learn from others.

In reading, class size has been reduced somewhat in third grade because Miss Carne, Mrs. Nesbitt, and the reading teacher each teaches a group. However, throughout the day Miss Carne has several difficulties, primarily related to control.

She believes three of the children to be strong leaders who compete for her attention and for the attention of the group by misbehaving. But she has no time to take them aside individually for a talk because of the other 32 children. She is afraid of losing the rest of the class, so she confesses she sacrifices the individual troublemaker for the good of the group. Miss Carne feels the three attention-seekers make life in her classroom a three-ring circus. When one isn't acting up, the others are. One usually triggers another's bad behavior because one wants attention, seeing the other getting some. She also feels there are not enough corners in the room to send all the children who misbehave. As stated earlier, when these children were in both first and second grade, the group was perceived as containing many difficult children. This perception was one reason why class size had been so small (19 to 20) at the beginning of the second-grade year.

Miss Carne further feels she cannot do "fun or messy activities with 33 because they're so hard to control; it's too confusing and too messy." She confesses that she resorts to paper-and-pencil work. She has eliminated art altogether. Miss Carne reports she is unable to check work immediately, to provide much reteaching, or to listen to individual problems.

As we leave Pine Springs School, Miss Carne stands in front of the room. Mrs. Nesbitt sits on the table near the window. Closely spaced rows and columns of 33 slant-topped desks consume most of the room. Columns are narrow; rows are narrower. As she teaches by the blackboard, going over the sounds "oo" makes, Miss Carne walks to and fro on her five-foot long path parallel to the blackboard, three feet away from it. She very rarely ventures down the aisles or around the periphery. Perhaps it is easier to control from this vantage point, or perhaps Miss Carne stands there because she refers to the blackboard so much. Perhaps she also feels her size prevents her from squeezing down the narrow aisles. Jerome wiggles. Evelyn stares out of the window at the trees behind the playground: they are just beginning to turn colors. . . . Emmet copies his spelling words yet another time and raises his hand to use the pencil sharpener.

Part III

California

When school opened in September, one second-grade classroom and one second–third combination classroom existed at Harrison School in Oakland, California. Class size was approximately 35 in each class, which was reduced to approximately 22 when a third class was created in late January. The original class size of 35 exceeded the guidelines established by the local school board. The creation of the third class in January was a reaction to an order from the administrative office in Oakland to reduce class size immediately, and forced the reduction earlier than planned. Dr. Nikola Filby, one of the authors, became the classroom teacher for the newly created class, providing an interesting aspect of collaborative research where one member of the research team became an active teacher in the study.

The classes participating in the study at Harrison School provided an interesting contrast of teaching philosophies and teaching styles. A further noteworthy contrast concerns factors such as teaching conditions, teaching styles, and characteristics of pupils found in the Virginia site as opposed to those found in the California site.

As an inner-city school, Harrison is confronted with many problems inherent in urban education. Large turnovers of pupils are observed, and a large number of students from poor families are performing below "grade level."

While Harrison School is urban, many similarities are to be found with Pine Springs School in Virginia. Both sites had large black-student populations. When the researchers visited both sites they found many aspects in common between the California site and the Virginia site.

In this section, the reader will learn about Harrison School and how two teachers organized for instruction and taught in the larger and smaller classes. The case-study reports provide important insights into aspects that can change when class size is reduced, and the many constraints imposed on the teaching situations that limit what can be changed when class size is reduced.

Chapter 11 provides an overview and a summary of what was found in the classes at Harrison School.

8

Harrison School

THE SETTING

At one time Harrison School was located in one of the most densely populated sections of the city. Squeezed between multiple-family dwellings originally built as two-family flats, the school itself was then at maximum capacity with every square foot being used. Other than the sidewalks and street, there was no place for children to play. Block after block, the two-story, wooden-frame structures shut off open space. A row of such tenement-like buildings stood on what is now the faculty parking lot of the school.

Redevelopment in Oakland cleared the land. Today, Harrison School stands on the fringe of a large green area at an intersection free of congested shops and stands. Modern apartment complexes have replaced many of the wooden buildings. A few of the older buildings with Victorian earmarks have been preserved and even relocated to this area.

Three blocks from the school, a west–east freeway terminates into its north–south counterpart. The same number of blocks in other directions, warehouses are interspersed with light industry, reminders that the neighborhood is still very urban and inner-city.

What has not undergone change is the economic condition of the families. Purchasing power is still minimal. Regular and full-time employment is rare, with the consequence that many families are on welfare. School administrators estimate that 30 percent of the parents are unemployed. Many children live in single-parent families; some live with grandparents or other relatives; some live with foster parents. Some families move fairly often, with the consequence that approximately 30 percent of the children enter or leave Harrison School during the school year. Some students leave the school and then reappear several months later.

Economic stress is often accompanied by feelings of tension, frustration, and hostility, which surface as outbursts of anger. Robbery and shootings are not uncommon.

An incident that occurred a few years ago has led to a policy that requires all classroom doors to be perpetually locked to prevent sudden intrusions by outsiders. Parents who wish to contact teachers for whatever reason go first to the principal, who takes steps to assuage tempers and resolve conflicts. The locked classroom door policy creates a minor interruption each time a visitor (the principal, a parent, a monitor from the office, and so on) needs to gain access to the classroom. After the knock at the door, someone in the class must move to the door and open the door. This happens about four times an hour.

The marginal poverty and accompanying attitudes notwithstanding, children come to school adequately clothed, some meticulously dressed. Parental concern for the education of the youngsters is also reflected in parental involvement, which extends from the conference in the principal's office to actual classroom participation by mothers. Close familial ties bind some members of the school and the community. Many children in the school have cousins either in their own class or in other classes. Some mothers and grandmothers volunteer in the classroom. Teacher aides are frequently related to pupils in the school, thus creating effective communication networks between families in the community and the school. Children are aware that their behavior in school is quickly communicated to their homes.

THE SCHOOL

The school building is two stories high and L-shaped. The school office is located at the joint of the L. Classrooms are located on either side of the long corridors. Wall space in the corridors is covered with bulletin boards, and each class is assigned to cover the space by its room with a changing display of student work. The primary grade classes are on the lower floor; grades four to six are on the upper floor. Our second graders get to climb the stairs for class trips to the school library, the science-preparation room, or the math resource teacher. Before and after school and at recess the halls are patrolled to make sure students stay on the playground and do not wander indoors.

Most children from the neighborhood attend the school. In addition, children qualifying for the ER (Educationally Retarded) and EH (Educationally Handicapped) classes come from outside the neighborhood. Also, Oakland has an open-enrollment policy which allows children to attend a school outside their neighborhood. Harrison School has a good reputation and parents sometimes elect to have their children attend Harrison. The parents of these children must provide transportation to the school. Approximately 15 percent of the children do not live in the neighborhood.

In all, 17 classrooms house 400 students. There are as many students in grades four through six as there are students in grades one through three. Fifty-five children attend kindergarten. Two prekindergarten classes funded by the state occupy additional classroom space. Ninety-five percent of the students are black.

While Harrison School is no longer located in a ghetto, its role of educating the disadvantaged still predominates, since a significant percentage of the school's resources for teaching come from federal and state monies that are assigned for the education of children from families in economically deprived areas. These funds augment district resources for the purchase of teaching materials, the hiring of classroom aides, and for the services of a visiting nurse, psychologist, speech therapist, and music education coordinator. These funds also help pay for a full-time librarian and resource teacher; both have responsibilities for assisting in the improvement of the reading program. In addition, during the 1978–79 year, outside funds allowed one teacher to work as a math resource teacher.

The most obvious result of extra funding is the employment of teachers' aides for nearly all classrooms. The paid aides make a significant contribution in two respects. First, the aides are an extra resource in the classroom. They provide help to children who need extra attention. They can also perform many support activities, such as preparing teacher materials. Second, as pointed out earlier, the aides are a significant link with families in the community. At Harrison School many of the aides' tenure at the school exceeds that of many of the teachers. The aides know the community well, having lived through its transition from ghetto to an urban development. A not-so-obvious consequence of the aides' seniority of service is their knowledge of the community's power structure. In many instances, they form a part of it just as they form their own support system within the school.

There are, in effect, two faculties at Harrison School. The two faculties usually work harmoniously because they have as a common concern the welfare of the children, although in thought and action this concern is sometimes expressed differently. For example, teachers are very conscious of the academic goals and ways of maintaining and obtaining them. Aides are supportive of this goal; at the same time, their main concern appears to be maintaining tight discipline through verbal rebukes and reminders of accepted behavior.

An issue not studied in our research at Harrison involves how pupils see and react to dual adults in the classroom. Whom do they see as *the* authority? The teachers and aides in the participating classrooms at Harrison worked diligently to create a unified and consistent set of rules and procedures to circumvent pupils from playing teaching adults against each other.

The Teachers

The two participating teachers are Ms. Taylor and Mrs. Monroe. Ms. Taylor teaches a second-grade class. Mrs. Monroe has a second–third grade combination class. In each class, enrollment at the beginning of the year was about 35 students. This was acknowledged to be an excessively large class size according to district and state requirements. In fact, the district decided in January to provide another regular teacher to alleviate class overloads in three classes, including these two. It was this district action that required a sudden change in our scheduled split date. After the end of January, class size was reduced to 22 for both Ms. Taylor and Mrs. Monroe.

Ms. Taylor came to Harrison two years previously when Mr. Evans, the principal, transferred to the school. She is widely recognized as an energetic and skilled primary-grade teacher. She has been involved in developing the Follow-Through program and acts as a demonstration teacher. Her Follow-Through classes are frequently observed by visitors throughout the country. A white person in a predominantly black school, she is totally respected as a teacher and as a person. She commutes over 60 miles daily to and from Harrison School. She does personal things in the community such as shopping or using the local laundromat so that people in the community see her outside her school role.

Mrs. Monroe, a black, is also a veteran teacher. She was educated in the South and holds a Masters degree in education. She has taught in the district for 20 years, although she lives in a nearby community and commutes 40 miles daily. Her most recent experience has been in the upper-elementary grades at Harrison School. She is now relearning the nature of teaching primary-grade children, a totally different experience from teaching upper-elementary-age children. At Harrison, this also means learning about the Follow-Through program.

Aides

Mrs. Reed and Mrs. Horne serve as full-time aides to Ms. Taylor and Mrs. Monroe, respectively. Both are blacks. They are experienced and have served for some time at Harrison School, but in both cases they are new to these particular classrooms. They seemed to learn quickly the roles the teachers wanted them to play as instructional assistants.

Principal

Mr. Evans, the principal, had taken over at Harrison two years previously. The principal's role in the school, according to Mr. Evans, is to maintain harmony. He sees himself as the head of a large family cooperating for the attainment of a common goal, which is the education of the children. He considers that members of the support staff, such as the custodians, share responsibilities for providing a learning environment for children. Promoting mutual respect among the members of his "family" is the principal's expressed objective. He articulates the concept this way:

> And I try to be sure that I'm going to respect you no matter what your status is. You're to respect others. I can be firm, but I try to (make the school) one in which we work as a team. Everyone plays a part in this school. That's the way I operate.

Mr. Evans sees the need of blending together the resources of school and community. A phone call provides the contacts for important information in the community, at district headquarters, parent groups, and so on. Knowing one's school community, when blended with subtle leadership, provides the opportunity for "good things to happen" in the running of a school. To accomplish this, Mr. Evans spends considerable time meeting with parents and community members or attending district meetings. He also has to handle the administrative work entailed in the state and federal programs.

Mr. Evans is seldom directly involved in the instructional program itself. Instead, he strives to create a situation in which teachers can work effectively and in which the goal of educating children is taken seriously by everyone. Toward this end, Mr. Evans believes in order and discipline in the school. When he arrived at Harrison two years ago, students could be found running through the halls. Now they generally do not. To achieve better discipline, Mr. Evans assigned hall monitors before and after school and at noon hour. He also talked with teachers about having students walk quietly and in line when entering and leaving the classroom. Mr. Evans himself is a symbol of order, especially to the younger students, who are still awed by the threat of being sent to the principal's office.

Mr. Evans does not regularly visit classes, listen to students read, or talk to teachers about their instructional program. He believes in a phonics approach to reading and therefore has insisted that the school use the Economy reading series, but he leaves the implementation of the program to the teachers. His job is to create a climate that supports learning. The teachers' job, behind their closed doors, is to teach.

The many roles of a school principal cannot be simply assessed. On one day we observe Mr. Evans visiting a class during the lunch period where he insists the pupils eat their lunch (fried chicken) with one hand, holding their other hand in their laps. Later that day he is found carrying a four-month-old baby in his arms so that the mother can have a conference with a teacher. It reminded us that schools and roles are complex and that hasty interpretations of what we would see could lead us to premature conclusions.

Parent Volunteers

In addition to salaried aides in the classroom, there is considerable parental involvement. From 15 to 20 parents a day report to the classrooms for the purposes of assisting teachers. The children stand to benefit. One more pair of ears to listen, one more voice to encourage and praise, another pair of hands to prepare materials, another adult to whom the children can relate—all have great advantages. One of the principal's objectives is to provide an abundant learning environment for the children. For example, teachers are encouraged to take children on field trips and excursions as a way of widening their horizons. Increased supervisory help, occasioned by the assistance of parents, makes excursions into the urban center more possible. Within the classroom, the teachers at Harrison School appear willing to assist the parents in learning their role as helpers.

SCHOOL-WIDE POLICIES

The Daily Schedule

The daily schedule of instruction is the same regardless of class size. One half of the class (the lower reading groups) arrive at nine o'clock for one hour of reading followed by a 10-minute recess at which time the other half of the class arrives on the playground. At 10:10 the whole class assembles on the school-yard and is met by their teacher who escorts them into the school building. The school day for the whole class starts with a 50-minute arithmetic period followed by a second 10-minute morning recess. After returning from the yard, 25 minutes are spent on either oral or written language development.

At 11:35, the second-grade teachers' aides wheel carts holding the nutritional program's hot lunch into the classrooms. Children take turns serving the lunch and spend half an hour eating and visiting in a relaxed period of socialization. At noon the children leave the classroom for a 50-minute free play period on the school yard.

The one hour which follows the noon recess is spent according to the day of the week variously on literature appreciation, science, music, social studies, physical education, or art. A 10-minute afternoon recess marks a transition into an hour reading period for the children who arrived at 10:00 (the higher reading groups). The school day is over for those who arrived for reading at 9:00. The "ten o'clockers" leave at 3:00 in the afternoon.

The schedule of a typical school day at Harrison School for the participatory second-grade classes would look like the following:

9:00–10:00	a.m. reading group
10:00–10:10	recess
10:10–11:00	opening exercises, math
11:00–11:10	recess
11:10–11:35	language arts
11:35–12:00	lunch in classroom
12:00–12:55	recess
12:55– 1:55	literature, science, social studies, music, art, PE
1:55– 2:05	recess
2:05– 3:05	p.m. reading group

The Curriculum

All classes in the school use the Economy Press reading series and the Heath math series. Both Mrs. Monroe and Ms. Taylor rely primarily on these materials for reading and math instruction. It is understood, however, that other materials and activities can be used to supplement the basic program, and each teacher does this in her own way. A number of supplementary materials are available to the teachers. In addition, the children go once a week to the library and once a week to science periods, which are preparation times for the teachers.

Primary-grade classes at Harrison also participate in the district Follow-Through program. In addition to providing instructional aides and free lunch, the Follow-Through program also carries a curricular theme—reading through literature. Children are exposed to literature such as folk tales through reading, listening to stories, or watching films. They respond by writing their own stories or plays, drawing pictures, putting on plays, learning songs or poems, and so on. Much of this instruction takes place during whole-class lessons but it is also sometimes done during reading periods.

9

Ms. Taylor's Classroom

THE "LARGER-CLASS" VIEW

The Physical Environment

Ms. Taylor's classroom is colorful and crowded with displays, materials, and people. Most of the wall space and all but one strip of chalkboard are covered with vocabulary charts, spelling guides, posters, and an array of children's mathematics papers and artwork. One chart illustrates and names different types of whales, a current topic of study. In another area of the room is a bar graph the children have produced to show a comparison of the number of birthdays among the students in each of the 12 months.

Many of the things on display are intended as resources to help the children with their work. For instance, Ms. Taylor has sprinkled cards with printed vocabulary words on them throughout the room, on the walls and door. She explains to an observer that she has used this approach to provide support to students who are working independently on creative writing, an important part of her curriculum. With 35 students to manage, it is difficult to help individuals right when they need assistance. Ms. Taylor encourages the students to help themselves by looking for information on the posters, charts, and word cards. The anticipated result is less student time wasted in waiting for help from the teacher or her aide. For help with mathematics, both a large number line and a counting chart are tacked up.

Wall space not given over to samples of the children's work or instructional guidelines is occupied by bookshelves and cupboards. These house a wealth of recreational reading material, a collection of phonograph records, manipulative materials, games, and a wide selection of textbooks. Ms. Taylor says that she would like to have the instructional and recreational materials on tables so that the children could browse through them. But space is limited and the stored materials are not easily accessible. Ms. Taylor must make the decision of which materials to pull out rather than giving the students the choice.

A fourth wall in the classroom consists of windows that look out onto a wide expanse of green grass. The spacious outdoor view contrasts sharply with the crowded conditions in the classroom. With 35 students, the teacher, and the teacher aide, there is not much space available for students to move about.

The students sit at tables clustered together in groups. Each group consists of eight or 10 children who form a "family." Each family has an identifying name chosen by the group members. For example, one group calls itself the "Bugs Bunny" family.

The tables are tightly packed and students often bump each other's elbows or chairs. It is difficult for individual students to find a quiet place to work without other people close at hand.

The next section of the chapter describes the teacher's instructional style and teaching strategies. A typical lesson is included to illustrate how the teacher handled the large class prior to the split.

A Typical Mathematics Lesson

A typical mathematics lesson has been selected to illustrate what life is like in the large class. At 10:00 a.m. the students who arrived for the early reading period are joined on the playground by the students who will remain at 2:00 p.m. for the late reading period. The whole class participates in a 10-minute recess period together before it is time to enter the classroom. At 10:10 a bell rings and the students line up on the playground. Ms. Taylor signals for the students to walk to the classroom.

The 35 children walk down the hallway, with some students straggling behind, visiting with friends in other classes. Upon entering the classroom, the students hang up jackets and make their way to regular, assigned seats. The children talk to one another freely, continuing conversations begun on the playground. Ms. Taylor enters the classroom with the children and goes to her desk, with several children following her to turn in homework or report something of interest.

Following the routine of flag salute, calendar, and lunch count, Ms. Taylor calls the students to attention for a group lesson:

"There's no point in starting until we're ready . . . Tisha, this is not the time to look at the book . . ." A student comes in late and brings her homework to Ms. Taylor. Ms. Taylor sees two children passing a note and picks it up. She says, "Amanda, your table isn't ready yet. The others are."

As the children slowly quiet down, Ms. Taylor tells them that they are going to work on 10s and ones. Ms. Taylor holds up a card with a two-digit number on it and asks what number is in the 10's place and what number is in the one's place. She says that the children need to work on this skill because they had trouble with a worksheet the previous day. Students are called to the front of the room to put 10s and ones in a pocket chart to make two-digit numbers. Most of the children get a chance to respond. Ms. Taylor makes a particular point of calling on a child who has been absent and missed some of the earlier lessons. While most of the 32 students pay attention to the lesson, 5 or 6 students do not. These students are restless and seem to be tired of waiting for their turn.

The next activity is a group lesson on number sequence. Ms. Taylor hands each child in the room a card with a two-digit number on it. She calls one child to the front of the room and then calls for "the two numbers that come before and the two that come after." As these children identify themselves, with help from their classmates, they come to the front and Ms. Taylor helps them line up in a row. The whole class then reads the five numbers in sequence. Four sets of numbers are done in this way.

As a follow-up seatwork activity, the children do a page on sequencing from the textbook. They are to fill in the missing numbers under several number lines. The format of the page is somewhat confusing because the children must notice a vertical pink line down the center of the page which divides separate "items." Several children keep counting straight across the page. As the children work on this page, they talk to each other. Ms. Taylor and Ms. Reed, the aide, check pages and give help. But there are still some children having difficulty. One girl cries briefly because she doesn't understand what to do. Another girl starts to work but gets stuck because she thinks she can use a number only once on the whole page. It is difficult for the two adults to give individual help as often as needed.

The students work at various levels of skill. Amanda finishes the page and asks to work on the chalkboard. When Ms. Taylor sees that she is not doing mathematics problems on the board, as she was told, Ms. Taylor gives Amanda some more advanced place-value problems, building on the day's lesson—"what number is 10 more than 59?" Meanwhile, other students have not finished the basic assignment when it is time for recess. Ms. Taylor collects the papers and has the children line up to go out to the playground.

Discussion. This math period illustrates a number of features common to instruction in Ms. Taylor's class. The basic lesson is conducted with a group, in this case the whole class. This group lesson includes several different activities designed to provide variety and to involve the students actively in the lesson: for instance, coming up to form a line of numbers in sequence. Following the group lesson, students complete a seatwork assignment. During this part of the period, students are allowed to talk to each other freely and there is considerable movement around the room as well. Ms. Taylor believes in the value of student interaction and tries to create an environment in which students work comfortably and cooperatively with each other. With 35 students, the amount of commotion sometimes seems excessive and the goal of a cooperative atmosphere is not always met.

The seatwork period also gives Ms. Taylor an opportunity to interact with individual students. During the group lesson, Ms. Taylor seems to respond to different students' needs, for instance, by being sure to call on a student who had been absent. But the seatwork period offers a chance for extended interaction. Ms. Taylor spends about five minutes giving math problems to Amanda because she knows Amanda could benefit from more advanced work.

But time with one individual necessarily takes away from time with another. While Amanda works on advanced math problems, other students do not seem to understand the basic assignment, or they work so intermittently that they never finish. Because she is very aware of students as individuals, Ms. Taylor regrets being unable to reach each student. She tries to find time to work with the low-achieving students; and Mrs. Reed, the instructional assistant, often works individually with these students. Ms. Taylor believes that it is especially important for these students to complete work successfully so that they will develop confidence in their abilities. But in the large class, low students are apt to become lost in the shuffle, until they draw the teacher's attention through misbehavior.

Classroom Management

Interaction and group cohesion.   One of Ms. Taylor's goals for her students is to provide a learning environment that allows them to interact freely in an informal, comfortable atmosphere. This goal is not accomplished easily with 35 pupils.

Ms. Taylor's goals and philosophy are revealed in both her verbal explanations and the way she runs her classroom. Ms. Taylor emphasizes language development, including oral skills. In addition to specific activities like plays and speeches, students develop oral language skills through talking to one another. Students are allowed to talk freely during periods of seatwork activity. Besides developing language skills, Ms. Taylor views this interaction as a way to promote student cooperation as they help one another with assignments. Ms. Taylor hopes that students will come to feel a bond with one another in something like a family atmosphere. This intention can be seen in her seating arrangement by clusters of tables, each of which is called a family. Ms. Taylor speaks fondly of her class two years ago, in which this family spirit became quite strong: "We truly cared about each other. If something happened to one person, the others would show concern and want to help."

Ms. Taylor does not talk the same way about this year's class. For one thing, she feels that this class is "noisier and more talkative" than in previous years. To an observer, the noise is often striking. It seems similar to an adult cocktail party, with many conversations going on at once. Both children and adults become accustomed to the noise, to some extent, but it still has an effect over the course of the day. One boy's comment is revealing; the circumstances are as follows:

> An art lesson is in progress and the children are talking freely as they struggle to assemble turkeys from a hanger and construction paper. Many children are moving around trying to get help. At one point there is a slight lull in the action and the noise level drops. Roger looks up in surprise and says, "Gee, it quiet in here."

It seems likely that the noise level interferes with effective concentration on schoolwork.

Also, Ms. Taylor finds that with this large class, inattention and misbehavior are frequent. Usually there are children who do not pay attention during a lesson, as described in the sample math lesson above. Ms. Taylor must decide whether to speak to them, ask them questions in order to bring them into the lesson, or ignore them temporarily for the sake of preserving the momentum of the lesson for the other students. Students can get "lost in the crowd," either through their own efforts or unintentionally.

On several occasions in the large class, the misbehavior of a few of the students has spoiled special events for Ms. Taylor and the class. When the class went to the park as a special outing, some children threw sand in each other's hair. When the class went to the auditorium for a "rhythms" period, several boys clowned around so persistently that the period was cut short. Incidents like these disturb Ms. Taylor and lead her to restrict the curriculum. Even within the classroom, individual student misbehavior disrupts lessons and adds a negative tone. Ms. Taylor notes that the students seem unaware of the consequences of their behavior: "There are so many fun things you can do with children. They don't understand that they are spoiling it for themselves."

Ms. Taylor responds to this classroom situation in a number of ways. She tries to understand why this class might be different from other years. One explanation is the maturity level of the students. A few of the children are relatively mature, with reasonable self-control and mastery of the school situation, but not always interested in schoolwork. (Boy–girl relationships are already a topic of interest to these students.) On the other hand, four of the children were only six years old in September, the age of first graders. These children were accelerated from kindergarten because they had strong academic skills, but in many ways they still act like typical six-year-olds. Ms. Taylor feels that in general the class is immature.

Ms. Taylor has tried a number of techniques to improve classroom behavior. Happy-face stickers were effective for about one day, she reports. She instituted "warm fuzzies," balls of pink fluff, as a reward to each family group if they quiet down quickly at lesson time. By the time one family has earned its fuzzy, another is having it removed again for misbehavior. One system that does seem to help is a system of table captains instituted in early December. Each family group has a captain, who is responsible for passing out and collecting pencils. If all the pencils are turned in at the end of the day, the captain gets a happy-face sticker. Students take turns being captain, with each turn lasting two days. Ms. Taylor notes that the students seem to respond well to this responsibility. She is pleased that members of a family help one another out, being sure that enough pencils are found so that everyone gets a sticker. When the students go to science, Ms. Taylor puts the captains in charge; the science teacher reports back that the students' behavior is improved. But Ms. Taylor feels that there is still room for further improvement.

More often than she would like, Ms. Taylor finds herself yelling at a student. It appears that she reaches the end of her rope in terms of noise, interruptions and misbehavior, then explodes. Most frequently she yells at a student and threatens to call his or her parents. She says that calling the parents is the one thing that seems to get through to these kids.

The problems caused by this large class affect Ms. Taylor's feelings of professional satisfaction. She says that it is frustrating to work with interest and involvement in the lessons. She wants the students to have successful learning situations, but feels pressured because too much time has to be spent on eliminating distractions and managing inappropriate student behavior.

The teacher aide reports that she goes home every afternoon with a headache. There are a number of students with problems in this class and she finds it difficult to meet all of their needs.

Individuality of students. Ms. Taylor works to develop group cohesion, but she also focuses on the needs of individuals within the group. She is very much aware of the learning styles of different students and she tries to respond to them as individuals.

In her journal Ms. Taylor makes numerous comments about individual students, particularly students about whom she is concerned, for instance:

> My concern with Dave is growing. I found through a discussion with the preschool teacher about a family matter that Dave did not trust us enough to tell us the truth. Perhaps that is a factor in his lack of progress. . . . Delores tried hard today to show me that she can work and does come to school to learn. . . . Randy can do many classroom activities only if an adult is nearby to guide him. . . . William does not like to be in the spotlight. . . . Brenden showed his extreme sensitivity today when he dissolved into tears after being accused of calling a child names . . . . Note: There isn't time to enter all of the interesting observations that happen from day to day.

In class, Ms. Taylor would like to reach each of her students. As seen in the sample math lesson, she calls on students in order to draw them into group lessons, particularly if they may be having difficulty. During seatwork, she has a chance to interact with individuals. Perhaps because of her interest in individual learning patterns, Ms. Taylor will often spend time working with a few students as they do the assignment. Of course, with 35 students, this means that some students do not get the help they need. Ms. Taylor looks forward to the smaller class so that she can reach more individuals:

> Randy will really show progress in the reduced class-size situation. He can do many classroom activities only if an adult is nearby to guide him. The smaller class size will free adults to spend that needed time with him. This is why I expect to see progress with him.

Self-confidence. Ms. Taylor is especially concerned about low-achieving students and about helping them to become self-confident learners. Twelve of the students in the class are reading in the pre-primer. One of these students, Marcia, has been tested to belong in a class for the Educable Mentally Retarded, but the mother has refused to authorize the placement. Instruction in the class is not individualized, beyond the level of four reading groups, but Ms. Taylor proceeds through the curriculum slowly and in depth and tries to enable each student to complete assignments successfully. She includes frequent reviews of basic concepts. And she is delighted to call attention to a student's good performance. For example, when Marcia finishes a page she did not think she could do, Ms. Taylor draws a smiling face on the paper and sends Marcia over to show Mrs. Reed the good work. Ms. Taylor and Mrs. Reed often call each other's attention to good work so that the child will receive praise and encouragement. While walking around the room checking work, Ms. Taylor makes comments like: "Look how smart you are to know which numbers make 15!"

For children of this age, the adults are important figures to be turned to for help and support. Ms. Taylor believes that it is important for a child to have a one-to-one relationship with an adult in the room. Both she and Mrs. Reed work closely with the students, particularly to get them going on a project; Ms. Taylor observes:

> Occasionally Randy withdraws and does not do the lesson, whatever it might be. Usually that's because it's something he's not very secure with. If I observe this going on, I can go over, talk to him, work with him, and assure him that I haven't assigned anything that he's not capable of doing—then he gets in and he does it.

As children develop confidence in their abilities, Ms. Taylor encourages them to become independent and self-reliant. She encourages students to seek help from each other as well as the adults in the class, and there are numerous examples of this taking place:

> "What's 14 take away 5?" asks Michael to which William replies, "I don't know," continuing with his work. "Here, count back," Amanda tells Michael with authority. Michael looks puzzled and Anita points to the 13 on the number line and says, "Like this. Back to 13 then 12, 11, 10, 9." Each time she counts, a finger is held up to keep tally of the number of times counted and finally saying with satisfaction as the fifth finger goes up, "See, you land at 9."

If Ms. Taylor believes that a child can do more on his or her own and is becoming too dependent on others, she may intervene. The following illustration demonstrates how Shawn is directed to self-reliance:

> "Shawn, I know you need Erica's help with some of the words in the story but today I want you to try and get the meaning of the story without anyone's help. In a little while, either Mrs. Reed or I will hear you read and can show you how to get the words without another's help." . . . Within a few minutes, Ms. Taylor stops at Shawn's desk and guides her through a reading of the story.

The room is also arranged to offer visual support to students, as described earlier. Vocabulary words are on cards and wall charts. In the math lesson described earlier, children were able to use a counting chart on the wall to do the sequence problems on their worksheet. But several children had to be reminded and encouraged by an adult to use this resource before they were able to work independently. Once again, the adult appears to be a critical resource, a resource in short supply with 35 students needing attention.

Patterns of Instruction

Grouping. All regular instruction in the classroom is organized around group lessons. For reading and spelling there are several different instructional groups. In other subject matter areas, most instruction is carried out with the whole class.

During the morning reading period, students work on both reading and spelling. For the first part of the period, Ms. Taylor works with one group using the spelling book. Mrs. Reed assists a smaller group of students who cannot work successfully in the spelling book and who receive extra practice with basic sight words and phonics. The second part of the period is spent on reading activities, with a different grouping structure. Ms. Taylor works with the lower group, which combines some of the children from the spelling-book group and all of the children who did word drills with Mrs. Reed. This group reads in *Tag,* a pre-primer and activity book which is a supplementary component in the Economy series. Many of these children went through the regular pre-primer in first grade, but Ms. Taylor believes that they cannot yet read well enough to move ahead to more difficult material. She did not want them to have to repeat the same book, so she made a special effort to get this supplementary pre-primer. The other three children in the morning period are reading in *Green Feet,* the primer. Mrs. Reed works with this group for oral and silent reading and workbook activities.

During the afternoon reading period, all children do the same spelling, but there are again two reading groups. A group of five students reads in the first-grade reader; a larger group is in the second-grade reader.

Types of lessons. Most instruction occurs in teacher-directed (or aide-directed) group lessons. Ms. Taylor uses the school-adopted texts in reading (Economy Press) and mathematics (Heath) for the major part of her instruction, and students progress sequentially through the texts. In reading, students regularly engage in oral and silent reading, discussion of stories, and the completion of workbook pages. But two other types of lessons are also typical and of importance to Ms. Taylor—response to literature lessons and creative writing.

The Oakland Follow-Through program in which Harrison School participates carries the theme of reading through literature. Ms. Taylor has worked closely with the Follow-Through program for a number of years and serves as a demonstration teacher. Visitors from as far away as the East Coast come to the classroom to observe demonstration lessons. Often these lessons will involve presenting a children's classic and responding to it in different modes. Ms. Taylor may read aloud a story such as ''The Three Little Pigs'' and guide the students in retelling the story. Some students may then rewrite the story while other students draw pictures to illustrate it. Often these lessons extend over several days. For instance, after this initial lesson on ''The Three Little Pigs,'' students may sign up for parts and put it on as a play. Several different teams of students may act it out so that many students get a chance to participate.

Not all work with literature relies on traditional forms or the "classics." Ms. Taylor chooses material that she believes will be of interest to the children and spark their enthusiasm, as, for instance, this humorous verse printed on chart paper:

Hey diddle diddle, the cat and the fiddle,
The cow jumped over the moon,
The astronauts laughed at the very idea,
And said, "You're a little too soon."

Ms. Taylor emphasizes creative writing because it combines reading, writing, and other language arts skills. Spelling words during creative writing requires students to use rules that also serve well in deciding words during a reading lesson. Decoding is subsequently involved in this writing lesson when children read their own original stories, some of which contain the new vocabulary, recognized either through sight or the application of phonics rules. Creative writing periods also allow for considerable interaction among the students as they assist one another with spelling and discuss what they are doing. After Ms. Taylor introduces a topic for writing, she often takes dictation from some students to help them get their ideas down while other students work on their own. With 35 students, including many nonreaders, some students get discouraged at the difficult task. If they cannot get help from the teacher, they may produce nothing.

Ms. Taylor also has an array of other activities in mind to do with students, but she finds herself unable to do some of these because of the large class size and the management problems she has with the class. As quoted above, she believes that there are many fun things to do with children, but that this particular class is spoiling things for itself. Her belief that she must fall back on more common, basic activities is reinforced by the psychologist, who visits the class and recommends, among other things (such as the successful strategy of table captains) that Ms. Taylor use more "busy work." This "solution" is hardly appealing to Ms. Taylor.

Directing a lesson. In group lessons, Ms. Taylor tries to involve the children in responding actively, as illustrated in the sample math lesson. She will often include several slightly different but related activities during the period in order to maintain the children's interest. In addition to holding the children's attention, she wants to have them thinking actively about the topic in a concrete and meaningful way. For instance, she emphasizes the concepts underlying subtraction by dramatizing the absurdity of the statement, "Two take away three":

Ms. Taylor asks Tanya and Amanda to stand up. "How many children do we have? (2) Can I take one child away, say Amanda?" (Yes) "Can I take the three children away—Amanda, Tanya, and Aurora?" (No) "Why not?"

Instead of writing on the chalkboard $2 - 3 = ?$ and going through an explanation about not taking a larger number from a smaller number, Ms. Taylor instead has had the children act out a situation where subtraction is not possible.

Even with these tactics, not all students are attending to the lesson at any one point. Some students can usually be observed tilting their chairs, whispering to a neighbor, playing with a pencil, looking around the room, wandering over to sit by Mrs. Reed, or even crawling into the coat closet.

Instructional Assistants

Mrs. Reed, the full-time instructional assistant, and Ms. Taylor seem like a compatible team in the classroom, in spite of the fact that this is their first year working together. Although Mrs. Reed helps out with general support activities such as cutting out letters for a bulletin-board display, she also works directly with small groups or individual children. In reading, she has regular assignments to work with particular groups. At other times of the day, she will often work with individuals who need extra help to get something done. Ms. Taylor and Mrs. Reed share an interest in the children as individuals, and in helping each child to succeed. Ms. Taylor states that "Mrs. Reed is a patient woman who is so able in dealing with children and able to bring the very best out in them."

In addition to Mrs. Reed, there are also a number of parent (or grandparent) volunteers who help out occasionally in the classroom. Ms. Taylor finds that these extra people do not always come reliably, so they cannot be counted on in the program in the same way that Mrs. Reed can, but they provide extra help for individuals when they are present. Sometimes as many as four adults may be present in the classroom.

Summary

Ms. Taylor is a teacher with a rich conception of teaching. The basic form of her teaching is fairly traditional—group lessons, many of which involve regular textbook materials. But she builds on this structure through classroom-management strategies that increase group cohesion while also recognizing individual differences. She incorporates a variety of different types of lessons, many of which involve active student participation. She encourages student interaction and cooperation. She is very much aware of individual student needs, and tries to provide guidance and support so that low achievers, in particular, can become successful, self-confident learners.

Ms. Taylor finds this particular class of 35 students to be very frustrating, and she looks forward to an improvement when class size is reduced. The class seems particularly noisy and prone to misbehavior. More often than she would like, Ms. Taylor is driven to the point of yelling a threat in order to bring behavior into line, although she has been trying a number of positive techniques, and the recent addition of family "captains" has brought some improvement. Because of the large size and the behavior problems, Ms. Taylor has felt limited in the instructional activities she could use with the class.

When asked to speculate about what might happen in the smaller class, Ms. Taylor writes the following in her journal:

My class would definitely be different with fewer students. This fact was brought home to me last week on a rainy day when nine students were absent. Observations on that day:

Children were quieter.

They were able to work together in small groups.

They seemed able to share more readily.

The attention span was longer. Directions could be given less times.

Both teacher and students found activities more enjoyable because disciplining was cut down.

(All was not perfect—broken cars.)

These observations confirm my feelings that 34 students (especially these 34 with their unique intellectual and personality make up) are too many in one classroom if you intend to give the children the opportunities to:

1. explore at centers

2. have a quiet place to read or work

3. have free time to extend their learning through books and games

4. have a one-to-one relationship with an adult in the room

5. use a multimedia approach to learning

6. use creative dramatics

7. use cooking

8. extend learning through art and science

At the end of January, the class size was reduced to 22 students. What difference does this make in the classroom environment and activities? The "smaller-class" case study in the next section provides the contrast to answer this question.

MS. TAYLOR'S CLASSROOM: THE "SMALLER-CLASS" VIEW

The Physical Environment

What differences occur when the class size is reduced from 35 to 22? The most visible difference is the physical environment. While the room contains the same array of visually stimulating material and student work, there is a new sense of openness. There are fewer tables in each of the four clusters, fewer students, and more space. The extra small tables have been placed under the windows. Some of the curriculum materials that were previously stacked in bookshelves have been spread out on the tables for easy access. With fewer students in the class, an observer feels he or she can see more of what is happening. The teacher probably feels the same way.

A Typical Mathematics Lesson

A typical mathematics lesson is described here to show a comparison between the larger and smaller classes. The day begins in the smaller class very much as it did in the larger class. The difference is that with fewer students, the procedures run more smoothly and quietly.

The students salute the flag and read the date placed on the chalkboard by the teacher. Ms. Taylor checks for homework brought in by the later-arriving students, takes attendance, and prepares the lunch count. After the morning ritual is completed, Ms. Taylor moves into the lesson. She begins simply by telling the students to write their "doubles." This is clearly a review concept, and students start in to work as Ms. Taylor hands out the paper. She continues to move around the tables monitoring as the students write and talk quietly among themselves.

Ms. Taylor encourages the class to use problem-solving techniques. For example, as the other students start to write, Michael and Tanya are looking for pencils.

Ms. Taylor says, "It's too bad our friends have not found Michael and Tanya a pencil yet."

Loi gives a pencil to Michael, and Tanya finds one under her chair. Ms. Taylor feels more comfortable using a group problem-solving approach with the smaller class. In the larger class, she was more likely to make a direct statement to a single child: for instance, "Michael, find a pencil."

The students work steadily. When one of the boys complains that his seatmate is copying from him, Ms. Taylor replies:

"Well, maybe he needs a little help, since he was absent for awhile."

She changes the connotation of "cheating" to "helping," perhaps to develop the idea of cooperation.

After about 10 minutes, Ms. Taylor stops the "doubles" activity and leads the class in a time-telling exercise. She holds up a large clock model and asks the students to write the various times she demonstrates. After the students write the time shown, the teacher asks them as a group to call out the correct time.

Following the time-telling exericse, Ms. Taylor tells the class that she is going to show them some cards and ask them to write answers to questions she will give them. Ms. Andreini holds up large models of Bicycle brand playing cards, two at a time. She asks the class to write the sum of the two cards on their papers. Ms. Taylor asks Chawn what it means to "write the answer." Chawn responds correctly and Ms. Taylor continues the lesson with these words: "I know this is an exciting game, but if Amanda hollers out the answer, then Dean doesn't get a chance to think." The teacher continues holding up cards and no one calls out any of the answers. After several combinations are shown, Ms. Taylor asks Latanya for the answer in order to check on her response.

Ms. Taylor seems to be able to monitor individuals more closely in the smaller class. Midway through the lesson she stops and says to Michael: "Michael, if you can't see, come over here." She asks Michael to call out the answer to the next question to see if he is able to follow along.

Ms. Taylor paces the mathematics lesson to provide for a variety of activities to maintain the children's interest in the lesson. She follows the card activity with an exercise in counting by twos. She directs the class to count by twos on their papers while she arranges a buff-colored newsprint sheet and fastens it to the front chalkboard. Ms. Taylor calls out the counting-by-twos answers and moves into the next activity, which is based on money.

Using a rubber ink-pad, Ms. Taylor stamps a nickel, a dime, a quarter, and a penny on the newsprint chart. She tells the class to write the value of what she has stamped on the sheet on their papers. Ms. Taylor stamps other values on the chart and the class continues writing. Some of the children talk among themselves and some actually call out the answers. Ms. Taylor does not tell the students to be quiet, but continues listing problems on the chart. All of the students write on their papers and seem to be involved with the lesson.

Ms. Taylor finishes her part of the lesson and tells the students to continue writing the answers on their papers. During the final 15 minutes of the mathematics period, the instructional pattern is highly individualized. Students who complete the chart work find other things to do. Some students go to a file cabinet in a corner of the room where individual folders are kept. Each student has one of these folders containing work assignments to be completed when all other work is done. These folders have been individualized to meet the learning needs of all students. Other students go to the board to do mathematics problems or choose activites from the bookshelves.

Activities are varied at the end of the class period. Small groups work together and individuals move about. The teacher moves about the room monitoring student work. The teacher-aide assists on the opposite side of the room.

When it is time for the mathematics period to end, Ms. Taylor says, "Now boys and girls, it's time to return to your seats." The students are told to leave a library book on top of their tables for the next period. Ms. Taylor asks the students to line up and walks with them out to the playground for recess.

Discussion.   In many ways, this lesson is similar to those in the larger class. The lesson begins with several different whole-class activities. It ends with students independently completing a whole-class assignment and then moving into a variety of individual activities. This particular lesson did not involve the textbook, but many lessons in the smaller class followed a similar format while using textbook materials. The major difference in the smaller class is that the lesson is developed more completely and successfully.

During whole-class activities, the students appear to be more involved and attentive than they were in the larger class. All the students seem to remember, for instance, previous lessons with "doubles," and they are all able to get to work on this activity. During recitation activities, such as the one with a deck of cards, Ms. Taylor is better able to notice and respond to individual cases of inattention, as she does with Michael. This and the other whole-class activities proceed quickly enough that there is more time for individual work at the end of the period.

In response to the increased opportunity for individual work, Ms. Taylor has now prepared a folder for each student. The work is selected to provide extra practice in needed skills in different curriculum areas. Students can do work from their folders whenever they have free time. But work in the folders is optional. While some students often turn to these folders, others choose different activities available in the class, including items displayed on the tables under the windows. There appears to be a greater diversity of activities in the smaller class, and more students have an opportunity to complete the basic lesson and move on to individual work.

Classroom Management

Interaction and group cohesion. Ms. Taylor's basic classroom management style, which could be described as a group-process approach, does not vary from the larger class to the smaller class. Ms. Taylor has an awareness of the needs of individuals. At the same time, she has a concern for developing group cohesiveness. Ms. Taylor attempts to build group cohesion by developing a spirit of cooperation among the students. She provides opportunities for students to work and talk together. The students are encouraged to help each other in solving problems, both academic and social.

Ms. Taylor feels that there is a clear difference between the beginning months of the year in the larger class and the final months in the smaller class. The smaller class is more cohesive and more comfortable. Student interaction proceeds more smoothly and Ms. Taylor can encourage cooperation and problem solving. Students are more involved in classroom lessons. This journal entry from Ms. Taylor summarizes the difference in interaction and group cohesion in the small class:

> I had a fifth-grade teacher in my room at lunch time today. It had begun to rain so the children had to stay inside for a period of time. He was just amazed at the ease with which they got to rainy-day activities, how quiet they were, how they didn't need direction from me—they were self-directed. They worked together well. Later on, as a reward for some good behavior, I took them to the park at which time again I could observe the way that they played together and get along together. I think that all of this has to do with the fact that they are a smaller group. They're like a family now—more than they can be with a larger class size.

How much of this difference can be attributed to class size? Ms. Taylor noted in the beginning when this class was larger that it seemed to be composed of more children with problems than she had taught in previous years. This group of children may have represented a particularly challenging set, but the large class size undoubtedly made it more difficult to deal with the problems presented. The situation was one in which the effects of class size were intensified. Not all large classes with this same teacher would present as many problems; but in a difficult situation, a large class size seriously limited the teacher's ability to cope.

Reducing class size did appear to allow for an improvement in the situation, but this improvement did not occur immediately. During the first month after the class-size reduction, Ms. Taylor was frustrated at the continuing management problems, especially those with Amanda. Over time, the smaller class size apparently allowed more teacher contact and encouraged more student involvement so that conditions gradually improved. This sequence of events is discussed further in Chapter 11, a discussion of the California site.

Individuality of students. By having a smaller number of students, Ms. Taylor is more aware of the needs of each one. She has more time to try different management strategies with students who may be experiencing behavior problems or learning difficulties. For example, Ms. Taylor reacts differently toward the same behavior manifested by two children.

> Amanda leaves the group and goes to the back of the room and pouts. Everyone else is responding in writing to questions being asked orally by Ms. Taylor. The lesson is a review of the sequence of events observed when seeds grow into plants. Amanda, sullen and sulky with head on her desk, looks up occasionally with thrust-out lips.

> At the same time: Brenden puts down his pencil, walks quietly to the empty desk near the window and stares aimlessly into space, giving no outward sign that he has any bad feelings about leaving the lesson.

Ms. Taylor ignores Amanda, yet says to Brenden: "Brenden, come on back and give the answers another try. I know you can do them."

While both children withdraw, Amanda's action is a familiar attention-getting antic. At first, the smaller class size encouraged Ms. Taylor to respond more often to Amanda's behavior, as she did to other individuals. But this only seemed to increase the frequency of Amanda's misbehavior. Now, Ms. Taylor has learned that it is best to ignore Amanda; besides, she knows Amanda can write the answers. On the other hand, Brenden has difficulty with paper-and-pencil assignments and retreats unless his efforts are acknowledged and he receives encouragement.

In the larger class, Ms. Taylor tried to pay attention to individual students. However, each child received attention less often. Ms. Taylor finds satisfaction in noticing individual children—how they learn, how they behave, the progress they are making. Her journal contains a wealth of evidence about how she is able to respond more fully to individuals when the class size is smaller:

> On the first day with the smaller class, Ms. Taylor wrote that "I am already seeing things that I was unaware of due to the large number of students—Tanya's oral reading needs strengthening."

"When there are 35 children in the class, I don't see them catch on and grasp things the way they do when we have 22 children. This is because Mrs. Reed, the aide, and I have added time to spend with them to make sure they get it. With a large class we have trouble spotting who isn't getting it and I'm not sure what to give for practice work. In a large class I don't see as many children feeling good and this is because we can't get to those children often enough who don't understand."

Ms. Taylor often discussed the progress of individual students in her journal. The following comments of hers about three students illustrate how academic progress is achieved under the two class-size settings.

William responds very well to adult attention. In a large class there is little of this to go around. Progress for William is not as great in a large class.

In a large class Donneatta's schoolwork drops off and her work is very, very slow. It is of good quality but there isn't enough of it when there are 35 children in class. With less children she shows progress by speaking out more in the reading group.

In a large class Brenden will tend to quit tasks if he thinks he can't do them. In a smaller class, we're able to support him and then he completes the task and feels good when he's finished.

Three other examples illustrate the special kinds of individual attention that Ms. Taylor is able to give in the small class that were less frequent in the larger class: as she describes it,

I am also able to work with the children on individual problems, little personality things that they need to correct to enable them to interact better with larger groups. I am pleased to see Dean, who up to this point, has spent 90% of his time minding everybody's business but his own, now really working on minding his own business. He's aware of when he's not attending to his own affairs and he's attending to somebody else's—I can bring this about with just a look at this time. I look at him, he says, 'I know, I'm not minding my own business,' and he settles down. This has been effective also with Amanda. You can't zero in on individual problems such as this with a large group of children because there are so many problems and so little time.

On other occasions individual help is targeted on academic performance.

Doris is having trouble with borrowing, as in a problem such as $31 - 17$. Ms. Taylor takes her aside when the other children are busy and with a box of blue cardboard cut-outs to represent pennies and dimes, she says to Doris: "Put out a dime." (Doris does.) "Now if I ask for seven cents from that dime, what do you have to do?" (Without saying anything, Doris changes the dime to ten pennies and waits. After a short pause, she hands Ms. Taylor seven pennies.)

This type of situation occurs more frequently in the smaller class because Ms. Taylor has time to pull individual students aside to give them special help. Sometimes, a more long-term individual activity is prescribed.

With fewer students, Ms. Taylor is able to monitor language skill development in the class. She notices that Audra, who writes fluently, is an incredibly poor speller. Ms. Taylor asks a curriculum specialist about Audra. The specialist suggests that Audra should develop her own dictionary of words that she misspells frequently and she should proofread her own stories using the self-made dictionary.

Self-confidence. While all students receive individual attention from Ms. Taylor, the low-achieving students are of special concern. It is these students in particular who seem to bloom under the smaller-class conditions, where they can receive the help and encouragement they need in order to do their work successfully and feel good about what they are doing.

In the smaller class Ms. Taylor is able to encourage children when they become "bogged down" on an assignment, as we have seen in earlier examples with Brenden. Ms. Taylor appreciates the opportunity to provide this help, as she states in her journal:

> When the class is large, Mrs. Adams (the aide) and I do not have extended time to go around and encourage the children. The able students get along all right but it is the less able students that are hard to reach in a large group. I find that when the class is reduced in size, the less able students are putting more time into reading because Mrs. Reed and I have the opportunity to go around and give encouragement. Children do not receive as much encouragement when the class is large.

At times, more than a little help is required. In the smaller class, Ms. Taylor is more likely to notice critical points in a child's development and to be able to provide special assistance. Often, Mrs. Reed is assigned to give extended individual help at these moments, as in the case of Randy. Ms. Taylor noticed that Randy was just at the stage of being able to do spelling dictation. She recorded this incident in her journal:

> He was able to take dictation last week for the first time . . . this week, he didn't seem interested in doing much of anything . . . I felt from his attitude that people were working with him at home but either he was learning the material and not letting me know . . . or he just wasn't learning . . . I called his family and that didn't produce any positive effects. I had Mrs. Reed take about a half an hour time with him this afternoon just privately between the two of them because Mrs. Reed is a patient woman who is so able in dealing with children and able to bring the very best out in them. She took this time, which she would not have in a large classroom setting. Randy spelled his words and earned a happy face sticker which he'll wear home today. When he's asked where it came from he can say, 'I spelled my words.' The parents feel good because they've helped him, Randy feels good because he's succeeded, and we feel good because we've been able to help a child hopefully begin to get over whatever hurdle it is that makes him see not doing his work as a positive thing.

Another special case is that of William. William missed six weeks of school early in the spring. When he returned, he found himself further than ever behind his classmates. To rebuild his willingness to try, Ms. Taylor and Mrs. Reed paid special attention to William, giving him chances to participate and do well, and praising his efforts. Ms. Taylor made sure William could answer some easy questions in the group. The following incident illustrates their approach:

> The class is doing a nutrition lesson. Students are marking answers in a booklet. William has a correct answer and calls out, "Mrs. Taylor, come here." Ms. Taylor checks his work and sees he has many correct answers. She praises his work and William beams. She helps him with a couple more, then says, "Mrs. Reed, you should see what this boy has done." Ms. Taylor pats William on the head. Ms. Reed comes over and puts C's next to all the correct answers.

The smaller class makes it possible to give this kind of individual attention immediately. William is encouraged to believe that he can do well, so he is more willing to keep trying.

Patterns of Instruction

Grouping. As in the larger class, instruction is carried out primarily in group lessons. With the reduction in class size, there are some changes in the grouping arrangements. For the morning reading period, grouping remains the same, but there is a shift in the afternoon reading period. Previously there had been two groups in the afternoon. One of these groups became so small that Ms. Taylor moved two students ahead to form a single group. Now all children work together for the initial activities, including basic phonics, story development, and reading of the story. Following this, Mrs. Reed works with a few students who need extra practice reading the day's story. This group rereads the story aloud. The remaining students remain with Ms. Taylor for extended comprehension activities. She can build on the day's story and introduce activities suggested in the teacher's manual.

In mathematics, the grouping patterns are somewhat more flexible. The whole class continues to move as a group through the second-grade book published by Heath. In the smaller class, however, Ms. Taylor is able to create small groups for extra instruction when the need arises. Ms. Taylor is able to monitor the small class more closely and sends individuals to work with the teacher's aide when they have trouble completing the day's assignment. Ms. Taylor also will teach a lesson to a small group, when some students are slower to grasp a concept on which the class is working.

Types of Lessons. Ms. Taylor used direct instruction with the total class when she had 35 students. At the end of each lesson, students were given an opportunity to work on individualized activities. However, there was a limited amount of time available for independent work because of numerous questions from the students and disciplinary interruptions.

With the smaller class, Ms. Taylor retains the same basic organization of presenting a lesson to the total group and using time at the end of the period for a variety of alternative activities. In the smaller class the total group lesson tends to proceed more smoothly with fewer interruptions, leaving more time for individual choices of activities at the end of the period.

The following description of a mathematics period illustrates the wide range of activities students participated in during the smaller class:

> Two children are at the chalkboard doing addition problems out of an old hard-cover third-grade arithmetic book. Three childen are gathered around an aide, having their work checked. Two childen are busily engaged in solving a math puzzle. Four children are completing worksheets from their folders. Four children are on follow-up activities resulting from a just-finished lesson with Ms. Taylor, and the remaining five children remain with Ms. Taylor to complete their understanding of a math skill.

A similarly wide choice of activities follows an afternoon reading lesson. Because only half of the class is present, fewer children are involved.

> Three children are reading silently from library books. Two are working together testing each other on spelling. One child is finishing the writing of a story. Two children have chosen to do puzzles. Two more are taking turns waiting to read aloud to the aide, Ms. Reed. And Ms. Taylor is listening to a child read orally for purposes of diagnosis.

Ms. Taylor is able to provide individual work folders for the 22 students. She did not have time to select materials and keep up with folders for 35 students. By having the folders available to the small class, students are more likely to use time left at the end of a lesson productively.

In addition to more opportunities for independent work on a variety of alternative activities in the smaller class, there are other advantages over the larger class. There are numerous ways in which the curriculum is enriched and strengthened, in addition to the extended comprehension activities in afternoon reading described earlier. For example, with the larger class, there were few field trips. Field trips engage the children's attention through firsthand experiences to provide the stimulus for follow-up activities in social studies, science, and the language arts. Ms. Taylor took the smaller class on several field trips, and comments:

> The trip to the P G & E Energy Expo Exhibit was relaxing and educationally very rewarding. The trip is something I never would have thought of doing with 35 children. Taking 35 children to San Francisco on public transportation would have been a most difficult if not impossible task.

> The trip to the Alameda State Beach is impossible to make with 35 children. The group has to be small to hear and see what the naturalist talks about. It is an excellent trip and one that imparts a great deal of knowledge and experience to the children. However, 35 children cannot be accommodated on such a trip.

Ms. Taylor also took this class on its first community walk after the class size had been reduced. The class walked to a construction area to observe a bulldozer being used. Following this walk, as for the other field trips, students wrote about their experiences. Ms. Taylor commented to observers that she found she was having the students do more writing in the smaller class. She had more time to discuss writing topics with children and more time to comment on student compositions.

In the smaller class there are also more opportunities for lessons involving the manipulation of objects. Ms. Taylor describes this activity with the smaller class:

> I was also able to let the children go to the centers, for example, the math and science center where they could experiment with measuring liquids. We were talking about pints, quarts, cups. They were able to pour water from one container to another so that they could actually see that 4 cups = 2 quarts—they saw it by actually doing it with the measuring of water. With 35 students I couldn't allow that type of activity to go on because it invariably ends in a mess and arguments and fights.

Probably because of this opportunity to measure things themselves, the students seem to understand the concepts better than in previous years, according to Ms. Taylor: "I feel for the first time that children aren't parroting back the information that I'm giving them, but that they understand when I show them a quart."

Another area of the curriculum that is enriched in the smaller class is student speaking before the group. Ms. Taylor offers the students an opportunity to participate in a unit on public speaking. Each student is responsible for giving a short talk. The remaining students form an audience responsible for listening carefully and offering constructive help to the speaker. Ms. Taylor had planned to spread the speeches over two days, but she finds the students so engrossed in the activity that they continue along so all students can participate the first day. The entire class listens attentively while each student has a turn to speak. Ms. Taylor is delighted that the unit goes so successfully.

Ms. Taylor is also able to offer more creative activities in the smaller class. She comments in her journal:

> I am able to do so much more with creative activities with a smaller class. Today we made rabbit puppets for Easter. The children named their puppets and before the art lesson was over each child was able to have his puppet introduce himself or herself to the class. Next week we will write stories or little plays that they will share in the puppet theater next Friday.

Directing a lesson. As in the larger class, Ms. Taylor plans group lessons to motivate students and involve them actively as participants. Ms. Taylor's typical approach to motivation is to appeal to her students' natural curiosity, fascination with puzzle-like activities, interest in dramatization and story telling, fondness for absurdities, challenge in finding dissimilarities, and their tendency to avoid boredom and monotony. In the smaller class, each student can have a turn to respond more often. Also, there is more opportunity for active experience with manipulative materials. The use of manipulatives is a hands-on experience which has some of the same intrigue as solving a puzzle.

Games that require the use of playing cards hold a particular excitement for these second graders. Undoubtedly there is a degree of identification with adults who have been seen to enjoy playing cards. With a deck of playing cards for each two children, Ms. Taylor teaches games that require the knowledge of the basic addition and subtraction facts and have such names as "Twenty-nine," "Sweet Sixteen," "A Hundred and One," and "Casino." The games replace repetitive, tiresome drills. Ms. Taylor uses the playing cards both in the larger and smaller classes.

Ms. Taylor appeals to students by stimulating their interest. During a reading lesson, she first gives background information to develop an interest in the story:

> "Have you ever been watching TV and had someone come along and turn it off in the middle of what you are watching?" (The response indicates an indentification with the situation.) "How did you feel on being stopped like that?" (The children answer, "angry," "mad," while some suggest a response such as "I'd tell my mother.") "Yes, you feel angry and mad and as if you want to do something. This story you are about to read is not about TV watching. But it does tell of some of the same feelings you have been talking about. Read by yourself and see those feelings. I'll be back in 20 minutes to talk with you about the story."

Again this is an instructional strategy that is used in both the larger and smaller classes. However, in the smaller class Ms. Taylor is able to spend more time on comprehension discussions with the students, in addition to other comprehension activities.

Summary

Ms. Taylor began the school year, 1978–79, with 35 second-grade students. During the first weeks of the school year, Ms. Taylor found this particular class to be more difficult to handle than classes from previous years. Perhaps its difficulty stemmed from a wide spread in reading skills, differences in maturity levels, or a combination of personalities; but these difficulties were exacerbated by the large class size. Both Ms. Taylor and her teaching assistant commented that this group seemed to have a larger-than-usual number of behavior problems, and they found the frequent misbehavior very frustrating. It seemed to prevent them from achieving the cooperative family spirit they desired, and also resulted in a curtailed curriculum.

Midway through the school year, class size was reduced to 22 students. Ms. Taylor's basic instructional style and classroom management approach remained the same. She maintained her focus on building group cohesion, recognizing individual differences, and developing self-confident students. However, the quality of life in the classroom improved tremendously when there were fewer students. Over a period of months in the smaller class, students became more involved in their work. The frequency of misbehavior appeared to diminish.

Ms. Taylor enjoyed a quieter, more relaxed teaching environment which allowed her more time to devote to individuals. She was able to plan individual work folders for the 22 students and monitor their progress more closely. There are numerous examples of special tutorial work with individual students. For all students, the curriculum was richer in the smaller class because of field trips, extended reading activities, more opportunities for choices of independent learning activities, and more opportunities for working with manipulatives.

10

Mrs. Monroe's Classroom

THE "LARGER-CLASS" VIEW

The Physical Environment

Even with 35 students in a mixed grades two and three class, Mrs. Monroe's classroom seems orderly and spacious. The physical environment contributes to this impression. The room, like many older classrooms, is high-ceilinged. Along one wall is a double row of windows that look out over a large open area of green grass. Within the room, the central floor space contains an arrangement of students' work tables. Two students work side-by-side at each table. The tables are arranged back-to-back in pairs, with space between each pair of tables. There is a wide aisle down the center of the room. At one end of the room are shelves and storage cabinets. The teacher's desk is centered in front of this area.

The remaining two walls are covered with green chalkboards interspersed with bulletin-board spaces. At the front of the room, which is predominantly chalkboard, the daily schedule is posted in one corner. The schedule lists activities for the entire day beginning with preplanning for the teacher and including activities for the class: 9:00–reading, and so on. At the other end of the chalkboard is a chart that reminds the students what to do when they finish assignments:

I check my work.

I enjoy my library book.

I complete other work.

I use flashcards.

I study spelling words.

I identify troublesome words.

I work with the reading game.

I work quietly with a neighbor.

To the right of the chalkboard is a bulletin board entitled, "Art." It measures about four and a half feet by six feet. In the center is a large, colorful design, obviously commercial; around three edges, children's work forms a neat border, with cut-outs, patterns, and white snowflakes on black paper. To the left of the chalkboard is another bulletin board that has a label saying, "Put your arithmetic to work." Below this are nine mimeographed worksheets, neatly and symmetrically spaced, framed by colored backing.

To the right of the classroom, on the wall opposite the windows, are a long chalkboard and a bulletin board above it. This chalkboard, like the others, is very clean. Over parts of the chalkboard hang four charts. One chart gives the classroom composition: the number of boys and girls in each of the two grades and then the total. One day in November, in the larger class, the count was 13 boys and nine girls in grade two and nine boys and four girls in grade three. Three other larger charts are for reading lessons. For example, one lists for "Word Study." The bulletin board above the chalkboard carries the question "Where Do You Live?" in large, artistically formed cut-out letters. Spaced around this message are framed, commercial maps of the metropolis, country, state, and city. Like all the room decorations, this display is carefully arranged and uncrowded.

Although Mrs. Monroe has allowed for open spaces in the classroom, she feels the pressure of housing 35 students. It is difficult to separate students the way she would like. One of her discipline techniques is to change seating or ask a student to move away from the group. As she expresses it, "there are not enough corners"; there are more children with behavior problems than places to put them. With fewer students and less crowded conditions, this might be less of a problem.

Key
R = Remedial students
A = Average students
I = Independent students

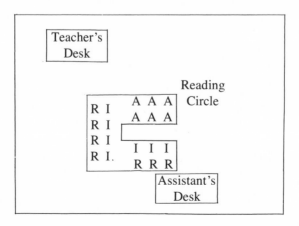

Mrs. Monroe also envisions a different seating arrangement when the class is smaller. She explains that she would prefer to have the chairs and tables in a "Horseshoe Party Arrangement." In this arrangement, she says, students could enjoy seeing each other's faces and company. Clean-up and game activities could be accomplished more easily. Also, this seating arrangement would provide for interaction between the independent and remedial learners. The independent learners could serve as role models as well as "study partners" for the remedial learners. A diagram of Mrs. Monroe's "ideal" arrangement appears on page 157.

A Typical Math Lesson

Description. Math is the first lesson of the day for the total class because of the staggered reading schedule. In the lesson being described, 32 children are present. Early reading students, who arrived at 9:00 a.m., have just had recess with late reading students who come to school at 10:00 a.m.

Mrs. Monroe goes to the playground to bring the children in. The first children walk into the classroom and find their seats with a minimum of confusion. Meanwhile, sounds of a scuffle can be heard out in the hall. Mrs. Monroe moves quickly to settle a dispute between two little boys who are pushing each other and arguing over their positions at the end of the line. Mrs. Monroe reports that this type of skirmish is a frequent occurrence with the long lines created by a class size of 35.

Mrs. Monroe escorts the stragglers into the room and they take their seats. There seems to be no confusion over where each student is expected to sit and the room is settled within a short time. As the students wait for class to begin, they quietly carry on conversations begun on the playground.

Mrs. Monroe calls upon one of the boys to lead the group in pledging allegiance to the flag. All of the students turn to the front of the classroom to face the flag. They place their right hands over their hearts and recite the pledge. When the salute is over some students, begin to talk among themselves. The teacher aide, Mrs. Horne, says, "Sshh, be quiet." The students sit down and are quiet.

Mrs. Monroe tells the class to get out their math books. She writes the page numbers for the second-grade assignment on the chalkboard. Most of the children begin to turn pages and find something to do. However, six or seven students talk to their tablemates rather than begin working. Those working in the third-grade book have not been given a specific page assignment, and there is more talking among this group, although some books do appear. Mrs. Monroe visually surveys the students and says, "We don't need any room for talking."

After the children start working, Mrs. Monroe uses attendance cards to call the roll. The students continue working, but glance up to respond when their names are called. Several students volunteer information about classmates who are absent.

After taking attendance, Mrs. Monroe begins a review lesson on telling time with the third graders. The second graders continue working independently. Mrs. Monroe holds up a large cardboard model of a clock face and has the students count by fives. She then calls on individual students to read particular times. Several of the students have difficulty telling the time.

While Mrs. Monroe works with the third graders, Mrs. Horne, the teacher's aide, sits at a table near the front of the classroom. Periodically, individual second graders walk up to Mrs. Horne to have their workbook pages corrected.

The third graders are sitting in two groups of six and eight. Students in the group closer to the teacher seem to pay more attention than the group that is farther away. As the lesson continues, fewer students seem to be paying attention. They glance around the room or play with their pencils.

Mrs. Monroe hands Mrs. Horne additional worksheet pages for the second graders and puts on a record about multiplication tables for the third graders. The voice on the record challenges the third graders to "Listen and call out the answers." The students generally listen as the voice on the record recites the table of fours. Some quietly call out answers; others do not. When the record ends, Mrs. Monroe moves to the chalkboard. She calls for three boys to come up to the board and work out problems they have heard on the record. The three boys compete to finish first. The remaining third graders sit and watch. Although they have not been told to, many second graders also watch the chalkboard activity from their seats.

The three boys complete the exercise and are told to erase their work and call other students to take their places. After several groups have worked at the board, Mrs. Monroe plays the phonograph record again. She then gives worksheets on multiplication to the third graders as a follow-up activity. As the students work, she moves around the room checking their answers. One student has finished an entire page correctly, and she says, "I can tell who was a good listener."

Four minutes before recess time, Mrs. Monroe tells the students that it is time to get ready for recess. She collects the papers of the third graders. Students put their books and pencils away. When the students are ready, she calls them to line up, then sends the line out the door.

Discussion.   Several features of this lesson are typical. Many revolve around the difficulty in managing separate lessons for the two grade levels. Mrs. Monroe comments in her journal that she does not try to give the second-grade and third-grade groups an equal amount of attention each day. On this particular day, she was directly involved in lessons for the third-grade group. But she had to be sure the second graders had something to do and she also had to oversee their behavior. In this case, the second graders had to read for themselves the directions for their task, or look at their neighbors, or ask Mrs. Horne for help. Mrs. Horne did not teach lessons, but often had to figure out directions on confusing worksheets so she could explain them to children who asked for help.

An alternative arrangement that Mrs. Monroe often used was to alternate between the two groups. This frequently meant that each group would receive a lesson and directions from Mrs. Monroe, but that one group had to wait five to 10 minutes before their lesson began. Even in the typical lesson described above, the third graders had to wait until after attendance was taken before their lesson really began.

Another typical feature is Mrs. Monroe's emphasis on basic skills, which is seen especially in the multiplication drill. She had previously taught upper-elementary grades and expressed frustration at children reaching that level and not knowing basic facts. She relied on a number of different formats for practice work—in this case, the record player, boardwork, and worksheets.

In spite of the difficulty of managing two groups, the math period runs fairly smoothly. The second graders usually find something to do (sometimes, listening to the third graders). The third graders wait reasonably peacefully. The children stay in their seats and are generally quiet. They may be doing the work wrong, or they may be giving the lesson less than full attention, but they are not disruptive. This, too, is typical of the classroom.

In the next sections of the chapter, specific aspects of the classroom program are described in more detail. The role of class size and possible changes are discussed.

Classroom Management

An observer entering Mrs. Monroe's room in November is impressed with the orderliness and quiet. During transition periods or between assignments, students talk quietly; once the lesson begins, the noise level drops. As a reminder that silence is expected, Mrs. Monroe might say: "I'm waiting for your mouths to close," or "We don't need any room for talking."

Students stay in their seats, except when taking their work to be checked. Following the hour-long noon recess, Mrs. Monroe provides an extra transition between the activity of the playground and the quiet she expects in the classroom: There is a five- to 10-minute rest period, when students put their heads down, relax, and close their eyes and mouths.

Of course, students sometimes become restless or talkative, potentially disturbing the class. Mrs. Monroe responds in one of several ways. During a transition, she may remind a student of what he should be doing, for example: "Scedric, get your book out."

If students become restless during a lesson, she will write on the board "P.M. Club." Students know that if their names to up under this heading, they will have to stay after school. An individual student may be told to move to another seat, with the explanation: "You're not ready for company."

Occasionally a student is sent to stand in the hall. During such incidents, Mrs. Monroe responds calmly and firmly. She never raises her voice.

It is perhaps Mrs. Monroe's demeanor which is one key to the room's smooth functioning. Like the classroom, Mrs. Monroe is calm and formal. She is dignified and speaks in slow, even tones. It is clear that she is in charge of the room. She is the teacher.

One aspect of this formal approach to teaching is a kind of distance between the teacher and the students. Teacher and students seldom chat casually about topics of interest. Students do not share their personal experiences in class. Instead, Mrs. Monroe interacts with the students as a class unit. Lessons tend to be taught to the class, or subcomponents of the class, rather than individualized, as will be discussed later. Interactions do take place between the teacher and individual students. Sometimes Mrs. Monroe is called upon by individuals to arbitrate disputes. She says about such situations that she "tries hard to be fair." She also offers some personal feedback to a student about his work. If a student completes a worksheet correctly, she is clearly proud of this and may comment: "You're doing real well."

A student who does less well may draw the comment: "Well, that wasn't very good. I guess you didn't do your homework last night."

Even individual comments like these clearly preserve the teacher–student roles.

Another factor important to the room's smooth functioning may be the regularity and predictability of classroom events. Regular patterns of activity are established. Students have assigned seats for reading groups and for other activities. All activities begin at the direction of the teacher. The same kinds of instructional activities appear repeatedly, as will be discussed in a later section. The children know what is expected of them. They know what will happen in the classroom. A stable, predictable environment has been created.

Although good order is maintained, Mrs. Monroe is very conscious of the potential for disruption and of the constant vigilance she has to exercise. She comments on the fights that break out at the end of the line coming in from recess. She also comments on the lack of space to separate children ("not enough corners"). Careful planning of the day's instruction has to be done so that the students always have something to do. Mrs. Monroe does not feel that she can get to know her students as individuals because she must keep the groups working and out of trouble. She feels the pressure of "staying on top of things" with so many students.

Patterns of Instruction

Types of lessons and use of materials. In reading, students are assigned to groups according to their level in the school-adopted basal reader series, which is published by Economy Press and emphasizes a phonetic approach to beginning reading. There are four groups, two in the morning and two in the afternoon. The range in reading-group levels is from *Green Feet,* the primer, to *Mysterious Wisteria,* a third-grade reader. Each child has a workbook to accompany the reader. Supplementary dittos are also available.

A typical lesson for a reading group includes silent reading, oral reading, and a workbook page or dittoed exercises. Mrs. Monroe reinforces the series' emphasis on phonics through a variety of phonics activities. She also emphasizes fluency and expression in oral reading, for instance, by reminding the students that they should read naturally, the way they talk. Sometimes, comprehension questions are asked following the group's oral reading. The comprehension questions that are asked generally require recall of information from the story rather than interpretation or relationship to personal experience.

Three variations occur in the reading schedule. On Mondays, during both the morning and afternoon reading periods, students go to the library. The librarian teaches a lesson on library skills, phonics, or reads a story to the class. The children may check out books. On Thursdays, Mrs. Monroe generally has supplementary written work to enrich the program and reinforce skills—for example, Dolch crossword puzzles. On Fridays, the students work in a reading kit published by Science Research Associates (SRA).

Mathematics instruction is organized around the textbook, published by Heath. Some students are in the second-grade book and some are in the third-grade book. Most students are working at grade level, but there are some second graders in the third-grade group and some third graders in the second-grade group. A typical lesson involves doing one or two pages from the math book.

Mrs. Monroe supplements the math book in a number of ways. She frequently brings in dittos. These present the material from the textbook in a somewhat different, often simpler, way and provide extra reinforcement for skills. Some dittos use a puzzle or game format designed to motivate children. Mrs. Monroe also uses games or contests in the classroom to provide variety and motivation. A common game is the "big T" game played at the blackboard:

$$
\begin{array}{r|}
\times\ 3 \\
\hline
6 \\
2 \\
5 \\
4 \\
\end{array}
$$

Three or four students start by writing the problems as shown above. They then compete to fill in the answers as soon as possible. A third kind of supplementary activity is the use of the record player. A multiplication-drill record is used both with the whole class and with groups.

At Harrison School, the Follow-Through program emphasizes literature and language development. Mrs. Monroe is new to the Follow-Through program because she has just moved to this grade level. She does not have as many materials and ideas for instruction in this area as she would like. A common activity is to read a story to the class, or play a story record, then have the children write about the story. Around Christmas, language workbooks published by Laidlaw are delivered to the school. Mrs. Monroe uses these books, moving through them in sequence. She also works on spelling, using the spelling workbooks, and views spelling as important practice for writing correctly.

Directing a lesson. Mrs. Monroe organizes her teaching around the curriculum materials. She usually focuses on how students are to complete a lesson rather than on a general introduction of the topic of the lesson. For example, in introducing a reading lesson, Mrs. Monroe directs the children's attention to a workbook page:

> Get your reading workbooks out and turn to page 22. I will read the words in the box at the top of the page. Put your finger on each word as I read it: 'aside,' 'ashore,' 'atop,' 'ablaze.' (Pause) What do all the words start with?

When the answer is given, Mrs. Monroe explains that words are formed by blending the sound of "a" with the word that follows to build the new word. Attention is directed to the bottom half of the page where sentences with blanks appear. The children are asked to complete each sentence on their own using the words in the box at the top of the page.

A typical math lesson begins with the directions for doing a workbook page. Once the children have found the correct page, Mrs. Monroe asks: "How many see those yellow arrows on the page? What are they really for?" The question is a rhetorical one because Mrs. Monroe explains that the arrows point to spaces where answers to addition problems are to be placed. One or two sample problems may be done on the board to clarify the directions, then the students go to work.

The main structure of Mrs. Monroe's lessons focuses on procedure rather than on content. Students are trained to follow directions, respond when asked questions, and to complete whatever work assignment is given. Mrs. Monroe does not attempt to engage student interest in a lesson by providing any type of set induction. She expects students to do the work and they do.

Monitoring and evaluating student work. During most lessons there is a period when students work independently to complete the assignment. During this time both Mrs. Horne and Mrs. Monroe help the students, check papers, and provide feedback. Mrs. Horne usually sits by the group she is working with; Mrs. Monroe often moves around from student to student. There is an almost constant need for individual attention and no way to get around to everyone. Some students do not know what to do on the page; others have finished already and want their papers checked.

This situation contributes to the amount of time students spend waiting. They wait for directions; they wait for the teacher's attention. Students are usually anxious to have their workbooks corrected right away. Frequently, Mrs. Monroe has to say, "Wait, it's not your turn yet." Children who have finished their work and who wait for Mrs. Monroe or the aide often become restless. They talk to other students, creating an increased noise level, or they get into arguments and minor scuffles. The chart posted in front of the room is in response to this problem. It lists things to do when work is finished (e.g., check my work, study spelling words). Children were not often observed doing these things. Sometimes they would work ahead in the book, not necessarily accurately. Mrs. Monroe was busy helping the rest of the class through the day's lesson.

When work is checked, the focus is on whether the answers are right or wrong. A student who completes a page correctly may be praised or allowed to be a "helper" for another student. A student who makes errors must correct those problems, if time allows.

Difficulty/pacing. Mrs. Monroe expects the students to cover fairly difficult material. Students are expected to progress regularly through the book. Some second graders who are capable workers are placed in the third-grade group for reading, mathematics and/or spelling. In creative writing, all students are expected to be able to write independently about a story.

The fact that some students cannot complete tasks successfully is accepted regretfully by the teacher. Mrs. Monroe comments that when she presents a lesson she looks for at least a few students to understand what to do. If some students get it, the others will eventually. Sometimes "eventually" seems to be forever. Mrs. Monroe is frustrated in December by how long it is taking the third-grade group to grasp the idea of regrouping. She knows from checking the papers that many students are not doing well. She reteaches the lesson using a ditto with simpler problems and a format that reminds the students to regroup:

$$
\begin{array}{r}
\bigcirc\ \square \\
35 \\
-17 \\
\hline
\end{array}
$$

She reviews the language of the ten's place and the one's place. But progress is slow. In reading, some students seem to reach a review page and not remember the words from previous lessons (if they ever knew them).

Class size. What aspects of these patterns of instruction might be related to class size? When asked to describe her ideal smaller class Mrs. Monroe writes that, "The curriculum wouldn't be different, but we could participate in many more enrichment activities . . . more reading activities—drama, role playing, action games."

She is also extremely aware of the difficulty of monitoring students to give help and feedback during seatwork. She writes that she would like to be able to do more one-to-one instruction: "Meeting individual differences is a full-time job. I feel if the class were smaller I could do much better."

Instructional Assistants

Mrs. Monroe depends upon the teacher aide to help maintain discipline and a quiet work environment. Mrs. Horne listens to oral reading, supervises and checks seatwork. She also prepares instructional materials. Mrs. Monroe usually tries to have Mrs. Horne work in one half of the room while she works in the other half. They may trade positions during the period.

During December Mrs. Horne is absent for a week because she has strep throat. There are no provisions for substitute aides and Mrs. Monroe has the entire class of 35 by herself. She finds the experience totally exhausting.

Mrs. Monroe sometimes uses one child to help another. But she tries to remain close to where the students are working so that she can monitor the tutoring.

Summary

The previous sections describe the classroom when it contained 35 pupils.What changes will be made when the class is reduced to 22 pupils? Mrs. Monroe envisions a different seating arrangement that is more conducive to student interaction. She looks forward to more room for separating pupils when necessary, but hopes that fewer discipline problems will arise. She does not plan changes in the basic curriculum or mode of instruction, but she envisions a number of possibilities for enrichment activities. She is also aware of students who need extra help to understand and complete assignments; she believes the smaller class will allow her to meet individual needs better.

Midway through the school year, the class is divided giving Mrs. Monroe 22 students. The next sections of the chapter describe the life in the smaller class.

MRS. MONROE'S CLASSROOM: THE "SMALLER-CLASS" VIEW

The Physical Environment

With fewer students (22 instead of 35), Mrs. Monroe's orderly classroom seems even more spacious. Fewer student tables occupy the center space. One table is moved over to the corner to create a Multiethnic center where some of Mrs. Monroe's materials relating to this theme are now displayed.

Mrs. Monroe appreciates having more room to spread students out. During reading, for instance, there are now only 10 or 11 students and to an observer the room appears almost empty. There is certainly space to isolate students when necessary. More space, along with smaller numbers, contributes to a calmer, quieter environment. On the first day, Mrs. Monroe notes in her journal that "The room is so much quieter."

Mrs. Monroe does not arrange the students' seats in a horseshoe formation as she speculated she might do. Perhaps she finds it difficult to use this arrangement in a split-grade (second/third) class, where she has students seated in grade-level groups, since much of the instruction is differentiated by grade level. Also, the seating arrangement may be constrained by consideration of the aide, Mrs. Horne. Mrs. Horne prefers to stay seated rather than walk around the room. Mrs. Monroe has tried to encourage her to move around but without much effect. So, in order to take advantage of the aide to supervise and provide help, Mrs. Monroe tends to seat a group of low-achievers at Mrs. Horne's customary table.

A Typical Math Lesson

Description. The following paragraphs describe a typical math lesson in the smaller class. The students enter the room and move quickly to their seats. The period begins, as before, with the flag salute led by one of the children. After the flag salute, Mrs. Monroe calls the roll and prepares the lunch slip.

Mrs. Monroe walks to the front of the classroom, writes "Second—pg. 211" on the chalkboard, and says, "Open your books, second graders. Open your book to these pages and don't say anything. Just have your book open when I come by." As the six second graders who are present flip through the pages in their math books, Mrs. Monroe confers with the aide, asking whether the children have worked on page 211. The aide, Mrs. Horne, responds, "Yes." Mrs. Monroe walks past the group of second graders and over to the flannel board, where she picks up several pieces of felt in the shapes of fractional parts of a circle.

Mrs. Monroe then turns her attention to the third graders. She walks over to the chalkboard and writes, "Third—pg. 251." The 10 third-graders get out their books and turn to page 251. It is a page of multiplication problems where basic facts must be filled into a matrix format:

$$\begin{array}{cc|c} 7 & 8 & \\ \hline A & B & 4 \\ C & D & 3 \end{array}$$

The students must copy the problems on a piece of paper and work out the problems by replacing the letters with the appropriate numbers.

After giving the page assignment to the third graders, Mrs. Monroe returns to work with the second graders in a group lesson. She draws the attention of the second graders by saying, "You do not need a pencil in your hand. Put your pencil down on the table." She begins the lesson by demonstrating some figures on the flannel board. She uses students' names frequently and seems very aware of which students are paying attention.

> Mrs. Monroe holds up a red circle. "What is this I have in my hand, Willie?" Willie says, "A circle?" Mrs. Monroe confirms it is a circle. Now, Mrs. Monroe holds up a blue piece which is one-half of the whole. She says, "Lakisha, what do I have in my hand? It's a part of a circle, isn't it class?" The children agree that the blue on the red is a half-circle.

Mrs. Monroe continues to form different figures on the flannel board, and quiz the second graders. Occasionally a third grader calls out an answer as well.

After a few minutes Mrs. Monroe moves the lesson to the chalkboard, where she writes fractions and asks the class to identify them.

As Mrs. Monroe is drawing a circle on the chalkboard, she says, "I'm waiting for Jack to get his mouth closed." Mrs. Monroe does not turn around but she has recognized Jack's voice. She divides the circle she has drawn into three parts. She says, "Now what parts do I have?" Someone answers, "A third." She says "yes" and writes the symbol on the board, the fractional form, one over three, $\frac{1}{3}$.

She draws a circle and divides it into four parts and says, "Now how many pieces do I have?" "Lakisha, how much do I have?" Lakisha doesn't know. Mrs. Monroe says, "Count." Mrs. Monroe helps Lakisha count some parts. Lakisha still doesn't give the answer. Mrs. Monroe goes to someone else and asks for an answer.

After Mrs. Monroe has drilled the second graders to her satisfaction, she asks the group to look at their workbooks. She says to the children, "Yesterday I didn't see that the work was being done correctly." She explains what the page calls for, then leaves the children to finish the page independently.

As the second graders complete their workbook page, Mrs. Monroe surveys the work being done by the third graders. She notices that some students do not understand the format of their multiplication problems and she draws a sample grid on the board with the answers written in. She does not immediately explain the grid, but instead returns to the second graders.

Mrs. Monroe hands out to the second graders a new ditto that requires them to match geometric shapes to the correct label. She focuses the students' attention by giving the directions, "You will see some words in big, bold letters. I want you to put your hand on those words. You're going to touch those words. Put your pencils down." She has students read the words aloud— circle, square, triangle, rectangle—then she leaves the students to complete the page on their own. It is now 10:35 and the students do not receive another assignment for the rest of the period. By 10:40 several students are finished and they are told to color in the geometric shapes.

After handing out the ditto to the second graders, Mrs. Monroe returns to checking the work of the third graders. She draws their attention to the grid drawn on the blackboard and explains to them that it is an example of how they are to write the problems:

In your book you're to find the answers where there are letters. I put the answers in to show you how. Now if you don't know the answers, it's because you didn't study enough at home.

For the remaining 15 minutes of the math period, Mrs. Monroe circulates around the room checking students' work and giving assistance. Mrs. Horne remains in her seat near the second graders and checks their work when they come up to her.

The third graders seem to have several types of difficulty with their work. Some students do not understand the format of the problem. Even after her group review, Mrs. Monroe has to supply individual directions to at least one student:

> Mrs. Monroe turns to two third graders and says, "You're working mighty slow. So you want to stay this evening? Are you having trouble? Show me the one that's giving you trouble." The child points. Mrs. Monroe bends over the child and shows her how to do this particular exercise. She comments that the child knows her multiplication facts, but doesn't understand how to set up the problems.

Other students do not yet know their basic facts. Some students refer to a chart of basic facts permanently displayed on the wall. One student comes to Mrs. Monroe for help and is told to get the multiplication tables from his desk. He returns with a calculator and is allowed to use it to get his answers.

Students do not appear to give each other much help. Sonny says aloud that he does not understand how to do the problems. Jacob, seated two seats away, responds "I do," but continues on without offering any explanation.

Although Mrs. Horne checks the work of the second graders, Mrs. Monroe also looks at these students' work. She discovers a confusion that several students have about how to label a figure that is rotated. She draws several figures on the board and questions the students to clarify the issue. As she looks at their work, Mrs. Monroe comments, "I can see the people who are doing perfect work here, Mrs. Horne."

With about five minutes remaining in the period, Mrs. Monroe announces to the third graders, "I will expect the third graders to finish at least 12, at least 12 of those squares." She continues to circulate around the room and work with individual students. At 10:57 she tells the students, "Fold the paper in half and put the folded paper inside the book. It is recess time." Both the third and second graders put their materials away and stand. Mrs. Monroe says, "You may line up quietly." Derrick, a large third-grade boy, picks up three of the class balls. He gives one of the balls to another boy. Mrs. Monroe says, "You do not pass out balls in here, pass out balls outside." All of the children quickly walk out of the room and into the play area outside.

Discussion. Many features of this lesson are strikingly similar to the math lesson described in the larger-class setting. Instruction is still oriented toward the textbook and toward basic skills instruction. (The third graders are still working on multiplication facts.) As before, a variety of supplementary materials are in use. In this case, Mrs. Monroe uses the flannel board and the chalkboard to present concepts to the students. She also gives the second graders a ditto to complement their workbook page.

As before, some problems arise from the difficulty of teaching two different instructional groups. The third graders do not receive much introduction to their page, and the unfamiliar format causes some confusion. Later in the lesson, Mrs. Monroe allows the second graders to spend time coloring so that she can have an opportunity to help the third graders. But despite these difficulties, the lesson seems to proceed smoothly. Students are generally quiet and there is little evidence of disorder.

The same calm, orderly environment was described for the larger class, but a difference is apparent to Mrs. Monroe. She notices that there are fewer behavior problems to take time from teaching and she feels that the smaller class has helped her attitude. She reports that she feels more relaxed and is more enthusiastic about determining strengths and weaknesses of pupils. She has more patience to explain to students who do not understand what they are supposed to do.

This greater capacity to deal with individuals may be reflected at two points in the math lesson. During the small-group recitation, Mrs. Monroe appears to try to call on students to draw them into the lesson and to be sure that they understand. With a smaller class, each student is likely to be called on more often (as shown also in the Virginia data), and this alone may be beneficial. In addition, Mrs. Monroe may be better able to keep in mind the needs of individual students. For instance, she knows that Lakisha "needs special help in math fundamentals" and she spends time working through a problem with Lakisha.

Attention to individuals also occurs when Mrs. Monroe circulates around the room as the students do seatwork. As in this sample lesson, she often spends time monitoring the students' work, offering assistance and feedback. With fewer students she feels that she can do this more effectively. This assistance may be seen in the sample lesson, for instance, when she cleared up the second graders' confusion about the rotated figure. In her journal, Mrs. Monroe makes the following comment:

> Since the class has been made smaller, I now have time to observe closer and to give more individual attention to the needs and problems found from pupils day by day. Before when the class was so large (35 to 39), it was an exhausting matter to explain the lesson assignments and see to it that each pupil was following directions.

Classroom Management

Mrs. Monroe's management style is to create a structured learning environment. Her classroom is a quiet place in which students are expected to pay attention during frequent periods of group instruction, to follow directions, and to complete assigned work on time. One observer in the classroom commented that "there is a very peaceful atmosphere" as the children work.

Mrs. Monroe does not alter her basic style of classroom management when the class is made smaller. The same basic routines exist that formed the core of classroom life in the larger class. The same comments are heard as Mrs. Monroe reminds the students that she is "waiting for (their) mouths to close."

It does appear, however, that management is accomplished more easily in the smaller class. Certainly Mrs. Monroe feels that this is the case. She has more room to spread people out and fewer people to keep track of. She reports that there are fewer fights at the end of the line. And she feels more relaxed and able to keep up with the demands of teaching. Mrs. Horne, the aide, also comments that the class is easier to deal with now, especially since some particular students with behavior problems (who used to be seated near her) have been moved to the other classroom.

This change in the teacher's feeling is most apparent during Thursday's "station day," when students use instructional games during the reading period (see the following section for further details). At this time, Mrs. Monroe seems especially relaxed and able to joke with students. The smaller class size apparently encourages the teacher to allow more informal activities such as games, although they are still carried out with direct adult supervision.

Patterns of Instruction

Types of lessons and use of materials. In looking ahead to the smaller class, Mrs. Monroe did not envision any changes in basic curriculum or instructional procedures and none occur. As before, group instruction takes place. For most subjects, there are two groups, divided roughly on grade-level lines. In reading, there are two groups in the morning and two in the afternoon. Instruction is organized primarily around the textbook, with a number of supplementary materials and activities. General patterns of organizing the class for instruction have changed little in the smaller class.

Mrs. Monroe did envision the smaller class as an opportunity to use a greater range and variety of enrichment activities such as "drama, role playing, and action games," and this does occur to some extent. The primary example observed in the classroom is the use of games on Thursdays during reading period. In the larger class, Thursday reading was an occasion for supplementary written work such as dittos which were passed out to each reading group and completed by the students individually. In the smaller class, more interactive games such as Bingo are included. The period is divided into 20-minute segments, punctuated by a kitchen timer, after which games are traded across groups. But the students still work in two groups, one with the teacher and the other with the aide, and the adults generally determine what games are played. A typical "Station Day" is as follows:

> Mrs. Monroe announces that it is Station Day and says "We want to get started right on time." She sets the kitchen timer to 20 minutes and tells the children to move to the part of the room to which they've been assigned. At one table, Mrs. Horne sits with three children who get out puzzles. At another set of tables, Mrs. Monroe sits with a group of seven children. She passes out envelopes of green markers for her group to use in playing a Bingo game with vocabulary words from the basal reading series. Mrs. Monroe calls out a word, and the students look quickly to see if they can find it on their sheets and cover it with a green square. When a student thinks that he has "bingo," he must read off the words to Mrs. Monroe so she can check that he has won. As the students play the game, they seem intent on what they are doing, but the room is still quiet.

> After the Bingo game, Mrs. Monroe leads her group through a variety of language-arts games. She introduces one game as "the homonym game." One boy is slow

in getting his markers. Mrs. Monroe says with a good-natured smile, "and who is the slowest one in this group?" She passes out cards to the groups and explains the rules. Once the game has begun, Mrs. Monroe leaves her group and takes several games over to Mrs. Horne's group. She reviews the rules of the Bingo game for Mrs. Horne.

As the activities continue, a great deal of enthusiasm persists with the games. When a child mispronounces or does not give the correct definition of a word, there is good-natured laughter and teasing. The children play a number of games and ditto-sheet activities. When recess time arrives, the students ask to stay in to play the games. They say that "We don't need recess." Mrs. Monroe laughs and says, "Oh yes we do."

Mrs. Monroe believes that this kind of day would not have been possible in the larger class. She explains that many of the games were not designed to accommodate groups as large as her reading groups in the larger class. But she may also be willing to tolerate more student action and exuberance with fewer students present.

Directing a lesson. Mrs. Monroe does not alter her method of directing students through a lesson. She continues to focus on giving directions and calling upon students to respond to probing questions. The difference in the small-class situation is that Mrs. Monroe now appears to call on each of the students more often during a lesson. In the large-class situation, there were simply too many students for the teacher to notice and regularly call on them. With fewer students Mrs. Monroe can involve all students in the lesson, often purposefully calling on students who are inattentive or may be having difficulty, as illustrated in the sample math lesson. Mrs. Monroe varies her attention to the students so that no particular pattern is followed and all of the students are subject to accountability.

Monitoring and evaluating student work. Mrs. Monroe presents a lesson to a group of students and notes how individual students respond. Follow-up to group instruction takes the form of paper-and-pencil activities. While the students work, Mrs. Monroe moves around the room to offer help and check papers. With a smaller class, she is able to work with each student more often. Students spend less time waiting. Mrs. Monroe feels she knows more about how students are doing. Here is how Mrs. Monroe expresses her feeling about teaching the smaller class:

> (In the large class) . . . at the end of the day I was so completely exhausted with that many people in the room and now I can walk around the room, get to everybody, and find out what I need to plan for the next day and that's most helpful to me. (I can) see if they have done what I have asked them to do and where they made errors and what step do I need to take next to correct the errors. Should I go over this lesson again, should I plan something completely different getting over the same point in a different way?

> Many times with the larger group I didn't always have time to do that because so much of the time was spent for discipline and I neglected getting around to what

they accomplished unless I stayed here very late in the afternoon . . . I did that quite a bit, but it was taking so much from me and now I stay sometimes but it's peaceful and I can plan ahead . . . to correct the mistakes I've seen as I walked around the room, as I worked with (students) individually.

Difficulty/pacing. As in the larger class, Mrs. Monroe continues through the curriculum, presenting group lessons from the textbook and helping as many children as possible to master those lessons. The sample lesson in mathematics in the small class is typical of the sequence that occurs. Concepts are illustrated for the group and directions are given. Mrs. Monroe then monitors the students' independent work, giving help and checking papers. Based on the response of the group, a decision is made about the next day's lesson—move ahead, re-teach, or provide additional practice. Often the latter two options are needed.

Because she can monitor student work more effectively in the small class, Mrs. Monroe feels that she has more complete and accurate knowledge of how the students are responding. She can make a more valid decision about how to plan the next day's lesson (and she has time to think about it). Mrs. Monroe seldom deviates from the group structure to prescribe special work or extra work for a student who seems to need it.

With the smaller group for lessons and the greater opportunity for individual contact, some students seem to make more rapid progress. Mrs. Monroe finds that Kevin is making progress in reading. He had been in the lowest group, a group of four, and he often wasted time with one of the other students in this group. This other student changed rooms and only two students were left in Kevin's group. Kevin seems to be attending better and performing better.

Other students continue to have difficulty. Lakisha needs help with basic math fundamentals. David was tested and recommended for a special class; his mother gave consent, but he was never moved. Several new students are added to the class and many of them are working at a low level. They are placed with a group and given individual help when possible.

Instructional Assistants

In the large class when there were 35 students, Mrs. Monroe used the teacher aide to assist students who were working independently, to help grade papers, to urge pupils to complete their tasks, to prepare instructional materials, and to assist the slower students.

The teacher aide's role does not change with fewer students. She is in the classroom to assist the teacher wherever she is needed, as in the following example.

Mrs. Horne is standing in the front of the room, ready to be of assistance. Mrs. Monroe says, "Mrs. Horne, they need help over here." Mrs. Horne comes to the back of the room, gets paper, and takes it to the third-grade students.

Mrs. Monroe discusses the teacher aide in an interview conducted after the class is reduced in size. She comments that things are much better in the small class because she can check on each child herself. She feels that only she can perform certain key teaching functions.

> . . . there are certain things I must do myself and I can't assign to her to do because I think there are certain things that I don't think she quite understands. At least I wouldn't put it off on her and there are many chores that I need to do personally. With a smaller class I have a little more time in which to do them.

Mrs. Monroe continues to use students as instructional assistants. When a student finishes a worksheet, Mrs. Monroe grades it. If the student gets the answers correct and seems to understand the lesson well, Mrs. Monroe may send him or her around to check other papers. Mrs. Monroe comments to an observer that she always rechecks any papers graded by students to avoid possible errors in marking. But her main intention in using student tutors is to provide additional help for other students to get them over the rough spots during seatwork.

Although Mrs. Monroe continues to use student helpers, the amount of tutoring does not appear to increase in the smaller class. Being a helper serves as a reward for top students rather than a regular method for assisting low students. This is true in spite of Mrs. Monroe's expressed belief in the value of peer help, for instance, as a rationale for the horseshoe seating arrangement. Perhaps peer interaction conflicts with Mrs. Monroe's desire for control, and even the smaller class, which we have seen allows her to feel more in control, is not enough to persuade her to increase peer interaction. Recall Mrs. Monroe's statement that she tries to oversee peer tutoring. Also, the following exchange shows the salience to her of order in the classroom:

> The observer asks Mrs. Monroe if the class had remained larger, would peer tutoring work as well? She replies: "I doubt it because there were so many children and so many problems popping up all over the room."

Summary

This chapter describes a teacher who began the school year with a class of 35 second and third graders and had her class reduced to 22 students at the end of January. There were changes that occurred as a result of the reduced class size, although many basic features of classroom life remained the same.

The physical environment of the class seemed more open and less crowded. The teacher was able to set up a multiethnic center using one of the tables previously occupied by students. However, her "ideal" arrangement of classroom furniture was not accomplished.

Classroom management seemed easier and less time-consuming in the small class. The lines did not stretch out as far and fights were fewer. There was more room to separate children. Mrs. Monroe commented that she felt more relaxed and did not have to maintain such a strong disciplinarian role. There are numerous examples taken from Station Day in which the teacher laughed frequently and seemed to enjoy being with her students.

The basic approach to instruction was largely the same in the small class as in the large class. Lessons were taught to groups, with an emphasis on basic skills. One new feature was Station Day, when the students played instructional games in small groups. Also, the teacher was able to monitor more effectively during seatwork. Mrs. Monroe felt that she was able to meet individual needs better when she had fewer students. She could get around the room to see how students were doing and she had more time to spend with them. This enabled her to give immediate help and also to plan more accurately for the next day's lessons. Both the teacher and teacher aide were less exhausted at the end of the day and stated that they seemed to get more accomplished during class time.

11

Discussion of California Site

Oh happy day, the class has been (relieved) of
11 pupils. The room is so much quieter. We
can give each pupil special help each period of
the day.

Mrs. Monroe wrote these words in her journal on the day class size was reduced. In California, class size was reduced from about 35 to about 22 students. Generally, both teachers felt positive about the smaller-class situation. One observer commented on the sense of relief just from reducing the number of bodies in the room. There was space to spread out a little bit without bumping into somebody.

We need to analyze more closely, though, the real changes that took place, or did not take place, when class size was reduced. In this chapter, we summarize the changes that took place in the classes of Mrs. Monroe and Ms. Taylor. In what ways were the changes similar or different in the two classes? What aspects of the context seemed to influence the changes that took place?

Behavior Management

In Mrs. Monroe's class, management seemed easier to her as soon as class size was reduced. She and Mrs. Horne, the aide, both commented appreciatively on the removal of several children who were perceived as possible discipline problems. As early as one week after the split, Mrs. Monroe wrote,

> Before the class was reduced we had so many behavior problems that took time from actual teaching . . . I feel sure it has helped my attitude and I can be more relaxed and relate on their level better.

It would be desirable to support this perception of the teacher's with quantitative observation data on student attention or instances of teacher disciplinary statements. As reported previously, complete quantitative data on student atten-

175

tion are not available for the California site. However, some of the records made by one observer, along with his anecdotal description, are informative. On the positive side, student attention appeared to be especially high during afternoon reading in the smaller class. Only around 10 children were present, and these children were reading at a second or third-grade level. With these 10 children and two adults, attention appeared to average over 90 percent. Additional positive evidence concerned the reduction in waiting time. It was common in Mrs. Monroe's class for the students to complete worksheets or workbook pages and have them checked by Mrs. Monroe or Mrs. Horne. In the large class, students stacked up waiting a turn. Mrs. Horne was heard to explain to one restless student, "I can only check one paper at a time." In the smaller class, this waiting time appeared to decrease.

Observation of student attention also revealed some limitations imposed by the classroom grouping arrangements. During morning reading, Mrs. Monroe divided her time between two groups of students, each sitting at a different table. The effect of the teacher's presence was readily apparent. When she was wroking directly with a group, attention was high. When she moved away, attention began to drop off. As a second example, the split-grade class resulted in Mrs. Monroe's establishing two math groups, each with a different assignment. Although the aide monitored the work of the group Mrs. Monroe was not with, the aide did not give lessons presenting the content of the assignment. Consequently, one group often had to wait for their lesson. This type of wait time did not appear to diminish when class size was reduced. Both of these examples point to the difficulty of managing more than one instructional group. They suggest that a reduction in class size which does not change the basic grouping structure cannot eliminate certain kinds of attention problems.

In general, classroom observers agreed with Mrs. Monroe's assessment that students were more attentive and caused fewer disruptions in the smaller class. Mrs. Monroe's statement that there were fewer fights at the end of the line is entirely plausible. This pattern would be consistent with that found in the data on student attention from the Virginia site. Students in the Virginia site were observed to be "on-task" more often in the smaller class than in the larger classes. It is important to note, however, that the biggest difference in Mrs. Monroe's class may have been in her perceptions rather than the events themselves. Even in the *larger* class, observers were struck by the quiet, orderly atmosphere. There never seemed to be many incidents of overt misbehavior. The question, then, is what seemed so different to Mrs. Monroe. One possibility is a reduction in the mental load required for the teacher to monitor and orchestrate classroom events. Kounin (1970) has creatively described the skills of a successful classroom manager, including "withitness," the ability to notice or even anticipate events so as to appear to have eyes in the back of the head. Mrs. Monroe seemed very aware of potential problems and would often act to forestall difficulty, for instance, by asking a student to move his or her chair back from the group to a separate table. With fewer students, there may have been less for the teacher to "keep on top of." Maintaining the same or even a higher level of student attention could be accomplished with less mental strain on the teacher.

In Ms. Taylor's class, the behavior management issue followed a different pattern. Ms. Taylor did *not* feel that classroom management improved immediately. In early February she wrote "it still seems just as difficult to get them to settle down." By the end of February, her statements were even stronger:

> My concern increases over my disappointment with the fact that behavior problems have really not minimized that much with the smaller class size . . . I still find as many behavior problems as I had before. The only way you can call it less is because there are 21 childrren instead of 35—so . . . you have 21 problems instead of 35 problems. However, in proportion to the number of children, the problems have not decreased.

Why did Ms. Taylor perceive the situation in this way? She acknowledged that the overall number of problems did diminish, but the situation did not feel any better. For one thing, attention rates were lower to begin with in Mrs. Monroe's class. Ms. Taylor was particularly frustrated by the amount of misbehavior in the larger class prior to the split. Perhaps the behavior patterns of the children and the teacher, as established in the larger-class phase, are not readily changed simply by reducing class size.

Ms. Taylor herself suggested that her manner of interacting with the children in the smaller class may have contributed to the lack of improvement. On February 1, she wrote "perhaps the smaller group is more familiar, whereas the larger one was more formal." This speculation is consistent with several things noticed by the observers. We have noted the contrast between Mrs. Monroe's class, which is more formal, and Ms. Taylor's class, which allows more complex and varied patterns of interaction, more movement, and more noise. Mrs. Monroe remained consistently formal in her basic approach and had relatively few behavior problems. Ms. Taylor, even in the larger class, encouraged informal interaction, within the framework of a fairly traditional organization of groups and activities. She tended to be aware of the students as individuals. In fact, evidence from observation suggests she was even more likely to respond to individuals than to groups when class size was reduced. This type of informality may have contributed to continued behavior problems in the short run.

An important specific case is that of Amanda. Amanda was a child prone to misbehavior, including teasing other children and "picking fights." Several of Amanda's friends left the class when the size was reduced and Amanda expressed unhappiness over this. Her behavior became worse after the split. Ms. Taylor noted on January 29, the day of the split, that "Amanda's behavior was much worse today," and on January 31 that Amanda was "still acting out quite a bit." On February 5, Ms. Taylor complimented Amanda for good behavior and Amanda then got into two fights and destroyed a classmate's art project. Amanda's behavior may well be a large part of the reason for Ms. Taylor's general statements about lack of improvement in classroom discipline.

The apparent solution to the problem of Amanda is especially instructive. By late February, Ms. Taylor expressed the problem as "Amanda . . . showing poor effects from added adult attention." Ms. Taylor had a conference with the school psychologist and they worked out a program of behavior modification. Essentially, the plan was "not singling her out as a student who receives a lot of special attention for her misbehavior; we treat her just like everybody else." By March 8, Ms. Taylor reported that this plan was paying off and that Amanda's behavior was better. From this point, Ms. Taylor stopped complaining about lack of improvement in classroom discipline generally and began to focus on more positive results.

So then, what pattern can we see? Ms. Taylor may have responded more to individuals in the small class and this may have contributed to maintaining or even increasing some negative behavior patterns. There is also evidence, however, that this same behavior on the part of the teacher, her capacity to respond to individuals in the small class, helped foster a slow but cumulative *improvement* in student attitudes, student attention, and student learning. From the first day in the small class, Ms. Taylor commented that she was able to notice more about individual students, respond to their needs and provide encouragement. For many students, this opportunity for positive attention from the teacher promoted task involvement and thus created an environment with fewer behavior problems. Ms. Taylor herself, when reflecting on her experience with the smaller class, described the circularity of effect:

> Pupil attitude improves in a smaller class size. As we picture the large class working on any given task, an observer sees several things. Some children are attending to the task despite noise and disruption. Other children are working, observing what is going on around them, and playing or talking. A good number of the children (as many as twenty-five percent) are not doing anything. The adults in charge are not even aware of the percentage of children not working on the assigned task unless they cause a disturbance. They are too busy trying to maintain order.

> Now we change the picture by removing one-third of the children from the group. At first the children are uncomfortable. Why? Suddenly they are all visible. The children that work all of the time or some of the time and the ones that never do any work at all. They can be seen by both adults and their peers. The discomfort is short-lived because suddenly they realize that they can get the teacher's attention and help when they need it. As they realize this, the children begin to enjoy the small class size. The twenty-five percent of the class that never worked before can now get the help that they need from the teacher or assistant and thereby gain the confidence that they need to do their work. The pride and self-esteem of these students is raised and now they can work at the assigned tasks because they "want to," not because they "have to." Positive parent contacts increase when parents see their children experiencing success and hear about it directly from the teacher who now has time to phone and report the *good* as well as the bad. School attendance improves as children no longer need to fear failure. The classroom has become a "safe place" because there is help for them.

Individualization

Both teachers felt that the small class enabled them to spend more time with each individual child. Since both teachers were constantly active during seat-work periods and moved around the room helping children, it seems logical that the reduction in class size should mean more time for each individual. A similar pattern was observed in Virginia and appeared in the coded observation of target students carried out in Virginia.

What did the teachers do with this opportunity for individual contact? For Mrs. Monroe these interactions focused on the group assignment. Students received directions, explanations, and feedback about their work in a more immediate and timely manner. Mrs. Monroe felt that this contact gave her more information about how students were doing and thus enabled her to plan better for the next day's lesson. She would know whether to continue ahead, review the lesson, or reteach the concept in a new way. Thus, teacher contact was not only of immediate benefit to the students, it also allowed a more accurate diagnosis of student needs which could result in the assignment of more appropriate learning tasks for the group.

Ms. Taylor also noted the opportunity for more individual teacher–student contact. She wrote often in her journal about the specific academic and emotional needs of individual children and about how she and Mrs. Reed, the aide, could better meet those needs. The case study describes numerous incidents of special help for individuals. For instance, when Amanda began to misbehave more often after class size was reduced, Ms. Taylor was able to seek out the advice of the school psychologist and try to apply it in the classroom. She wrote that ''I'm having the time to spend trying the various attitudes she suggested might work . . . I couldn't have taken the time to work with her especially if I had many other children that needed the same kind of attention.'' We have seen that in this case the solution was less teacher attention, but Ms. Taylor needed an opportunity to try different techniques and find the best way of dealing with that particular child. The smaller class provided this opportunity.

A more typical example might be one of help and encouragement on an academic task:

> . . . Robert, although he does not write alone, he dictates to me and then I write for him and he copies it. He is coming now and telling me, ''Come on and help me, I have something to say.'' Earlier on in the year, when there were so many children to bother me and ask questions at the time he wanted to talk, he just didn't bother to write anything.

This example is like the type of teacher–student interaction in Mrs. Monroe's class in that it involves a group assignment, story writing, and assisting students in carrying out that assignment. It is different in that Ms. Taylor talks more about one child's particular pattern of behavior and changes in that pattern over time. These patterns are independent of planning and conducting basic group instruction. They are, perhaps, variations on the theme. The case study describes several individual students, including a boy who missed a month of school, a new student who was non-English-speaking, and several students with learning difficulties. Her awareness of individual learning patterns allowed Ms. Taylor to look for times when students seemed ready for growth spurts and try to take advantage of these opportunities. In addition to her own time, she could ask Mrs. Reed, the aide, to spend extra time with a student at this point. The incident with Randy and spelling words, reported in the case study, is an example of this.

It should be noted that Ms. Taylor tended to be aware of students as individuals even in the large class. For instance, during one math period, in the larger class, as students were doing seatwork following a group lesson, Ms. Taylor spent a few minutes giving more advanced problems as boardwork to a student who finished early. She spent some of her time in this way even though other students still needed help with the basic assignment. This suggests that she both knew what the student needed and valued the individual student's progress as well as that of the group. The difference in the small class is that she could deal with individuals more effectively.

Curriculum. In both classes, the basic curriculum, textbooks, instructional grouping, and activities, remained the same after class size was reduced. As in Virginia, there were some constraints on the teacher's choice in these matters. Both the reading and math textbook series were mandated by the principal. However, the teachers in this school felt relatively free to implement the curriculum as they chose. The principal seldom visited the classroom; doors to the rooms could be closed. Mrs. Monroe and Ms. Taylor began the year with somewhat different approaches to the curriculum and the smaller-class situation allowed them to develop their individual approaches more fully.

For Mrs. Monroe, the smaller class offered additional opportunities for enrichment of the curriculum. In particular, Mrs. Monroe liked to use games and puzzle-type dittos to reinforce basic skills, provide variety and increase motivation. She did this in the larger class, for instance, with math speed contests on the board. Also, on Thursdays, in reading, she used materials such as reinforcement dittos or crossword puzzles which were passed out to the students in each reading group. In the smaller class, Mrs. Monroe felt able to use more instructional games such as a bingo-type game with new vocabulary words and a homonyms game. Mrs. Monroe explained that many of these games were designed to be played by only a small number of students at one time. However, even in the larger class each reading group unit had no more than eight students; games like bingo could conceivably be played in groups of this size. The teacher may have been more willing to allow the action and noise of group games when the class size was smaller and discipline was perceived as less of a problem.

Ms. Taylor also enriched her curriculum, and in ways that involved greater activity on the part of students. She took more community walks and field trips.

She made greater use of hands-on materials in math and science. (Details were given in the case study.)

Ms. Taylor also expanded the curriculum in two other ways. She set up individual work folders for the children. These folders contained worksheets to reinforce recent instruction or give individuals extra practice in areas of weakness. Children could use these folders during free time when they had finished the group assignment. Ms. Taylor felt that she was able to keep up with the work of correcting and maintaining the individual folders because of the smaller class size.

Second, Ms. Taylor included more in-depth comprehension activities for her afternoon readers. She was able to do this in part because of a shift in grouping patterns. With only two students left in the reading group, she moved these students ahead so that all afternoon students would read the same material. She then set up new subdivisions within this large group so that everyone did the same basic lesson, but some students received extra practice on oral reading with Mrs. Reed while others did extended comprehension activities with her. If she had decided to maintain the two original instructional groups, Ms. Taylor would have been unable to spend more of her time as an instructor on extended comprehension. The fact that she chose extended comprehension rather than moving through the material more quickly reflects a basic belief of hers. Ms. Taylor commented once that through the course of her years of teaching she has come to believe more and more strongly in the value of developing lessons thoroughly and in depth.

Summary

We have seen some similarities and some differences in the responses of the two California classes to the class-size reduction. In general, behavior management seemed easier, although the pattern of improvement differed. There appeared to be fewer instances of misbehavior and greater student involvement in lessons in the smaller classes. Both teachers appreciated the opportunity to give more help to individual students and felt that this individual contact made them more aware of how each student was doing, although they verbalized and acted on this information in somewhat different ways. In the areas of curriculum and instructional strategies, each teacher continued the same basic approach to instruction that she had used in the larger class, but with some modifications. Both teachers included more opportunities for active student involvement such as games, field-trips, and hands-on activity. In general, each teacher began the year with her own established set of educational views and practices, developed through many years of teaching. When class size was reduced, the teacher's general approach remained the same, but the teacher was able to implement that approach more fully and more effectively.

Part IV

12

Quantitative Data

Are students paying attention in class? How much of the time do they attend to academic work? How much of the time do they wait for help? Do they pay more attention in a smaller class, where they can get more time with the teacher?

Questions like these were clear from the beginning of the study and lend themselves to quantitative measurement. Other issues emerged during the study which also suggested numerical analysis. For instance, one California teacher wondered if students were absent from school less often in the smaller class. Where appropriate, events were counted to yield numbers as one piece of evidence about classroom processes and how they changed when class size was reduced.

This chapter presents all the quantitative data available from one or both sites, including sections on student behavioral measures, student achievement, and supplementary data. Some of these data have already been reported as an integral part of the case studies. Quantitative evidence is assembled here for ease of reference and comparison across the two sites.

It is important to put this chapter into perspective in the book as a whole. We feel that the quantitative data are important but that they are only one type of evidence which should be considered along with the case-study descriptions, interpretations, and appraisals in order to form conclusions about what happened in the two sites. The chapter is placed late in the book in order to encourage viewing the data from this perspective.

A special caution is urged in regard to the data on student achievement. The primary focus of this study was *not* on student achievement. Instead, we sought a detailed description of classroom processes that would lead to a better understanding of how classrooms work and of the constraints imposed by class size. It is not our intention to underplay the importance of achievement, however. The reader wishing more information about the positive relationship between achievement and class size should consult *School Class Size: Research and Policy* (Glass, Cahen, Smith, and Filby, 1982).

Student Behavioral Measures

One major set of data concerned student attention and related variables. The methodology chapter describes data-collection strategies. The data reported here were collected through a time-sampled observation of target students. The observer would look at the first student, record the nature of his involvement in the lesson, then locate the next student and do the same for him. Student behavior is reported in four categories—engaged–academic, waiting for teacher help, off-task (inattentive), and down time (no assignment given). Where students were doing seatwork, the observer also noted whether or not the teacher was in contact with the student, for instance, checking his or her work. Details of the observation categories and procedures are given in Appendix A. Other measures described in Appendix A were gathered but are not reported here, generally because events were very infrequent and reliability of measurement was low.

Observation in Virginia was conducted during three reading periods and two mathematics periods in the larger-class phase and four occasions each in reading and mathematics in the smaller-class phase. There were six target students in reading and six in math. In the California site, the need to reduce class size earlier than scheduled made it impossible to obtain enough larger-class data for reliable measurement, so only Virginia data are reported.

For each student on each day we calculated the percentage of time-sampled records on which a particular behavior was occurring. For instance, during a one-hour reading period, Michael might be observed 20 times. On 15 of these times he might have been coded as engaged—academic. Thus 15 of 20, or 75 percent, of the records are engaged–academic. In other words, Michael was attending to the task about 75 percent of the time.

Data were summarized for each category first by calculating the median percentage for each student across observation days within each time period. For instance, if Michael's attention rates during the three observations of reading in the larger-class phase were 75 percent, 58 percent, and 52 percent, he would have a larger-class median score of 58 percent. The within-pupil distributions of observation measures were non-normal and we therefore chose the median as the most representative measure of "average." These student-level medians are reproduced in Appendix B.

As a second level of summarization, we pooled the data for all students in each time period and calculated a number of measures of central tendency and variability, which are reported here. As was pointed out earlier, we faced limitations in the data-gathering schedule in Virginia and we were totally unable to obtain enough systematic observational data in Oakland due to the mandated order to reduce class size before the agreed-upon date. Because of the limited amount of data available, we have not attempted to use sophisticated procedures to analyze several matters. For example, the limited amount of data did not permit us to analyze separately the engagement for reading nor for mathematics. The data, therefore, may hide some potentially important subtleties but we feel there is insufficient evidence to perform these logical analysis extensions with adequate confidence. Therefore, our "larger-class"–"smaller-class" analyses have pooled data across subject-matter areas and teachers. The analyses do allow us to summarize central tendency and variability of important

TABLE 12.1   Reliability of Paired Observation Measures (Virginia Site)

Measure	N of Children Measured	r_{xx} (Single Day)
Attention to academic task	18	.86
Waiting for help	18	.53
Off-task	18	.83
No assignment—waiting	18	.70
Contact with teacher during seatwork	15	.65

measures at the "larger" and "smaller" class categories and to estimate the change in these measures when class size was reduced in Virginia.

The reliability of observational measures is reported in Table 12.1. The reliability coefficients reflect paired observations. To illustrate: for the variable "attention to academic tasks," the two observers recorded, in a time-sampling framework, whether 18 children were or were not attending to the academic task. The attention rates for the 18 students during a single academic period were then correlated, yielding a coefficient of .86. The same procedure was used for the other measures shown in Table 12.1. It is important to note that these coefficients are based on a single-day sample. Data were later aggregated across days for each student (as reported in Appendix B) and across students. This procedure leads to more reliable measures, since sums of measures are more reliable than the parts making the sums. Therefore, the reliability coefficients shown in Table 12.1 should be considered as lower-bound reliability estimates of the data reported.

A further note on reliability is to be found in the field notes of one observer in California. While he was making general observation of the classrooms, he made informal assessments of class engagement rates (the number of children in the class engaged). His notes tell us the difficulty of accurately counting the number of students before the split and how much easier it was to reliably count the number of students engaged when class size was reduced.

From the work in the Beginning Teacher Evaluation Study (BTES), it was hypothesized that a reduction in class size would lead to an increase in the important components of academic learning time. These components include the amount of engagement or the attention that students pay to academic tasks. Corresponding reductions were expected in the amount of time that students would be off-task or waiting for help, or waiting for a new assignment. These states can be viewed as nonproductive time in the classroom (i.e., the student is not working on academic tasks related to academic goals). Furthermore, from BTES it was theorized that more frequent teacher–pupil contact would occur, which could provide the opportunity for increased teacher knowledge of student performance levels and which, on the average, could lead to a higher quality of instruction being given to the pupils. The BTES philosophy was built on the assumption that changes in classroom learning environments, teaching

TABLE 12.2   Data on Percent of Time Pupil is Engaged–Academic (N = 12)

	Larger Class	Smaller Class	Difference	Statistical Significance of Change (One-Tailed Test)
Mean	56.6	74.6	18.0*	t = 4.1
(Standard Deviation)	(18.9)	(13.4)	(15.2)	p < .001
Standard Error of Mean	5.5	3.9	4.4	
Median	59.5	80.0	13.0	
Standard Error of Median	9.5	3.8	6.1	
Biweight	56.7	79.6	17.1	

*Mean Percent Difference (Difference/Larger) = 31.8%

procedures, and student learning behaviors were necessary conditions for increased levels of pupil achievement. As it was hypothesized that a reduction in class size would lead to increased quality of teaching, data were gathered and examined to test the hypothesis. Data are presented for the percent of time target pupils were engaged academically (Table 12.2), waiting for teacher help (Table 12.3), off-task (Table 12.4), in a "down time" condition (Table 12.5), and having contact with the teacher during seatwork (Table 12.6). All these tables present information for the "larger" and "smaller" class conditions, and change observed across the two conditions.

The summary measures in Tables 12.2 through 12.6 are computed directly from the data in Appendix B. An examination of the student-level data in Appendix B reveals that in many cases the data are not normally distributed. Therefore, several different summary statistics were computed. These statistics differ in the way they weight different values to obtain a measure of central tendency or "average" and a measure of variability. In addition to the classical summaries of means and standard deviations, we have reported medians and a relatively new average or measure of central tendency called a "biweight." The latter is a robust statistic, meaning that it is not highly influenced by measures that lie far above or below the average ("outliers") which can seriously over- or underestimate the mean and standard deviation. This robustness is achieved by giving less weight to outliers and more weight to numbers closer to the average (see Mosteller and Tukey, 1977). The median is probably well known to the reader. It is the point in a set of scores or numbers where one-half of the numbers lie above the point and one-half of the numbers lie below the point. In addition to displaying measures of central tendency and variability, we have provided standard errors for means and medians. These can be used to establish a "confidence band" around these averages. The reader inter-

TABLE 12.3   Data on Percent of Time Waiting for Teacher Help (N = 12)

	Larger Class	Smaller Class	Difference	Statistical Significance of Change (One-Tailed Test)
Mean	8.8	4.8	− 4.0*	t = −1.35
(Standard Deviation)	(9.9)	(7.1)	(10.4)	p < .10
Standard Error of Mean	2.9	2.1	3.0	
Median	8.0	0.0	−8.0	
Standard Error of Median	6.4	4.0	2.6	
Biweight	8.2	0.0	0.0	

*Mean Percent Difference (Difference/Larger) = −45.5%

ested in alternative analyses of our data has the opportunity of working with the basic data shown in Appendix B.

Table 12.2 reports data on student attention ("engaged–academic"). In the larger class phase, the mean attention rate was 56.6 percent. In the smaller-class phase, attention increased to 74.6 percent. If a difference score is calculated for each student (smaller minus larger), the mean of these difference scores is 18.0 percent. With parametric statistics such as the mean, this mean difference is the same as the difference between the means, 74.6 − 56.6. (This equivalence does not hold for the nonparametric statistics—the median and biweight.)

To talk about a difference of 18 percent doesn't fully describe the magnitude of the improvement that occurred. Another way to consider it is in relationship to the original engagement rate. If the mean difference (18.0 percent) is expressed as a percentage of the larger-class baseline (56.6 percent), then the percentage of improvement is 31.8 percent. This figure is reported at the bottom of Table 12.2 and subsequent tables.

The final column in Table 12.2 reports the statistical significance of the mean difference score. Because we had a directional hypothesis, that "smaller-class" conditions would yield improved performance over the "larger-class" conditions, a one-tailed correlated "t" test was utilized. Based on data from the 12 target students, the probability of the difference being attributable to "chance" findings was less than one in a thousand. In other words, both practically and statistically, there was a major improvement in student attention when class size was reduced.

Other rows in the table indicate other measures of central tendency—the median and the biweight. In general, the same message is apparent in all three measures: there was a dramatic improvement in attention when class size was reduced. The fact that these measures do not correspond exactly with each

TABLE 12.4   Data on Percent of Time Students Off-Task (N = 12)

	Larger Class	Smaller Class	Difference	Statistical Significance of Change (One-Tailed Test)
Mean	11.7	7.7	−4.0*	t = −1.45
(Standard Deviation)	(11.7)	(11.6)	(9.6)	p < .09
Standard Error of Mean	3.4	3.3	2.8	
Median	10.0	2.5	−3.5	
Standard Error of Median	4.0	3.8	2.3	
Biweight	9.7	2.2	−2.9	

*Mean Percent Difference (Difference/Larger) = −34.2%

other, and that the median difference does not equal the difference of the medians, results from the non-normal distribution of scores. It was this non-normality which encouraged us to offer alternative measures. But the best way to understand the data may be to examine the individual student scores in Appendix B. For example, a plotting of the academic–engaged measures ("smaller" against "larger") shows that pupils with the lowest engagement rates in the "larger-class" situation showed the greatest amount of positive change in the "smaller-class" situation. For instance, students 7 and 10 changed from 38 percent attention to around 80 percent. This finding may be partially attributed to the classical statistical phenomenon known as "regression to the mean." But it may also illustrate the fact that some students will be attentive even in the larger class while other students will not. The smaller-class conditions may particularly change the behavior of students who are inclined toward inattention. In the remainder of this section, we try to tease out some of the sources of this increase in attention, using both the other quantitative records and our field observations.

Table 12.3 shows the summary data for percentage change in waiting for teacher help. The mean difference in waiting for help was four percent (a 45.5 percent decrease or improvement). The median percent decreased from eight percent to zero percent (larger class to smaller class). Variability of the measures was large in relationship to the averages. Some readers may feel that the value of "t" (−1.35) with an associated p value of .10 may not deserve serious attention as a positive indicator. We do not take all of the "classical" statistical interpretations as seriously as some. To some scientists p values must be .05 or smaller. For exploratory work with small samples we feel that significance levels can be more relaxed—perhaps even p values of .10 through .20 can be considered as having a positive message to transmit. To us, the important message in Table 12.3 is that wait-time decreased when class size was reduced. This is one source of the increase in attention.

TABLE 12.5   Data on Percent of Student Down Time (N = 12)

	Larger Class	Smaller Class	Difference	Statistical Significance of Change (One-Tailed Test)
Mean	13.9	0.0†	−13.9*	t = −3.71
(Standard Deviation)	(13.0)	(0.0)	(13.0)	p < .002
Standard Error of Mean	3.8	†	3.8	
Median	9.5	†	−9.5	
Standard Error of Median	5.2	†	1.7	
Biweight	8.4	†	−8.4	

*Mean Percent Difference (Difference/Larger) = 100%
†All data values were zero; therefore there was no variability across scores.

Off-task behavior is reported in Table 12.4. The results parallel those shown in Table 12.3. Students off-task behavior decreased approximately 34 percent when class size was reduced.

Table 12.5 displays some very interesting summary data on changes in percent of down time for target students after class size was reduced. Under the "larger-class" condition, students spent an average of 14 percent of the time with no assignment. The median percent was 9.5 and the biweight was 8.4. Observation during the "smaller-class" condition showed that none of the 12 target students were observed to be waiting for an assignment. A dramatic finding, we believe, but a nightmare to a classical statistician. (With no variability on a measurement the classical hypothesis test strains to meet its mathematical assumptions!) We feel the data here strongly show the effects of class-size reduction—100 percent reduction in downtime.

The last set of data from formal observation are shown in Table 12.6.

The percent of time pupils have contact with the teacher increased from a mean of 2.5 percent to a mean of 4.8 percent. The reader will note that pupil–teacher interaction was small in the "larger-class" condition but almost doubled in the "smaller-class" condition. Large variability across the measures relative to the mean creates a serious problem in reaching "classical" levels of significance, but the 92 percent increase in pupil-teacher contact from "larger" to "smaller" conditions deserves attention as a positive indicator.

The reader may be concerned about how small these numbers are. Even in the smaller class, a student interacted with the teacher only five percent of the time during seatwork. One needs to examine the observed percentages in light of a theoretical average based on the number of students in a class. For example, if a teacher circulates during the entire seatwork period and splits his or her time equally among 20 pupils, each child would receive five percent of available time, ($1/20$). With 13 pupils, each child would, on the average, re-

TABLE 12.6 Data on Percent of Time Pupil Has Contact with Teacher During
Seatwork (N = 12)

	Larger Class	Smaller Class	Difference	Statistical Significance of Change (One-Tailed Test)
Mean	2.5	4.8	2.3*	t = 0.79
(Standard Deviation)	(4.5)	(7.5)	(10.1)	p < 0.22
Standard Error of Mean	1.3	2.2	2.9	
Median	0.0	0.0	0.0	
Standard Error of Median	2.6	2.6	2.6	
Biweight	0.0	0.0	1.3	

*Mean Percent Difference (Difference/Larger) = 92%

ceive eight percent of the available time ($^1/_{13}$). These numbers will be reduced if the teacher does not circulate routinely. Of course, the teacher may not divide time equally. If the teacher devotes additional time to one pupil in a class it will force a reduction in the time a teacher gives to another pupil. Brown and Saks (1980) refer to the concept of "jointness" in understanding time allocations in classes. "Jointness" is when the resources made available to one pupil influence time allocation to other pupils. It would be interesting to know whether a teacher with a smaller class divides time equally or perhaps spends a lot of time tutoring some students while others need and receive less contact. The data in Appendix B suggest that this latter circumstance may apply, although not enough data were collected for reliable assessment of individual students on this measure. As we continue our research in classrooms, we will need to better understand, and perhaps value more, small and subtle changes in pupils.

In summary, we feel the data presented in Tables 12.2 through 12.6 provide convincing evidence that the quality of instruction improved when class size was reduced.

The reader is cautioned here about two things. As mentioned elsewhere, increases in the quality of teaching, student behaviors, student performance, and so on can be attributed to maturity rather than to reductions in class size. Later in the school year the teacher may know more about the students and be more comfortable with the students than in the earlier parts of the year; this condition, rather than a reduction in class size, could be the major contributing factor to the positive indicators shown in Table 12.2. A counterargument to this concern is the finding in BTES that there were *no* general increases in attention levels over the course of the year (Fisher, et al, 1978).

A further caution is against dismissing relatively small changes in some of the data displayed in the tables. We call attention to the growing belief that changes in many pupil behaviors, qualities of teaching, and even student achievement, are typically small. This does not mean that they are meaningless, however.

It is unfortunate that the conclusions from the data on student behaviors from the Virginia site could not be checked by replication with data from the California site. As pointed out earlier, a premature splitting of the classes did not allow us to gather enough systematic observation to estimate data reliably for the variables in Tables 12.2 through 12.6 for the California site. However, insights from the California field notes complement the coded data from Virginia.

From the field notes of researcher Cahen, we learn that engagement of pupils in a group is high when pupils expect and receive teacher attention. The engagement rate drops appreciably when the teacher is forced, or chooses, to attend, even for a brief period, to other children away from the group with which she or he is working. The engagement rates pick back up when full attention is again paid to the group at hand. It was also observed that engagement appeared to be higher (informal assessment) when group size was made smaller after the split. It appeared that this increase might be a function of children expecting more frequent turns; they also didn't have to wait as long to have their papers examined or to wait in a long queue for help. As one aide before the split responded to pupils in a long line waiting for help, "I can only correct one paper at a time."

We also observed the "proximity" factor, with regard to its relationship to pupil engagement. In group activities, pupils closer to the teacher generally appear to be more engaged. Pupils who slip away to the perimeters of the group frequently exhibit low engagement and remain this way until moved closer to the teacher. Smaller class sizes offer the teacher better options, such as smaller instructional groups and closer distances between teacher and pupils, which are believed to have a positive influence on pupil engagement in academic tasks.

Achievement Measures

In this section we will report change in pupil achievement in reading and mathematics between December and May for the Virginia and California sites. We will also display a further comparison of Class Size Project data against data based on students in BTES. The tests used in the study reported here were used and developed for the BTES study. Using the same tests allows for some comparisons between BTES achievement patterns and those observed in the Class Size and Instruction Field Study.

Achievement was measured in four domains—decoding, comprehension, subtraction–speeded, and arithmetic word problems. Because of the difficulty of the comprehension test for entering second graders, a synonym test was used for the December testing in place of the comprehension test used for May

TABLE 12.7 Achievement Scales—Reading

Test Name	Description	Examples	No. of Items	Reliability Wntr., Spring
Decoding	The student must identify the word containing the correct consonants and vowels to name a picture. Includes consonant blends and digraphs in initial and final position. Also, includes long vowel final "e" pattern and long vowel sounds of common digraphs.	 tuck thuck (truck) (cake) cack coke goot got (goat)	32	.92, .94
Synonyms*	The student must identify the word with the same meaning as an underlined word.	wash the dog A. chase (C.) clean B. love D. walk	16	.84, NA
Comprehension*	The student must read a story and answer multiple-choice questions about events, relationships between events, and main ideas.	Mary felt scared walking through the dark woods. . . . How did Mary feel? A. happy B. mad (C) afraid	23	NA, .83

*"Synonyms" was given in December as a pretest for Comprehension in May.

TABLE 12.8 Achievement Scales—Mathematics

Test Name	Description	Examples	No. of Items	Reliability Wntr., Spring
Subtraction Speed Test	Tests the student's ability to recall basic subtraction facts rapidly. The time limit is 1½ minutes.	$\begin{array}{r} 8 \\ -5 \end{array}$ 2 4 ③ 13	14	.85, .85
Word Problems	Tests the student's ability to solve word problems that involve addition and subtraction (with and without re-grouping), the joining of equivalent sets, partitioning of sets, time, and money. Problems are read aloud to the students.	Susan baked 25 cookies. Gregg and Lisa ate 15 of them. How many cookies are left? 15 ⑩ 5 20	15	.49, .71

testing. Sample items for the achievement tests are shown in Tables 12.7 and 12.8. These tables show reliability coefficients for the scales administered in the winter and spring.

Data for the BTES sample and the Virginia and California sites are shown in Table 12.9. The BTES results are based on the testing of 139 second graders. The Virginia and California data reflect the testing of 38 and 53 students respectively. For each site and for the BTES data set the median percent correct was computed and this score appears in Table 12.9.

It can be seen that the December scores are higher for the BTES group than for the Class Size group on synonyms and word problems but not on decoding and subtraction–speeded. (An informal examination of the description of the BTES population suggests that this group had a higher average social class level than the students tested in the Virginia and California sites.) Table 12.9 also shows that achievement increased from December to May testing. In both sites, students were learning. The next question is—how much? Comparing the BTES findings to those from the Virginia and California sites reveals that the Class Size sites generally showed greater gains than BTES on the two arithmetic tasks but not on the decoding and comprehension tasks. It should also be observed that change was not consistent across test domains in Virginia

TABLE 12.9 Achievement Scores—Median Percent Correct (Standard Errors in Parentheses)

Test Name	Time of Testing	Sample			
				Class Size	
		BTES	Cal.	Vir.	Total
Decoding	December	63	58	77	67
		(03)	(10)	(07)	(05)
	May	84	77	95	86
		(02)	(07)	(01)	(04)
	Difference	21	19	18	19
Synonyms	December	29	13	27	23
		(04)	(05)	(06)	(04)
Comprehension	May	48	28	54	41
		(06)	(06)	(08)	(06)
	Difference	19	15	27	18
Subtraction Speed Test	December	36	43	52	43
		(02)	(03)	(06)	(02)
	May	52	55	76	66
		(05)	(04)	(06)	(04)
	Difference	16	12	24	23
Word Problems	December	29	11	20	11
		(02)	(03)	(05)	(07)
	May	40	47	38	40
		(04)	(03)	(07)	(03)
	Difference	11	36	18	29

TABLE 12.10 Achievement Outcomes (Percentage of Students with Higher Scores than Predicted from BTES Data)

	Sample		
Content Area	Total	California	Virginia
Decoding	54%	47%	63%
Comprehension	35%	26%	47%
Subtraction	60%	53%	71%
Work Problems	55%	57%	53%

and California. The observed gain in decoding was about equal for the two sites. However, the Virginia scores approached 95 percent correct on the May testing, restricting the limits of growth or gain. The Virginia site showed a relatively large May score on comprehension when one takes into account their performance on the December administration of synonyms. The Virginia site also showed a relatively large change score on the subtraction–speeded test. The California school showed a relatively large amount of positive change on the arithmetic word-problems test.

Having the opportunity to take advantage of BTES data, we decided to attempt a further look at the relationship of growth in the class-size sites compared to that displayed by the students in BTES. A mathematical technique, called regression analysis, allowed us to make estimates of May performance for each Class Size student based on his or her performance on the December testing. Using data from BTES, a mathematical regression equation was calculated that predicted the level of performance in May as a function of a student's performance at December. The equations from BTES were then used on the Class Size data. We could then compare the actual score obtained for each Class Size student against the score predicted from the mathematical model generated from the BTES data. Each Class Size student now had a score which could be positive, zero, or negative, depending upon the relationship between their actual score in May compared to the score predicted from the BTES mathematical model. If a student did better in May than predicted, his or her residual score would be positive. Likewise, if the student did worse than predicted in May, his or her score would be negative. If the student did exactly as predicted, the residual score was zero.

Using a residual score for each student in the Class Size study, the percentage of students with positive residual scores was computed. Table 12.10 shows the percentage of students in each of the sites on each of the four content areas who achieved higher scores than those predicted from December scores based on the BTES prediction model. For example, on decoding, 47 percent of the students in the California site obtained higher scores than predicted. Sixty-three percent of the students in Virginia scored higher than predicted on this test. If the Class Size students were equivalent to the BTES population, one would expect 50 percent of the scores to exceed predictions. Upon examination of Table 12.10 it can be seen that of the eight measures reported (four content areas by the California and Virginia sites) five out of the eight measures are greater than 50 percent. In other words, on these five measures more than half of the students tested in the sites exceeded a score in May predicted from their performance in December.

To help interpret the percentage of students in Virginia and California who exceeded their predicted spring test performance, a 95 percent confidence band has been put around the 50 percent expectancy level established through the BTES data set. The standard error of a percentage of 50 based on the 139 BTES students is estimated to be .042. The 95 percent confidence band around the value of 50 percent then becomes 41.7 as the lower limit to the band with 58.3 percent being the top level of the band. These values can be used to better interpret the percents reported in Table 12.10. For Virginia the percentages on decoding and subtraction exceed those predicted from BTES data. For California, the word-problems test comes extremely close to surpassing the expected level from BTES. On the negative side, Oakland's performance on comprehension fell far below the expected level.

In general, it was observed that achievement gains were positive in the Virginia and California sites.

It is important to obtain as much information as possible from the teachers concerning their interpretation of why test scores might have been high, low, or generally as predicted. In the Oakland site, one of the teachers stated that there was a discrepancy or a mismatch between the type of comprehension activities she was using in her classroom and the type of achievement performance we were testing on our comprehension test. In the Virginia site, the frequent use of paper-and-pencil test-like tasks may have contributed to high achievement scores. It was observed that Virginia students typically took two to three tests each day as part of their reading group work. Furthermore, Virginia teachers proceeded further through the textbooks than pupils typically did in previous years, when class size was larger. The fast group in mathematics, for instance, finished the book in early April.

Supplementary Data

In addition to gathering achievement and systematic pupil behavior data during the course of the study, we had two opportunities to gather some additional information. The first idea was generated by an observation of one of the teachers in the California site. During a meeting of the teachers and the researchers, one teacher wondered whether attendance was greater in the smaller-class situation than in the larger. Upon further thought she believed that it quite possibly was, and suggested we make a comparison of the attendance figures for her class (1977–78 year versus the 1978–79 year). The school administrative staff cooperated in making the attendance information available. The plot of the percent attendance by school months is shown in Figure 12.1.

FIGURE 12.1   Oakland Site Attendance Data—1977–78 versus 1978–79

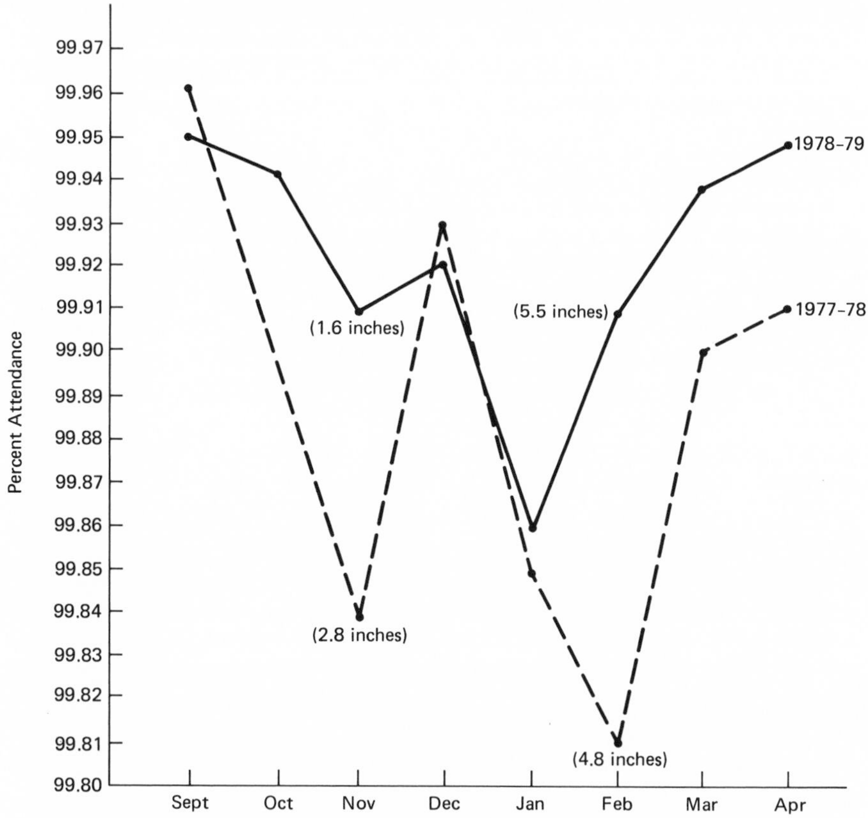

The reader's attention is directed to the month of January which gives the point after which the larger class was reduced to the smaller-size class. It can be seen that the attendance continued to drop during February in 1977–78 but rose during February in 1978–79. A difference also shows up, however, in November. We were aware of the fact that rainy weather conditions have a great deal of influence on pupil attendance. We obtained from weather records the inches of rainfall for the key months of November and February. These are shown in Figure 12.1. It can be noted that 1.6 inches of rain fell in November of 1978 and 2.8 inches of rain fell in November of 1977. Five and five-tenths inches of rain fell in 1979 in February and 4.8 inches of rain fell during the same month in 1978. This shows that attendance improved in spite of heavy rainfall in February of 1978–79.

We caution the reader that the choice of scale used in reporting the percent attendance as shown in Figure 12.1 greatly influences the perception of the plot of data shown. While the data generally support Ms. Taylor's hunch that at-

TABLE 12.11 Teacher-Talk During Math Lessons (Virginia Site)

	Anderson		Hopkins	
	Large	Small	Large	Small
1. Gives directions—academic procedure	10	5	8	2
2. Gives directions—management	11	7	5	12
3. Criticizes, justifies authority, demands attention	28	20	12	23
4. Other teacher-talk—academic	33	31	43	9
5. Other teacher-talk—affective	1	1	0	0
6. Confusion	5	1	4	10
7. Pseudo-silence	9	16	19	21
8. Student-talk	3	19	9	23

Entries are percentages of time during a 20-minute lesson.

tendance was better after class size was reduced, the important issue is that a participant researcher has attempted a conceptualization of evidence about the phenomena under study.

The researchers in Virginia attempted to utilize, on a limited scale, some additional objective information about "teacher-talk" during mathematics and reading lessons. This issue arose because of an emerging impression of the amount of time spent on discipline in the larger class size. An instrument developed by Flanders was adapted to obtain some additional quantitative evidence about types of teacher talk. Table 12.11 shows this data for Anderson's and Hopkins' classes during the larger and smaller phases of the study. The data are based on somewhat limited time sampling because they were gathered during one or two 20-minute lessons during each phase of the study. Some parts of the data reported in Table 12.11 suggest that positive changes took place: for instance, there was an increase in student talk. Time spent on criticizing, authority justification, and attention demands (category 3) did not change consistently. The results shown in Table 12.11 are not intended to be definitive in any way. They illustrate an attempt to obtain additional understanding of change possibly related to class-size reduction.

In conclusion, we believe we have provided evidence that reductions in class size can positively affect important aspects of student behaviors and teaching processes. In the smaller classes, students were more attentive and had more contact with the teacher during seatwork. We found the achievement gain trends to be generally positive but not overwhelming in magnitude. There is no guarantee that changes such as dramatic gains in achievement scores can be expected when a single change in schooling, such as reduction in class size, is induced; other factors also contribute to or impede gains in achievement test scores. Lastly, test performance reflects only a sample of the things children learn in school. There is a suggestion that attendance improved in the smaller classes and that students talked more during lessons.

13

Conclusions

After all of this, what do we know about the nature of instruction, and the role played by class size? In four primary-grade classrooms, we reduced class size in the middle of the year. In Virginia, class size was reduced from 20 to 13; in California, from 35 to 22 (with smaller group sizes due to instructional aides and a staggered schedule). What happened when class size was reduced? The preceeding chapters have described in detail changes occurring in each classroom and have discussed the experience at each school site. Now we want to step back to consider what happened generally. How consistent were the results from one school to the other, from one class to another? What themes emerged and were developed? What do the results reveal or emphasize about the nature of schooling? What areas can be suggested for further research to expand our understanding of schooling and its outcomes?

As with any enterprise as complex as education, the answer to what happened is not simple or easily evaluated. We are reminded often of the image of a glass half-full of liquid. The glass is both half-full and half-empty; the interpretation depends on one's perspective. In this case, it depends on one's ideal of what should happen in education and on one's expectations about how change can occur in complex systems. Changes did occur when class size was reduced. Teachers and students were generally happier and more productive in the smaller classes. These changes are important and meaningful. On the other hand, the process of instruction looked very much the same, regardless of class size. The machinery functioned more smoothly, but the design of the machine remained the same. For those with a different vision of education, this result may be discouraging. The experience gave us a more complete and vigorous understanding of the many factors that operate to shape the nature of education. Class size is but one of these factors.

In this chapter we will summarize and discuss general trends in the changes that occurred when class size was reduced. We will consider alternative explanations for these changes and ways to reconceptualize the "class size" issue. Finally, we will discuss factors which influenced and limited the amount of change across the two sites.

What Changed

The case studies provide a detailed picture of specific changes in each class-room when class size was reduced. Although the specifics sometimes vary, there was general consistency across classes in many of the kinds of things that changed or did not change. Three areas are discussed here—behavior management, individualization, and the curriculum.

Behavior management. One theme that emerged concerned behavior management—getting students' attention and keeping them engaged in learning activities. All teachers were concerned about control and felt that the smaller class size made discipline easier. In the teachers' views, they could spend more time "teaching" instead of "policing." The data on student attention support this assertion; students paid attention more of the time when class size was reduced.

This outcome seems to be a straightforward consequence of the reduction in numbers. Fewer people were "lost in the crowd" when group size was reduced. Each student had a chance to participate more in group lessons, either through having more turns or through having longer turns. The teacher was better able to keep track of what students were doing and involve them productively in the lesson.

In further work it might be useful to analyze student participation in greater detail. While students may generally have an opportunity to participate more often when group size is smaller, other factors are also likely to be involved. For instance, the turn-taking routines used by the teacher are likely to influence the opportunities for student turns. In reading groups, "round robin" ordered turns are often used, and in this situation group size would be directly related to the length of time each student reads. In other lessons, turn-taking may seem to be more "random," but in fact is likely to be nonrandom, and group size may affect some students more than others. If a teacher calls on volunteers or on high-ability students, then the fewer of these students there are, the more time each of them will get. But quiet students or low-ability students may continue to be nonparticipants. On the other hand, the teacher's turn-taking routines may themselves shift along with group size. In a large group lesson, the teacher may rely on volunteers or high-ability students in order to keep things moving along. In a small group, where control is perceived to be easier, the teacher may feel she or he can take time to draw all students into the lesson. Teachers might also change the nature of questions. In larger classes, teachers might ask questions evoking short responses; in smaller classes they might ask more open-ended questions or permit students to elaborate on responses more than they could in larger classes.

Similar to student participation in group lessons is the issue of student contact with an instructor during seatwork. In this part of our study we found that as the number of students decreased, contact time for each student generally increased. From BTES, we know that contact time is strongly related to student attention. Students are more attentive when they have more frequent contact with an instructor. Again, this aspect is a matter of sheer numbers. A teacher's time split 13 ways yields more for each student than a teacher's time split 20 ways. But, just as with student participation, the teacher's monitoring routine may be an intervening variable. If the teacher moves around the room, the teacher's attention may be more or less evenly distributed. Even if the teacher does not actually talk to each student, the effect of surveillance may be present. If the teacher sits at a desk and students come for help or to have their work checked, the effects of group size may be more uneven: the lines will be shorter for those who seek help, but those who do not seek out the teacher will be less likely to benefit.

Physical space, along with class size per se, seemed to influence student attention. In the larger class, students were sometimes a long way from the teacher: attention was most likely to suffer under these conditions. In group lessons, students on the fringes of the group were more likely to be inattentive than students seated closer to the teacher. When students lined up to come in from recess, one teacher commented on the fights that broke out at the end of the line, away from her vigilant eye. When class size was reduced, students could be brought physically closer to the teacher when this was desirable. This kind of close proximity was a permanent feature of Mr. Jameson's quarters in the erstwhile bookroom, and student attention rates were quite high in his room. On the other hand, there are times when it is desirable to have enough space to spread people out. Some teachers physically separated from the rest of the class students who were becoming disruptive and needed time out. There were also occasions when students needed a quiet space in order to concentrate better on their work, especially when doing seatwork. Neighbors close by could be a distraction. When class size was reduced in the regular classrooms, there was more space to spread people out; this appeared to contribute to higher attention, as long as the teacher could maintain surveillance.

We have noted before that the improvement in discipline and student attention, while real, may have been larger in the teachers' minds than in observable behavior. Mrs. Monroe had an attentive class to begin with, and still she noticed an improvement. In the Virginia site, the data on teacher-talk suggest that the teachers still spent a considerable amount of time monitoring behavior, even in the smaller class. This phenomenon is especially revealing of the nature of life in classrooms. As Phil Jackson (1968) has described, a major feature of life in classrooms is crowds. He emphasizes the student's perspective—the student must learn to subordinate his or her desires to the routines of the class; the student must learn to wait for a turn. From the teacher's perspective, the job is to manage a crowd—to coordinate the work of many people, to negotiate among the desires of many different people, to keep anyone from having to wait too long. This is a huge management job. Jackson observed that a teacher might have as many as a thousand interactions with students in one day. To keep all of these interactions in mind is extremely taxing. Even the 1000-interactions figure does not fully describe the problem, because the teacher is aware not only of the student(s) he or she is working with but also of the other students needing help or supervision. So, mentally, the teacher is reminded of all the students. Kounin (1970) has discussed this in terms of teacher "withitness," having eyes in the back of the head. With fewer students, the load on the teacher is reduced. Each individual student receives more teacher attention and becomes correspondingly more involved in class work. But over and above this, the teacher has less to keep in mind. In particular there is less competing for attention outside the sphere of what he or she is doing at the moment. This is what is represented in the heartfelt relief of Miss Anderson's statement: "There is more of me left at the end of the day."

Individualization.   A second theme concerned individualization. The teachers in this study viewed the smaller class size as providing an opportunity to meet student needs better. This is a common expectation among teachers (Wright, et al, 1977) and also reflects the nature of dealing with crowds. The teacher is aware of the individuals that comprise the class. She or he knows that they differ from each other in any number of ways—John likes to read mysteries, Samantha lacks confidence in her ability to read at all, Robert needs practice on consonant blends, Erika is quiet and doesn't participate often in group lessons, George's behavior has to be monitored closely. The question is how to run a classroom in the face of all this diversity. Which differences are important enough to require different instructional techniques or curriculum? How much differentiation of instructional programs can the teacher manage? Once the teacher plans the instructional program, diversity remains. How can the teacher help all students to learn the assigned material when Janice was absent for two days, Sarah has problems at home, Anthony seems not to grasp the new concept, and Rachel has mastered the material and is eager to move on? To one degree or another, the teacher must balance all these issues as she or he plans instruction from day to day. There is almost no end to what the teacher could do, given sufficient time, energy, support and resources. But all of these are limited, so something always remains undone. The hope is that reducing class size will provide an opportunity to do more for each student and leave less undone.

The changes that developed reflected one kind of individualization but not another. Little changed in the basic curriculum or mode of instruction. Students in all classes were grouped for instruction in reading and mathematics, and group instruction continued, with some modifications, even in the smaller classes. The curriculum itself was not individualized.

This result should perhaps not be surprising. Faced with the complexity of a classroom, each teacher develops routines and procedures that provide structure for both teacher and students. Out of a history of training and classroom experiences within the context of school policies and expectations, a teacher molds an approach which is comfortable, familiar, and acceptable in that school. Even if some aspects of the program do not seem ideal, a total change in approach represents a major undertaking. Educators who study staff development and change processes emphasize that change comes slowly, requires commitment on the part of the teacher, benefits from support within the school, and may require specific training in new techniques. We purposely declined to advocate specific changes. The time frame of five months in the middle of the school year meant little time for advance planning. The time frame also required a change in a system that was already operating; in other words, teachers had established certain ways of interacting with the larger class and the students in it. Although the smaller class size did appear to make teachers more confident of their ability to manage behavior, they did not attempt individualized programs, even though they all expressed a concern for individual needs.

What teachers did do, however, was provide more individual contact time in support of the ongoing program. Each teacher was able to get around to students to provide help when needed, to give feedback, and to encourage students to do their best. While most of these contacts involved academic work, teachers were also able to take time just to chat with students and find out about their feelings and interests. In this way, each teacher acknowledged the individual while still maintaining the group.

Curriculum. As we noted above, group instruction in reading and mathematics remained the dominant form of instruction. The content of instruction continued to be determined primarily by the textbooks. Especially in Virginia, the curriculum was viewed as pages to be covered in the text. As discussed in Chapter 7, this may have been due in part to school-system policies as well as teacher skills and beliefs.

In a number of ways, however, teachers were able to cover the curriculum more effectively. Because students were more attentive, lessons proceeded more smoothly and quickly. With the extra time this smoothness provided, teachers could cover more material. Sometimes they moved through the curriculum more quickly. At other times they expanded each lesson in greater depth. Also, teachers were sometimes able to emphasize different aspects of the curriculum: for instance, by spending more of their own time on things they considered important, such as Miss Anderson's story-reading sessions.

For the most part, changes in the curriculum could be considered enrichment. Things were added that had not been done previously, and the additions were generally not integrated into the core reading and mathematics curriculum, subjects that determine whether students pass. Some of these changes were additions to the daily program. For example, in the Virginia school the principal and teachers used this study as an opportunity to introduce three afternoon programs—Peabody language development, DUSO guidance and social development, and science. All children were able to take part in these three new curriculum areas. Other changes involved less instructional time but provided variety to enrich the basic program—free time to explore different activities, instructional games, poetry reading, and field trips.

It should be noted that these enrichments to the curriculum may not be reflected in evaluations of class-size effects. Typically, achievement tests in reading and mathematics are used to evaluate outcomes. This narrow definition of achievement overlooks learning in other academic areas, areas which may be valued by consumers of education. Also, many of the enrichment areas are intended to promote positive attitudes, enthusiasm, and overall learning skills. These factors may have long-term effects not in evidence on short-term achievement tests. Research in education may be misled by its focus on short-term achievement outcomes.

Alternative Explanations

It is important to note that the changes that occurred were not necessarily *caused* by the class-size reduction. For one thing, the smaller class condition always occurred later in the year, when second graders have attained more maturity and teachers have had more time to establish effective classroom routines. In other words, things may visually look better later in the year. A counterargument can be made on the basis of BTES data. In BTES, student attention rates were measured throughout the year from October to May for second and fifth grade students. No overall change in attention rates occurred from the first half of the year to the second half (Filby and Cahen, 1978). This suggests that neither student maturity nor teacher routine-setting leads to greater student attention as the year progresses. Instead, classroom behavior patterns tend to be established fairly early in the year (Anderson and Evertson, 1978).

People who hear about this study may also raise the issue of a "Hawthorne effect." Were changes due to a temporary increase in effort, which would diminish over time? Teachers were encouraged to take advantage of the smaller class and thus put some energy into making changes. They also experienced the relief of a sudden reduction in class size, which increased their enthusiasm. As teachers become acclimated to a new class size, they might make fewer changes. "Large" and "small" are relative concepts, and some teachers accomplish more than others in any given class size.

In response to this argument about teacher enthusiasm, the nature of the changes must be considered. None of the changes reflected major additional effort on the part of the teacher. Rather, it seemed that easing the constraint of class size allowed the teacher to do better what she or he was already inclined to do. Most of the changes that occurred could be described as modifications or improvements *within* the teacher's existing style and plan of instruction. Teachers did not change their basic approach, but they were able to implement that approach more fully and effectively. Such improvements would presumably endure over time.

We could even speculate about greater changes over time. When the teacher knows she or he will have fewer students for an extended period, she or he may get past the stage of sheer relief and have time to plan and experiment with more extensive changes.

Grouping Arrangements, Not Class Size

These results provide a concrete understanding of the phenomena behind Glass and Smith's finding that achievement improves dramatically only when class size is reduced below 15 pupils. In this study, we entered this range, and the school life of each child improved only to a small degree. The teacher's time and attention must still be split many ways. In addition, finances make it difficult to provide even this degree of improvement on a grand scale. For these reasons, it would be useful to shift and broaden the focus of investigation in future work. Instead of class size, perhaps we should investigate grouping arrangements and alternatives for organization at the school and classroom level which provide small-class conditions for some of the children and/or for part of the school day.

For example, the daily schedule can be manipulated to vary class size for parts of the day. In the California school, a staggered schedule was used; one half of the class was present during periods of reading instruction. Other scheduling alternatives would involve combination-grade classes such as K–1, with a longer day for the first graders, or keeping some students late on some days in an "extended-day" concept. In addition to scheduling arrangements, personnel resources can be used in various ways. Team teaching allows teachers to manipulate group size from very large to very small. Resource teachers, specialists, aides, and parent volunteers all expand the teaching staff. Peer tutors can also be used. These and other alternatives need to be described and investigated in order to use resources efficiently while still providing expanded opportunities for small-group instruction.

Factors Limiting Change

Chapter 7 discusses a number of factors in the Virginia situation which may have served to maintain the existing instructional program in spite of the class-size reduction. These factors include contextual constraints, teacher knowledge and skills, and teacher beliefs and attitudes. By comparing the experience in the two different sites, we can evaluate the relative impact of these different factors.

Chapter 7 provides a strong sense that class size is just one of many elements forming the context in which a teacher must operate. Other important aspects of the context include school size, textbook policies, promotion policies, school schedule, and principals' beliefs and actions. Many of these factors were different in the two sites. For instance, the Virginia school was small and the principal regularly "made the rounds," visiting the classes or walking the halls, while the California school was large and the teachers could more easily retreat behind closed doors. While textbook selection was determined at the school level in both cases, teachers in Virginia were tightly constrained by the mandated assessment tests and the promotion policy while teachers in California had more freedom to adapt or supplement the curriculum. The school schedule in Virginia included no recess periods while the schedule in California included abundant recesses. In Virginia the teachers traded students during the day, thereby requiring that the time schedule be tightly maintained and reducing the opportunity for projects and activities integrating different subject areas. In California the teachers had a self-contained classroom all day, although not all students were present all the time.

In spite of these differences in context, the response to the class-size reduction was very similar in the two sites. This similarity suggests that, in most cases, specific contextual factors were not the primary constraint on change. For instance, Virginia teachers were required to give assessment tests and they all did so, including Mr. Jameson, although this took a lot of time during the reading period. In California, use of the textbook was less specifically mandated, and these teachers did show more variation in the kinds of reading activities they used in both the larger and the smaller classes. But the amount of *change* in reading curriculum was not very different. Even with fewer constraints present, the California teachers did not make major modifications.

This result directs our attention to the other factors discussed in Chapter 7—teacher knowledge and skills, and teacher beliefs and attitudes. Each teacher had developed an educational program with which she or he was familiar and comfortable and which that teacher believed was acceptable in the school. Even changing several aspects of the context might not be enough to produce changes in that program unless the teacher envisioned and desired a different kind of program and was willing to work for some time to establish the new program. These are issues for professional development and teacher education.

Part V

14

Implications for
Conducting Research

The purpose of conducting this study was to learn more about the effects of class size on classroom practice. In that attempt, however, we also learned a great deal from and about the research process itself. This chapter addresses some of the issues we became more cognizant of and suggests possible implications for conducting future studies in classrooms.

DESIGNING THE STUDY

What is the best way to study how class size affects instruction? With this initial question, the process of designing our study began.

Choices had to be made early. Should we study a large number of classrooms somewhat superficially or a small number of classrooms in greater depth? We realized that with a large number, some people might view our study as more "credible"; however, others might find more merit if we described a few settings in detail. How would our decisions affect the generalizability of our findings?

As previous chapters reveal, we chose to study a small number of classrooms. We wanted to be able to note the nature of changes resulting from reduced class size, including those occurring over time. Extensive observation, then, was necessary, but possible to manage only if few classes were studied. Also supporting this decision was our belief that long-term familiarity with classroom life is necessary for understanding the complex process of teaching and learning, and matters affecting teaching and learning in smaller and larger classes. In addition, we wanted to avoid the anonymity, the "data by mail order" which results in many studies that cover a "large N of classes"— children tested, classes observed, but no one knows the teachers and students by names and faces!

We also chose to reduce class size rather than observe teachers who already had smaller or larger classes. We hoped to develop such a keen understanding of what occurred for the larger classes that when classes were reduced, changes related to class size would be more apparent. We believed differences between naturally smaller and larger classes would be due to other variables in addition to class size, so that a comparison of such classes would reveal less about the effects of class size on teaching and learning.

A number of factors affected the design and therefore the findings of our study. One factor was the seemingly minor issue of space. In order to form a third second-grade class, we needed schools with a room to spare. In neither site was this an easy task. If we had had more choices in site selection, we might have chosen a school where the two teachers were not as similar to one another as were Miss Anderson and Mrs. Hopkins.

System-wide decisions also affected the study. In California, for instance, district pressure resulted in reducing class size earlier than we had planned: this prevented the California team from gathering certain evidence; as a result, later comparisons could not be made.

Available resources further affected the directions the study could feasibly take. A forty-percent cut in the project budget occurred during the field-study year; this cut limited the study in terms of personnel, time, and cross-country travel to visit the other team's classrooms. Resources, then, determined how many researchers and research sites we could involve in the study and how often we could meet to discuss and interpret our observations.

As we became involved in the study, questions emerged that may have implications for designing future studies. For example, we wondered how many observers are needed to see ''all'' the critical events in the classroom, how we balance looking at the group versus target students, and whether photographs, video-tapes, and audio-tapes can supplement what we see and hear as observers. Other researchers might have pondered different questions, but these seemed particularly intriguing to us and were the topics of several lively discussions.

In reflecting on the design of our study, we are aware that, under different circumstances, the study would have developed in other ways. Other findings may have been revealed about the effects of class size on instruction. We wonder, for example, what we might have found out if the study had begun at the beginning of the year instead of in the middle, or if this had been a longer study, involving the same teachers and classrooms for more than a year, or if some classes had started larger and gotten smaller while others reversed that procedure, or if greater intervention about teaching strategies had been incorporated, and so on. Perhaps an added benefit to the findings of a research study is the generation of further questions and issues to ponder. Certainly our study provided this for us!

Incorporating Two Approaches

The teams from each site brought differing research expertise to the study and initially had different frames of reference with regard to ways of collecting evidence. For example, the California team had more experience with the Academic Learning Time (ALT) model. The Virginia team had more experience with developing field notes and doing educational criticism. This necessitated our spending time teaching one another, clarifying our language, research questions, and procedures, and discussing our views of what was important to observe or measure. Visits in each site and lengthy discussions gave us the opportunity to learn and try the methods. We asked each other many questions at this stage: "What do you write in field notes? Where do you look in the classroom?" "Okay, I understand the categories on this observation form, but how do you tell if a child is 'academically engaged'? What if she or he seems off-task but answers correctly?"

During this process, labels such as "quantitative researcher" and "qualitative researcher" became less important as we recognized our shared concerns about education and our desire to understand more fully what happens in classrooms. We realized that to answer our many questions, we sometimes needed to describe in words, sometimes in numbers; at times we needed to focus on processes, at times on products. This is not to say we lost our individual identities as researchers or became the same, but rather that we became more aware of the complementary nature of many of our procedures and used this knowledge to enrich our study.

Perhaps the most marked distinction of the teams occurred not in conducting the study, but during the writing phase. The Virginia team used evocative language to describe the classrooms and wove appraisal into the narrative. An informal writing style characterizes the Virginia chapters, with the authors often using *we* in hopes of communicating more personally with the reader. The California team chose a more direct writing style, reporting all evidence before offering their evaluation.

The difference in writing styles raised several questions for us and may be important for other researchers to consider: Does the dissimilarity of style affect the continuity, comparability, and clarity of reporting the findings? Is it possible to reach some compromises and, if so, how? In teaching methods of research, should we teach writing style too?

We resolved these problems by responding to each other's critiques verbally and revising our writing as much as was personally acceptable. We had no way of knowing early in the study that writing about our findings might be an issue. In future studies, writing style might be a worthwhile topic to include during initial discussions, in order to lessen the possibility of conflict and to lengthen the time to discuss the issues. We also hope readers will write to us about our cases, particularly regarding the problem of style.

CONDUCTING PARALLEL STUDIES

What does it mean to conduct *parallel* studies? Does this merely depend on the similarity of sites? What else must be considered in order to compare the findings of each setting?

Although thousands of miles separated the two sites for the class-size study, the research in each was similar, focusing on the same research questions, using the same research methods, observing the same grade-level classrooms, and following the same general procedures.

Obviously, establishing total parallelism would be impossible. For one thing, our frames of reference were different in that we knew different things about schools and had different experiences as teachers, researchers, or parents of children attending public schools. Furthermore, certain features of our research sites were dissimilar. For instance, the California team observed in an urban school, the Virginia team in a rural school. The teachers involved had varying years of teaching experience, and the schools enrolled different numbers of students in their classes. Furthermore, contextual influences in each setting differed, thus having an impact on the study. In California, the reduction in class size took place earlier than planned due to school-system pressure. Although this particular constraint didn't occur in Virginia, others did. Instructional time was lost, for instance, because of extensive practice for Christmas and May Day festivities, long-standing and expected community traditions.

Although we made some decisions early in the study about the approaches to use for specific questions, we found we also needed to evolve certain methods as required. For instance, in the Virginia site we became intrigued by the origin, nature, and effects of the numerous interruptions during instructional time and began recording field notes about those events. This concern was expressed to the California team, and they also started attending to it. Additionally, wondering about the authoritarian atmosphere in one classroom led us to use a modified version of the Flanders Interaction Analysis to obtain data about types and amount of teacher-talk. In the California site, the research team became aware of the possible increased school attendance of children in the small classes, began recording this information, and searched through previous attendance records to determine changes.

Instead of totally prespecifying the research design, then, we allowed part of it to develop in process. This flexibility permitted us to consider new questions along the way, creating a richer portrayal of the classrooms studied. In order to maintain as much parallelism as possible, we kept each other informed of these emergent issues, in case they might be important to consider in the other setting also.

Parallel studies might be an appropriate way to study many educational questions. Some researchers, for example, might wonder about various ways junior high schools make the transition to middle schools. That is, they might wonder how the school changes in terms of exemplifying a particular concept of middle schools rather than merely changing in terms of the grade levels included in the school. Others might be interested in how teachers in different parts of the country adapt the same curriculum materials. Still others might focus on various schools' responses to legislative mandates such as PL 94-142. Parallel studies provide the opportunity to examine the same question or issue in a number of settings and to illustrate possible influences on, and explanations for, educational practice, such as state mandates or other regional differences. Researchers must give careful thought, though, to what *parallel* means, to ways of achieving it, and the extent to which it is beneficial within a particular research design.

WORKING AS A TEAM

The class-size study was a team effort. This was not easy to accomplish across a continent, but we worked hard to maintain a team spirit throughout all phases of the study. Although one team member began the research as a graduate student, others had had varying years of experience as researchers, and one directed the project, somehow we evolved into equals. Several factors seemed to enable us to accomplish this.

In our early meetings we worked toward establishing feelings of equity and trust within the group. No one stated this as a goal; it merely developed. It was an important development, too, since we had to rely so much on each other's long-distance reports and trust them. Perhaps we accomplished this through our informal brainstorming sessions where everyone had a chance to be heard, or by realizing we needed to learn from one another, and by doing so. Or perhaps because we planned some time for relaxing over drinks and dinner! In any event, the team "clicked," and that benefitted the study.

We maintained the team effort by communicating frequently, usually talking on the phone or sending each other brief memos of ideas. The most beneficial way, though, was a site visit. We found it extremely helpful to spend a few days immersing ourselves in discussions of the study and to see one another's classrooms. These sessions helped us maintain the parallelism we sought and always stimulated ideas and enthusiasm. In fact, more visits would have been helpful in considering various interpretations of our findings and in clarifying any discrepancies, but this was impossible due to the reduction in our funding.

Working together as a team helped us realize the benefits of being able to examine an issue from various perspectives. We were able to critique each other's findings and analyses and to consider together the range of meanings and implications of the study.

INVOLVING TEACHERS AS COLLABORATORS

In designing the study, we planned for the teachers to be research partners, providing the insider's view about the effects of class size on instruction. Several issues developed from this attempt.

We became aware that the choice of a teacher as a research collaborator is an important one, and we need to allow enough time to select teachers and their classrooms carefully. The type and degree of collaboration can influence the research process and findings. Of the five teachers in our study, one ended up participating more fully than the others. She began by keeping a very detailed journal, but became more and more interested in the study, raised issues, and eventually wrote about her research experiences. The other teachers participated in a more limited way, mainly helping to gather evidence or to explain some influence on their teaching.

Certainly it takes a reflective, articulate person to study and describe his or her own teaching, but a richer portrayal of the classroom is possible with such a perspective. Spending time with several teachers before asking someone to be involved might help identify those able to assume that responsibility, and might be a way to involve teachers with different teaching styles and different types of classrooms, if this diversity is considered important to the study. Furthermore, during these initial contacts, the teacher could be helped to realize more fully what the final written version of his or her classroom might be like. Reading examples of other classroom accounts might explain the range of possibilities and give the teacher a stronger basis for deciding whether or not to become involved. Preparation is important, as one of the teachers in our study wrote.

> There are both benefits and liabilities facing any classroom teacher or teaching team that decides to participate in a research project. These need to be anticipated and carefully weighed before a decision to participate or not is rendered. If the decision is not carefully made, then frustration will ensue. The teacher will feel imposed upon, and the research team will not collect adequate data.

Obviously, though, no matter how thorough the preparation, complete realization of the role of collaborator can only occur through involvement in the study.

We also realized that teachers' roles as collaborators may differ during the various phases of the study. For example, the teachers had the chance to add to the list of research questions and to suggest ways of gathering evidence, but for the most part the outside researchers made these decisions. The more active role for the teacher was in helping to conduct the study and to interpret the findings. This may be due, in part, to how teachers view themselves professionally. Teachers who view themselves as controlled by the system may be hesitant to become active participants. Researchers designing future studies might want to work with the teachers to discuss roles and to decide at what points and in what ways collaboration about the study will occur. Furthermore, some teachers may want to assume a more active participation as the study progresses and they become more comfortable with a new professional role. Collaboration is a time-consuming effort, and finding ways to provide release time for teachers to talk with researchers and other participating teachers is a difficult but necessary issue to resolve if greater teacher involvement in research is to occur.

A number of other issues can be raised about collaboration, issues about decisions at various stages of the study, about reporting the findings, about anonymity for teachers versus recognition (and possible job risk), and about developing relationships and their effect on unbiased findings. (For a fuller elaboration of these and other issues, see Kyle and McCutcheon, forthcoming). The benefits of collaboration, as we discovered throughout this study, indicate that these issues need to be addressed and are worth the effort involved in doing so.

SUMMARY

Just as the findings about class size increased our understanding of this facet of educational practice, conducting the study helped us be more aware of ourselves as researchers, and of issues related to research efforts. It is our hope that, in some way, others may benefit from our experiences.

15

Implications for Teaching and Schools

What does this study imply, and what issues does it raise about improving the quality of teaching and schools? Clearly, with fewer students the potential is there to allow the teacher to devote more time to individual pupils, to reteach, and to check quickly the individual's work. Order is easier to maintain; therefore teachers are able to teach for a greater percentage of the time, and they feel more relaxed. Students have more turns, receive more personal attention; equipment is not spread as thinly and students generally increase their achievement more than in larger classes, as reflected by test scores.

One implication of the study, then, is to try to conceive of ways of reducing class size. Given the difficulties associated with the funding of education, it is clear that class size will not be reduced "across the board" throughout the entire day. Perhaps educators could consider the grounds on which to reduce class size for parts of the day. This occurs now for many students below grade level in reading, and those with special needs. Should we reduce class size for all students for those subject matters deemed most important? In which subjects, at what particular times of the day? Or should class size be reduced only for certain students? Policy papers related to class-size issues (Glass, Cahen, Smith, and Filby, 1982) bring different points of view to the issue of class size, and may be helpful to administrators and teachers as they consider appropriate courses of action.

The problem is one of organizing the school so the teacher is not responsible for overseeing work or monitoring behavior while working with another group. How can some students be "gainfully employed" while class size is reduced for others? While many possibilities exist, a few are listed below:

In Hawthorne Elementary School, a few students from kindergarten and first, then second and third, then fourth and fifth grades are released for arts or physical education classes, reducing the size of the group remaining in each classroom for other instruction.

In Avalon Middle School, students engage in school-related work in the community two mornings a week, and are in school all other times. The staff has scheduled this work-study to arrange for smaller classes for everyone in language arts classes.

At Longwood Elementary School, trained aides oversee the seatwork of all students not involved in active instruction. Before school in the morning, the teachers explain that seatwork to the aides and coach them in their skills.

School people are encouraged to brainstorm and deliberate about means for reducing the size of instructional groups for those subject matters and students where such reduction would be of great benefit.

Another matter related to these studies concerns teachers' and administrators working alone. For example, Mrs. Fleming (see Chapter 3) lamented her lack of anyone to turn to for help with professional matters. The nearest university was 40 miles away, the library carried few education journals, and assistance in solving problems seemed impossible to obtain. This was also true for the teachers. To whom might educators turn for commiseration or help with professional problems? Teachers and administrators in this study, like most across the nation, worked alone. How could they break down the separating walls and encourage communication among each other? How can a community be established, one in which teachers and administrators see themselves as working together to provide an excellent education for the years their students attend school? How can educators revise textbooks, develop appropriate curriculum materials, analyze curriculum guides, deliberate about the aims of the school, develop policies, and attend to other matters collegially to enhance growth and development of their programs, selves and students? Enhancing a spirit of professionalism, of excitement with the processes of education is important, it seems, to counter boredom, frustration and "burn-out" in addition to dealing with problems. Perhaps through cooperative vision and action, a school climate that will be supportive of excellent education can be established. How might Miss Anderson have changed her disciplinary tactics, had she been in such an environment? Might Mrs. Monroe have questioned the level of work she required of children? Raising issues and having a large pool of talent for consultation might prove helpful to a relative novice like Mrs. Hopkins. How might Mr. Jameson's differing views and criticisms of school policies and practices have been put to a useful purpose?

Many teacher centers seem to serve the purpose of addressing particular issues and taking advantage of the varying talents of their members. A school staff committed as a group to improving the quality of education could conceivably evaluate one another's teaching, coach and teach one another about appropriate skills, and solve problems for their unique situation. Meetings with clearly outlined problems to be addressed, curriculum development projects, ad hoc committees, professional discussions in the staffroom or at administrative meetings, and other courses of action would be necessary. These developments call for a high commitment to professionalism on the part of educators, and for a different sort of relationship with colleagues than is found in many schools and school systems, but the difficulties we face in schooling are not likely to be addressed alone or without this commitment. Several examples of problems successfully addressed by groups of teachers may be helpful.

Science teachers from Fairweather High School and Oak Bay Middle School met to relate their programs to one another's. The middle school science curriculum focused on process, while the high school's focused on content and hence was disjointed. A curriculum development project, funded by what would have been used to purchase textbooks, resulted in a new syllabus, cataloguing existing materials and purchasing new materials for the schools.

King Elementary School teachers, administrators, community members and parents developed a schedule whereby students interested in particular areas such as the arts, computers, creative writing, geology and animal life met in small groups with various people from the community and school for study several times weekly.

Several teachers at Shady Cove School met to plan ways of improving the school climate, then divided the chores and implemented them, meeting several times to reshape plans and discuss how the plans were faring.

It is probably too much to expect all staff members to be involved, yet a core of people working together may be able to improve matters in a way not possible if each worked alone on the venture. In the studies presented in this book, for example, such groups might have helped teachers conceive of ways to take advantage of small class size to reshape instructional practices for the benefit of all. Other matters alluded to in these studies which groups of teachers might address concern decreasing the number of interruptions, improving the nature of seatwork, and considering alternative discipline strategies. Indeed, many issues were raised in these studies.

For example, policies and practices clearly influence the curriculum and instruction in classrooms, and many of these influences may not be foreseen by policymakers. For example, promotion and testing policies brought about great adherence to the reading textbook in Pine Springs School although the textbook curriculum probably does not work for all students. How can policies be stated in such a way that they provide for certain sorts of control, yet educators can act appropriately on their professional responsibility of instructing students? Additionally, the pervasive concern about control and discipline at Pine Springs School may have perpetuated certain sorts of practice and may also have influenced Mrs. Monroe's choices of activities. How can we confront ourselves with our own practice, examine it, experiment with and develop more appropriate strategies for control to free our choices of activities, transforming them into those that are educationally sound? How might we move from teachers' control over student behavior to a more internalized students' control over their own behavior, which might be more appropriate in our society at large? Another set of issues concerns scheduling. When scheduling is done by separate subject matter areas, supported by separate textbooks for each subject matter and by the promotion policy and report card, how does this influence integration among subjects? For example, if separate times, texts and grades are allocated to spelling, language and reading, it is reasonable to believe that it may be difficult for teachers to help students see connections among the three. Integration among subjects seems important in order to facilitate students' learning, as does integration between what students learn in school and their out-of-school lives. Facilitating such connections may help students find relevance in their studies.

In short, attention might be given to creating different sorts of opportunities for learning in various ways. We say we believe students are different from one another, that they learn in different ways and have different interests, strengths, and needs. Policies and school-wide practices have the effect of setting the context, the limits within which planning and practice can exist. How might we develop policies to facilitate professional planning that considers matters such as individual differences, various appropriate forms of control, and supporting the learning of many students? What sorts of processes within the school could be developed to support teachers' growth and their ways of dealing with such matters, and to engage in constructive reflection and honing of practice?

Finally, improvement in schools cannot be expected to be rapid, large-scale or dramatic. Improvements happen slowly, are small in scale, frequently almost invisible (See Sarason, 1971). We hope for too much if we believe a change in one aspect of practice (such as the schedule, adopting a different mathematics text, or decreasing class size) will profoundly change the nature of education in a particular classroom or drastically improve the achievement of the students. Changes are more likely to be small, but noticeable. These small accomplishments are important, for, taken together, they might comprise what we would consider to be a larger-scale improvement. Gathering evidence about such small-scale accomplishments for purposes of research, praise, and public relations is an important endeavor. The venture of improving the quality of schooling is long-term, takes a high degree of commitment and concerted effort, support from many sources, and constant reexamination. Maintaining the status quo is safe, easy, and comfortable, yet those of us who are professionally committed to a high quality of education find ourselves uneasy, for we know that schools could be better places, students could learn more, and we could be better educators.

References

Adams, R. and Biddle, B. *Realities of teaching: Explorations with video tape*. New York: Holt, Rinehart and Winston, 1970.

Benedict, R. *Patterns of culture*. Boston: Houghton Mifflin, 1924.

Biggs, E. and MacLean, J. *Freedom to learn*. Ontario: Addison-Wesley, 1969.

Brown, B. and Saks, D. Production technologies and resource allocations within classroom and schools: Theory and measurement. In R. Dreeben and J. Thomas, (Eds.), *The analysis of educational productivity (Vol. I): Issues in microanalysis*. Cambridge, Mass.: Ballinger, 1980.

Coble, H. M. Some new insights on class size and differences in teacher/pupil performance in the various subjects. *Central Ideas*, 1968, *19(3)*, 1–7.

Emmer, T. E., Evertson, C. M., and Anderson, L. M. Effective classroom management at the beginning of the school year. *Elementary School Journal*, 980, *80*, 219–231.

Filby, N. and Cahen, L. *Teaching behavior and academic learning time in the A-B period (BTES Technical Note V-1b)*. San Francisco: Far West Laboratory for Educational Research and Development, 1977.

Filby, N. and Cahen, L. *Teaching behavior and academic learning time in the B-C period (BTES Technical Note V-2b)*. San Francisco: Far West Laboratory for Educational Research and Development, 1978.

Fisher, C. W.; Berliner, D. C.; Filby, N. N.; Marliave, R.; Cahen, L. S.; and Dishaw, M. M. Teaching behaviors, academic learning time, and student achievement: An overview. In C. Denham and A. Lieberman, (Eds.), *Time to learn*. Washington, D. C.: National Institute of Education, 1980.

Fisher, C.; Filby, N.; Marliave, R.; Cahen, L.; Dishaw, M.; Moore, J.; and Berliner, D. *Teaching behaviors, academic learning time and student achievement: Final report of Phase III-B, Beginning Teacher Evaluation Study*. San Francisco: Far West Laboratory for Educational Research and Development, 1978. (ERIC # ED 183 525)

Geertz, C. *The Interpretation of Cultures*. New York: Basic Books, 1973.

Glass, G V. Primary, secondary, and meta-analysis of research. *Educational Researcher*, 1976, *5*, 3–8.

Glass, G. V.; Cahen, L. S.; Smith, M. L.; and Filby, N. N. *School class size—research and policy*. Beverly Hills: Sage Publications, 1982.

Glass, G. V., and Smith, M. L. *Meta-analysis of research on the relationship of class size and achievement*. San Francisco: Far West Laboratory for Educational Research and Development, 1978.

Jackson, P. W. *Life in classrooms*. New York: Holt, Rinehart and Winston, 1968.

Kounin, J. S. *Discipline and group management in classrooms*. New York: Holt, Rinehart and Winston, 1970.

Kyle, D. and McCutcheon, G. Collaborative research: The concept and its potential for curriculum studies. *Journal of Curriculum Studies*, in press.

McCutcheon, G. Educational criticism. *Journal of Curriculum Theorizing*, 1979, *1*(2), 18–23.

McCutcheon, G. On the interpretation of classroom observations. *Educational Researcher*, 1981, *10*(5), 5–10.

McKenna, B. *Measures of class size and numerical staff adequacy related to a measure of school quality*. Doctoral Dissertation. New York: Teachers College, Columbia University, 1955.

Mosteller, F. and Tukey, J. *Data analysis and regression*. Reading, Mass.: Addison-Wesley, 1977.

Newell, C. A. *Class size and adaptability*. New York: New York Bureau of Publications, Teachers College, Columbia University, 1943.

Olson, M. N. *Identifying predictors of institutional quality: an examination of eleven internal classroom variables in relation to a school system criterion measure*. Doctoral Dissertation. New York: Teachers College, Columbia University, 1970.

Porwoll, P. *Class Size: A summary of research*. Arlington, Va.: Educational Research Service, 1978.

Richmond, H. *Educational practices as affected by class size*. New York: New York Bureau of Publications, Teachers College, Columbia University, 1955.

Ryan, D. W. and Greenfield, T. B. *The class size question*. Toronto, Ontario: Ontario Ministry of Education, 1975.

Sapir, E. The unconscious patterning of behavior in society. In D. Mandelbaum, (Ed.), *Selected writings of Edward Sapir*. Berkeley: University of California Press, 1963.

Sarason, Seymour B. *The culture of the school and the problem of change*. Boston: Allyn and Bacon, 1971.

Smith, M. L. and Glass, G. V. *Relationship of class size to classroom processes, teacher satisfaction and pupil affect: A meta-analysis*. San Francisco: Far West Laboratory for Educational Research and Development, 1979.

Tukey, J. *Exploratory data analysis*. Menlo Park, Calif.: Addison-Wesley, 1977.

Wright, E. N.; Shapson, S. M.; Eason, G.; and FitzGerald, J. *Effects of class size in the junior grades*. Toronto: Ministry of Education, Ontario, 1977.

APPENDIX A

Instructions For Rating Student Engagement/Interaction

One form was used to record information about the class as a whole and about selected individual students in the class.

Individual Students

Each row on the form was used to record what an individual student was doing at one brief, specific moment in time. Four to six students could be observed on the same day. The basic procedure was to look at the first student, take a mental "snapshot" of the student, then record information on the form about this sampled moment (this took about 45 seconds), then look at the second student, decide what he or she is doing, and mark that down. After one complete cycle through the set of students, we started over again. One complete cycle took about three minutes.

Some information provides a basic setting for instructional events. This information was recorded only when it changed. For instance, the *time* was recorded only at the beginning and the end of a continuous sequence of coding, or when other setting information changed. The *content,* reading or math, was written down only at the beginning or when it changed. The *group size* was done the same way.

Time, content, and group size gave basic setting information. The next basic category was the organizational structure. We wanted to make a distinction between *groupwork,* when groups of students were working interactively with each other and/or with the teacher on a single task, and *seatwork,* when students were working independently, at their own pace, possibly on different tasks. (More will be said later about defining these categories.) A given activity was either groupwork or seatwork, and different kinds of information were coded depending on the organizational framework:

Groupwork. One kind of general information about the group was recorded—whether or not an *adult* was present with the group (Teacher, Other Adult, or None). This information was recorded at the beginning and when it changed, rather than every time. Two other kinds of information were checked off on each row. The first was *"oral turn."* This category recorded whether or not the student was responding out loud in the group. It allowed us to estimate how often a student had a turn to respond in the group. We checked one of the four categories—choral response, individual response, hand raised, or not responding at the moment. The second category was student *engagement*—is the student paying attention? There were seven categories of engagement, as defined below. We checked off the one(s) that applied.

Seatwork. One kind of information was recorded about seatwork—the degree of supervision from the teacher or another adult. We wrote in the degree of supervision, high, medium, or low, at the beginning and when it changed. Two kinds of information were checked off on each row. First was *contact*. Often during seatwork students worked completely on their own without having any verbal interaction with anyone. If the student was involved in verbal interaction, we checked off the person involved. Otherwise, we checked off "No." Student *engagement* categories were the same in seatwork as in groupwork.

Class Engagement Measure

Every 15 minutes, we stopped and took a class-level measure of student engagement. The seven categories of engagement were the same as the categories used for individual students. We recorded the time when the estimate was made and the number of students that fell into each of the seven categories. At the bottom of each column we wrote the total number of students in the class at the time. (This total helped us make sure that no students had been skipped.)

Coding Categories

Time. Time, in minutes (*e.g., 9:14*)
Content. Reading (R) or Mathematics (M)

Reading includes reading-related activities that make some use of printed words, such as writing stories, spelling, or grammar, as well as a variety of reading activities such as reading a book, doing a worksheet, listening to a phonics lesson, discussing the meaning of a word or a story, and so on. Reading does *not* include purely oral language activities such as sharing ideas or the teacher reading a story to the class when the students cannot read along. In some way, the student should be reading something.

We started coding when it seemed that general transition time was over and the reading or math lesson had started: for instance, after the students came in from recess, settled in their seats, and the teacher said, "Get out your math books." We noticed that the lesson may have begun some time before all students were working productively.

Group Size. We wrote the number of students working in the same setting—groupwork or seatwork (see definitions following).

Groupwork/Seatwork. The major difference between these two organizational structures is one of pacing. In seatwork, the student works independently, at his or her own pace. Students might be given the same assignment to do, or they might each be working on something different, but they can go at their own rate. During seatwork, a student might interact with *one* other person; for instance, the teacher might check a student's work and give him or her feedback, or a student might ask another student how to spell a word. If more than two people are interacting, it is groupwork. In groupwork, the pace is determined by the group (or by the teacher leading the group). Often, activities in a group will be oral. Sometimes the group will do written work "together," one problem at a time. In groupwork, the student is not supposed to go at his or her own rate, but is supposed to move with and be part of the group.

Adult. Is there an adult, teacher, or aide working with the group?

(T)—*Teacher* working with the group
(O)—*Other* adult working with the group
(N)—*No* adult working with the group

Oral Turn. Usually in groups people take turns talking. We wanted to know how often a particular person gets a chance to talk. When we looked at the student, he or she was doing one of four things, in terms of *participation* in the group:

Choral Response (CH). Several students are asked to respond out loud together (e.g., read a poem, read a word, or recite addition facts).

Individual Response (I). The student you are looking at is having a recognized turn. The student might be asking a question, answering a question, explaining how to do something, or offering a comment.

Hand Raised (H). The student has his or her hand raised to indicate willingness/interest in having a turn.

No Turn (No). The student you are looking at is not having a turn. Probably the student is supposed to be listening to someone else. The student might be writing an answer or waiting; that is, it might not be anyone's turn.

Supervision. During seatwork, teachers differ in how closely they supervise what the students are doing:

High (H). The teacher is directing the activity; for example, the students are copying spelling words off the board and the teacher is watching the group, making sure all students are moving along, occasionally giving directions to the group as a whole. OR: The teacher has the students sitting in a circle around him or her while they work in their workbooks, so he or she can interact frequently with each child.

Medium (M). The teacher is available to the students or is walking around monitoring, but control is less direct or frequent.

Low (L). The teacher is generally unavailable; for instance, the teacher is working with reading group while the children you are watching are doing seatwork. (The teacher might occasionally monitor or be available in an emergency.)

Contact. During seatwork, is the student talking to someone else or listening to someone else or looking at someone else's work: in other words, does the student have some contact with someone? If so, who?

Teacher (T).   The teacher might check a student's work or the student might show his or her work to the teacher or ask a question.

Other Adult (OA).   As above, but an aide or parent volunteer.

Student (S).   The student might interact with another student.

No Contact (No).   The student is working on his or her own (or not working, but independent).

Engagement.   What is the student paying attention to?

Engaged–Academic (EA).   The student is paying attention to an academic task, such as:

• reading a book
• doing a worksheet
• playing a reading game that
  requires reading
• listening to the teacher explain how to do word problems
• answering the teacher's question
• listening to another student answer the teacher's question
• listening during another student's turn in reading circle
• checking answers against an answer key

Engaged–Procedural (EP).   The student is paying attention to some procedural activity that supports the academic task, such as:

• passing out or collecting papers
• getting out books
• sharpening pencils
• listening to directions
• putting a heading on a paper
• marking a score on a score sheet
• setting up a game

Engaged–Rules (ER).   The student is paying attention and the content is rules or classroom management, for instance:

• The teacher is talking to the class about the need to be quiet.
• The teacher is praising the target student for sitting still and looking up.
• The teacher is reprimanding the target student for being out of a seat.
• The teacher is marking student points on a chart for good behavior.

Waiting for Help.   The student is "stuck" and waiting for help. It would be appropriate for the student to have his or her hand up. The student might put up a help sign or show in some other way the need for help.

Off-Task (O).   The student is not paying attention, but is being quiet and not disruptive, for example:

• daydreaming
• drawing a picture instead of listening

Misbehaving (M).   The student is not paying attention and is doing something potentially disruptive, such as:

- playing around with another student
- knocking over his or her chair
- talking to a friend (not about the task)
- walking around the room

Down Time (D). The student is waiting because, for the moment she or he does not have anything specific to do: for instance, when the student finishes early or has not yet been given an assignment.

For all areas other than engagement, only *one* code is appropriate at a single moment. For instance, the student doing seatwork might have contact with the teacher or another adult or a student, but not two people at once. For engagement, *more than one* code might be needed to describe a particular situation. In particular, a student who is waiting for help or in down time will also fall simultaneously in one of the other categories. Probable combinations are as follows:

W + EA   The student is waiting for help on one problem but goes on to do the next one.

W or D + O   The student is quietly sitting and waiting.

W or D + M   The student is waiting and also misbehaving.

	Time					
EA-R/M						
EA-oth						
EProc						
ERule						
Wait						
Off						
Misb						
Down						
Total						

Date:

Teacher:

Observer:

Day Typical?
Yes No*
(Circle)

* If no, why?

Student	Time	Con-tent R/M	Size	Groupwork							Seatwork			Notes
				Adult TON	Turn CH I H	Engagement No EA EP ER W O M D	Sup HHL	Contact T O S	Engagement No EA EP ER W O M D				

Instructions For Rating Student Success Rate

One thing that we wanted to know about was the nature of the content students were working on and how successful they were in their work.

Recording success rate is not like recording engagement/interaction because content does not usually change as quickly as engagement/interaction. Often a student will spend from five to 15 minutes on the same general activity. What we wanted to do was make *one* entry for each activity for each target student. We used *one* line for each activity.

For each activity the following things were recorded:

Time Start.   When did the student start working on that activity? (e.g., 10:06)

Time Stop.   When did the student stop working on that activity? (e.g., 10:21)

No. Same Task.   How many students in the class were given the same assignment? Write down the number of students. Not all the students need to be working on the task at exactly the same time. For instance, students could be told to do two workbook pages: some students could work on one page first and some the other, some might not even get to page two, but all students were given the same assignment. The idea was to understand the degree of individualization of content.

Task/Content.   What is the student working on? At the left-most edge of this space, please identify the general content area by circling R for reading/language or M for math. Then describe the activity in more detail, for instance, reading a book, writing a story, spelling test, reading comprehension questions, meaning of words, addition speed test, addition problems with regrouping (carrying), number patterns, word problems, and so on.

Success Rate.   How well can the student do the task? Check one:

High-fluent (H+).   The student responds accurately and correctly, except for occasional careless errors, and the student seems to respond quickly and fluently. The task is easy for the child.

High-effort (H−).   The student responds correctly, but it seems to take the child some time and effort to do so.

Medium (M).   The student does not completely understand the content and makes some errors, but the student responds fairly readily and does not seem to find the task too hard.

Medium/Hard (M−).   The student knows enough to work on the task, but makes many errors and seems to find the task difficult.

Low (L).   The student does not know how to do the task!

Note: We found in BTES that our students, on the average, spent about half their time on tasks they could do correctly (H+ or H−). Low success was rare, but important.

Confidence. How confident are you in your rating of success level? Check High (H), Medium (M), or Low (L).

Sometimes we did not have information from which to judge success level, for instance, in a group situation where the target student never makes an overt response, or when the content changes quickly. We tried to make our best estimate on each activity, but also knew how confident we were of our estimation.

There is a lot of leeway in when and how to determine the rating of success level. We were not always able to tell from the child's performance in a group, but the child might later be doing a seatwork assignment on the same content, from which we could tell what the previous success rate should be. We attempted to use all of our information to rate each activity. As we got to know the individual children, we knew from past work how easy or hard a task was for the child. But we were careful not to assume too much. We looked at the child's work carefully. If we needed to, we asked the child to show us how he or she worked out a problem, or to read aloud to us. If the child was not working, it might have been because she or he didn't understand what to do; we asked the child to show us what he or she was supposed to do.

Class Low Success

Every 15 minutes, we stopped and surveyed the class. How many students seemed to be lost, that is, to be in the "low success" category? We wrote down the time, the number of students experiencing low success, and the total number of students in the class at the time. We remembered that a student might be making marks on the paper but might still be conceptually lost. It might take a couple of minutes to go around the room and look for low-success situations.

SUCCESS RATE OBSERVATION FORM

Date:

Teacher:

Observer:

Day Typical?
Yes   No*
(Circle)

* If no, why?

Class
Low Success:

Time	Number Low lot.

Student	Time Start, Stop		No. Same Task	Task/Content	Success Rate				Confidence			Notes
					H+	H	M	L	H	M	L	
				RM								
				RM								
				RM								
				RM								
				RM								
				RM								
				RM								
				RM								
				RM								
				RM								
				RM								
				RM								
				RM								
				RM								
				RM								
				RM								
				RM								
				RM								
				RM								
				RM								
				RM								
				RM								
				RM								
				RM								
				RM								
				RM								
				RM								

APPENDIX B

Median Percent of Observations Where Target Student Displayed Categorized Behavior

Target Student	Engaged–Academic			Waiting for Help			Off-Task			Down-Time			Contact With Teacher During Seatwork		
	L	S	Change	L	S	Change	L	S	Change	L	S	Change	L	S	Change
1	89	87	-2	0	0	0	0	0	0	0	0	0	0	9	9
2	37	44	7	9	0	-9	28	39	11	11	0	-11	0	17	17
3	67	77	10	8	0	-8	11	7	-4	7	0	-7	9	0	-9
4	53	84	31	22	0	-22	3	0	-3	25	0	-25	0	0	0
5	67	81	14	0	0	0	17	11	-6	7	0	-7	0	0	0
6	56	68	12	8	0	-8	8	17	9	8	0	-8	11	0	-11
7	38	83	45	25	17	-8	0	0	0	38	0	-38	0	5	5
8	75	86	11	0	14	14	0	0	0	13	0	-13	0	0	0
9	63	81	18	25	12	-13	13	5	-8	13	0	-13	0	5	5
10	38	79	41	0	14	14	13	0	-13	38	0	-38	0	0	0
11	71	71	0	0	0	0	9	0	-9	7	0	-7	10	0	-10
12	25	54	29	9	0	-9	38	13	-25	0	0	0	0	22	22

L = larger class condition
S = smaller class condition

233

Index

Academic Learning Time (ALT). 5, 212–13
Achievement measures, 193–98
  mathematics, 195
  outcomes, 197
  reading, 194
  scores, 196
Achievement tests, 5, 17, 205–6
Active participation, students', 17, 97, 120–21, 151–53
Adams, R., 222
Aides, teacher, 207
  Harrison School, 129, 130–31, 139, 143, 146, 164–65, 172–73
  Pine Springs School, 55, 95, 109–10, 117
Aid to Families with Dependent Children, 36
Anderson, L. M., 222
Anderson classroom, 44–70
  clerical tasks, 46–47, 56–57
  instructional activities, 47–52, 57–60, 64–65
  interactions, 52–55, 65–68
  interruptions, 68–69
  management, 48, 60–65
  physical environment, 45–46, 56
  summaries of, 55, 69–70
Artwork, 50, 75, 120
Attendance, student, 10, 185, 198–200
  taking, 46, 56, 73, 82, 92, 158, 166
Attention, student, 5, 16, 138–39, 159, 166, 175–78, 202–3
  instructions for rating, 227–28
  quantitative data, 185–86, 189–90, 193
Attention-seekers, 123, 148
Awareness, teacher, 5

Basic Goals in Spelling, 92

Beginning Teacher Evaluation Study (BTES), 5, 17, 187–88, 192, 193, 196–98
Behavior, student, 16–17, 47–48, 60–65, 67, 84–85, 98, 106–7, 113–14, 116, 123–24, 138–39, 148, 169, 175–78, 202–4
  instructions for rating, 227–28
  measures, 185–93
Behavior modification, 29, 66
Belief system, 121–22
Benedict, R., 27, 222
Berliner, D. C., 5, 222
Biddle, B., 222
Biggs, E., 120, 222
Blacks, 28–29, 130
Brown, B., 192, 222
Budget restrictions, 3, 129

Cahen, L., 5, 6, 8, 9, 18, 25, 185, 193, 218, 222
California. See Harrison School
Changes, Pine Springs School, 111–24
  belief and attitude, 121–22
  context of, 111–19
  skill, 119–21
Choices, allowing students to make, 69, 93–94, 146
Chores, classroom, 72, 81, 92
Christmas pageant, 41, 109, 117, 121, 214
Class Size and Instruction Program, 4–5, 193, 196–98
Clerical tasks
  Anderson classroom, 46–47, 56–57
  Hopkins classroom, 73, 80–83
  Jameson classroom, 92–93, 107–8
  Monroe classroom, 158–59, 166
Clusters, seating, 118, 135
Coble, H. M., 7, 222

Coded observation, 7, 16–17
Collaborators, teachers as, 215–16
Columbia University, 7
Community relations
  Harrison School, 128–29
  Pine Springs School, 38, 41, 117
Comprehension, 193, 194, 196–98
Contact with student, teacher, 5, 52–54,
  65–67, 78–79, 88, 107–8, 148–51,
  161, 164–65, 167–68, 177, 179–80,
  202–3
  instructions for rating, 224–28
  quantitative data, 186–92
Creative writing, 142, 153, 164
Crime in schools, 127–28
Curriculum, 85–86, 132–33, 180–81
  conclusions about, 205–6, 219–20
  expanding, 65, 86–87, 152–53, 180
  hidden, 28–29

Data, quantitative, 185–200
  achievement measures, 193–98
  behavioral measures, 185–93
  supplementary, 198–200
Decoding, 193, 194, 196–98
Developing Understanding of Self and
  Others (DUSO), 62–63, 67, 205
Dewey, John, 29
Discipline, 42, 54, 66–67, 84–85, 98,
  106–7, 113–14, 116, 138–39, 174,
  175–78, 202–4
Dishaw, M., 5, 222
Documents, school, 24
"Down time," 52, 78, 87
  instructions for rating, 229
  quantitative data, 186–87, 191

Eason, G., 7, 223
Effect size, 6
Emmer, T. E., 222
Engaged-academic (EA), 5, 16, 67–68, 89,
  97, 122, 176
  instructions for rating, 224–28
  quantitative data, 186–90, 193
Environment. *See* Learning environment,
  Physical environment
Evaluation of student work, 51–52, 63–64,
  77–78, 87, 120, 171–72
Everton, C. M., 222

Evidence, collecting research, 12–13,
  16–25
  achievement tests, 17
  coded observation, 16–17
  field notes, 18–23
  student work, 24
  teacher discussions, 23–24
  teacher journals, 24–25
External factors, 90
  interpreting, 29–30
  research questions on, 12

Families
  of Harrison schoolchildren, 127–28
  of Pine Springs schoolchildren, 36–38,
  117
Far West Laboratory for Educational Re-
  search, 4–5, 9
Feedback, 5, 161, 163, 164, 205
Field notes, research, 18–23
Field trips, 152, 180, 205
Filby, N., 5, 6, 8, 9, 15–16, 18, 25, 125,
  185, 218, 222
Findings. *See* Research conclusions
Fisher, C. W., 5, 222
FitzGerald, J., 7, 223
Flanders Interaction Analysis, 214
Flash cards, 93
Follow-Through Program, 130, 133, 141
Freedom to Learn, 120

Games, 134, 154, 162, 170–71, 180, 205
Glass, G. V., 5–8, 17, 185, 218, 222, 223
Glass-Smith Curve, 6
Good-workers chart, 47, 58
Green Feet, 141, 161
Greenfield, T. B., 7, 223
Groups
  managing, 48, 60–65, 76, 84–85, 120,
  141–43, 147–48, 160–61, 169–70,
  175–78, 202–4, 206–7
  organization of, 51, 63, 76–77, 86–87,
  141–43
Groupwork, 141–43, 146, 147–48, 151,
  176, 204–5
  instructions for rating, 224–25
  small group, 5, 57, 78, 86, 119, 146,
  169, 207
Guidance program lesson, 59–60, 67

Harrison School, 125, 127–81
 aides, 130–31, 139, 143, 146, 164–65,
  172–73
 behavior management, 175–78
 curriculum, 132–33, 152–53
 Monroe classroom, 156–74
 parent volunteers, 131, 143
 principal, 130–31
 research approach, 14, 21–23
 schedule, 132
 setting, 127–29
 Taylor classroom, 134–55
 teachers, 129–30
Hawthorne effect, 206
Hidden curriculum, 28–29
Hopkins classroom, 71–90
 clerical tasks, 73, 80–83
 instructional activities, 73–78, 83–88
 interactions, 78–79, 88–89
 interruptions, 79–80, 89–90
 management, 76, 84–85
 physical environment, 72–73, 81–82
 summaries of, 80–81, 90

Implications
 research, 211–17
 for teaching and schools, 218–21
"Indicators of Quality," 7
Individualization, 5, 12, 85–86, 92, 102,
  107–10, 119, 136, 139, 146, 148–50,
  179–81, 204–5
Instructional activities, 120–21
 Anderson classroom, 47–52, 57–60
 Hopkins classroom, 73–78, 83–88
 Jameson classroom, 94–103
 Monroe classroom, 161–65, 170–72
 research questions on, 10–11
 Taylor classroom, 141–43, 151–54
Interactions
 Anderson classroom, 52–55, 65–68
 conclusions about, 202–3
 Hopkins classroom, 78–79, 88–89
 instructions for rating, 224–28
 Jameson classroom, 106–7
 Monroe classroom, 163–64, 167–68
 quantitative data, 186–92
 research questions, 11
 Taylor classroom, 136, 137–39,
  147–51, 177, 179–80

Interpretation, research, 26, 27–30
 external considerations, 29–30
 patterning, 27–28
 social meanings, 28–29
Interruptions, 10, 112
 Anderson classroom, 68–69
 Hopkins classroom, 78–79, 88–89
 Jameson classroom, 94–96, 108
 Monroe classroom, 161
 research questions on, 12
 Taylor classroom, 152

Jackson, P. W., 203, 222
Jameson classroom, 91–110
 homeroom, 92–94
 interruptions, 94–96
 lunch duty, 103
 mathematics lesson, 94–98
 reading lesson, 98–103
 science lesson, 103–5
 style, 106–10
"Jointness" concept, 192
Journals, teacher, 16, 24–25, 61–62, 97,
  143–44, 148–49
Judgments, making, 30

Kounin, J. S., 68, 176, 222
Kyle, D., 9, 18, 223

"Larger-class" view
 Anderson classroom, 45–55
 Hopkins classroom, 72–81
 Monroe classroom, 156–65
 Taylor classroom, 134–44
Learning centers, 57, 73, 82, 85, 219
Learning environments, 3–4, 8, 169
Lessons, types of, 48–51, 61–63, 75,
  85–86, 141–42, 151–54, 161–63,
  170–71
Logistical arrangements for research,
  13–16
 dividing classes, 15
 hiring teacher, 15–16
 selecting schools, 13–14
 selecting target students, 14
Low-achieving students, 139–40, 150, 202
Lunch duty, 103

McCutcheon, G., 9, 18, 24
McKenna, B., 7, 223

MacLean, J., 120, 222
Management skills, 5
  Anderson classroom, 48, 60–65
  conclusions about, 202–4
  Hopkins classroom, 76, 84–85
  Jameson classroom, 106–7
  Monroe classroom, 160–61, 169–70, 175–76
  Taylor classroom, 137–41, 147–51, 177–78
Marliave, R., 5, 222
Materials, use of, 48–51, 61–63, 75, 85–86, 94, 141–43, 161–63, 170
  creative, 82, 86, 120–21, 153, 165, 180–81
  recreational, 134
  research questions on, 11
Mathematics, 42, 47, 57–58, 74, 83–84, 135–37, 145–47, 151, 158–60, 166–69, 205–6
  achievement scales, 195
  teacher-talk during, 200
May Day celebrations, 41, 117, 121, 214
Meta-analysis, 6–8, 17
Methods, class-size study, 9–31
  approach to research, 12–25
  developing research team, 9–10
  generating questions, 10–12
  processes, 26–30
  writing, 26
Microscopes, use of, 93, 104–5
Monroe classroom, 156–74
  aides, 159, 164–65, 172–73
  clerical tasks, 158–59, 166
  instructional activities, 161–65, 170–72
  management, 160–61, 169–70, 175–76
  mathematics lesson, 158–60, 166–69
  physical environment, 156–58, 165–66
  summaries of, 165, 173–74
Moore, Rob, 18, 24, 25
Moore, J., 222
Morale. *See* Teacher satisfaction
Mosteller, F., 223
Multiethnic center, 165, 173
Mysterious Wisteria, 161

Newell, C. A., 7, 223
Noise level, 137, 160, 165, 176

Observation, coded, 7, 16–17
Off-task behavior, 190, 191, 227
Olson, M. N., 223
"On task." *See* Engaged-academic
Open-enrollment policy, 128
Oral reading, 49–50, 62, 161–62
Order
  at Harrison School, 131, 161
  at Pine Springs School, 42–43, 113–14, 121–22
Organization, teacher, 51, 63, 76–77, 86–87, 141–43
  research questions on, 11

Pacing student work, 164, 172
Pageants, school, 41, 108, 117, 121, 214
Paired observation measures, reliability of, 187
Paper-and-pencil activities, 50, 63, 78, 81, 88, 124, 148, 171
Parallel studies, 213–15
Parents
  of Harrison schoolchildren, 127–28, 131, 143
  of Pine Springs schoolchildren, 36–38, 117
Participation, active student, 17, 97, 120–21, 151–53
Patterning, 27–28
Peabody Language Development Kit, 86, 120, 205
Peer tutoring, 173, 207
Phonics, 48, 115, 151, 161–62
Phonograph records, 134, 162
Physical education, 50–51, 75
Physical environment
  Anderson classroom, 45–46, 56
  Hopkins classroom, 72–73, 81–82
  Jameson classroom, 91–92
  Monroe classroom, 156–58, 165–66
  Taylor classroom, 134–35, 144
Pine Springs School, 33, 35–124
  Anderson classroom, 44–70
  beliefs and attitudes, 121–22
  children and adults at, 36–39
  context of changes, 111–19
  Hopkins classroom, 71–90
  Jameson classroom, 91–110
  order, 42–43, 113–14

promotion policy, 42, 108, 114–15
research approach, 14, 15, 18–21, 27–28
schedules, 39–41
setting, 35
textbook adoption and use, 41–42,
 75–76, 88, 92, 112, 114–15, 120,
 122–23, 220
Playgrounds, 35, 75, 135, 160
Policies, school-wide, 207
 Harrison School, 132–33
 Pine Springs School, 111–19, 121–22,
 220
Population, student
 Harrison School, 127
 Pine Springs School, 36
Porwoll, P., 7, 223
Principal, school
 Harrison School, 130–31
 Pine Springs School, 37–38
Problem solving, 57, 67, 145
Promotion policy, 42, 108, 114–15, 207,
 220
"Proximity" factor, 193
Public Law 94–142, 214

Quantitative data, 185–200
 achievement measures, 193–98
 behavioral measures, 185–93
 supplementary, 198–200
Questions, research, 10–12

Racism, 28–29
Reading, 42, 47–48, 58–59, 74–75,
 84–85, 87, 98–103, 141, 151,
 161–63, 205–6
 achievement scales, 194
Research approach, 12–25
 achievement tests, 17
 coded observation, 16–17
 dividing classes, 15
 field notes, 18–23
 hiring teacher, 15–16
 selecting schools, 13–14
 selecting target students, 14
 student work, 24
 teacher discussion, 23–24
 teacher journals, 24–25
Research conclusions, 201–8
 factors limiting change, 207–8

grouping, 206–7
 specific, 202–6
Research data, 185–200
 achievement measures, 193–98
 behavior measures, 185–93
 supplementary, 198–200
Research implications, 211–17
Research plan, 4–8
 background, 4–7
 outline, 8
Research processes, 26–30
 appraisal, 30
 description, 26–27
 interpretation, 27–30
Research team, 9–10, 215
Resources, school, 3, 129
Responsibility, student, 82–83, 92
Richmond, H., 7, 223
Riverview School, 37
Role playing, 120, 122, 170
Roll call, 46, 56, 73, 82, 92, 158, 166
Ryan, D. W., 223
Ryle, Gilbert, 28

Saks, D., 192, 222
Sapir, E., 27, 223
Sarason, Seymour, 223
Scales, achievement, 17, 193–98
Schedules
 Harrison School, 132
 Pine Springs School, 39–41, 103–4,
 116–17, 121
School boards, 3
School Class Size: Research and Policy,
 185
Schools, selecting, for research, 13–14
Science, 40, 103–5, 205
Science Research Associates (SRA), 162
Seatwork, 5, 40, 81, 107, 136, 139, 164,
 174, 180
 instructions for rating, 225
 quantitative data, 186, 191–92
Self-confidence, 139–40, 150–51
Self-evaluation, student, 78, 87, 120
Sexism, 28
Shapson, S. M., 7, 223
"Smaller-class" view
 Anderson classroom, 56–70
 Hopkins classroom, 81–90

"Smaller-class" view (*continued*)
  Monroe classroom, 165–74
  Taylor classroom, 144–55
Small groups, 5, 57, 78, 86, 119, 146, 169, 207
Smith, M. L., 5–8, 17, 185, 218, 222, 223
Socialization, student, 89, 205
Social meanings, 28–29
Space, classroom, 92, 100–101, 113, 118–19, 134, 144, 156–57, 165, 203
Spache Readability Formula, application of, 114–15
Specialists, teacher, 36, 99, 118
Spelling, 42, 92, 141, 163
"Station Day," 170–71, 174
Student-student interactions, 52–54, 67–68, 79, 89, 136–37, 147
  research questions on, 11
Style, teaching
  formal, 160–61, 177
  informal, 106–7, 177
Subtraction speed test, 193, 195, 196–98
Success rate, student, 5
  instructions for rating, 230–31
Sunburst, 114–15, 117
Synonyms, 193, 194, 196–97

Tag, 141
Target students, 14, 15–16
Tasks, appropriate, 5
Taylor classroom, 134–55
  aides, 143
  instructional activities, 141–43, 151–54
  interactions, 137–39, 147–51, 177
  management, 137–41, 147–51, 177–78
  mathematics lession, 135–37, 145–47
  physical environment, 134–35, 144
  summaries of, 143, 154–55

Teacher satisfaction, 201, 206
Teacher-student interactions, 44–45, 54, 65–67, 78–79, 88, 106–7, 147–51, 161, 163–64, 167–68, 177, 179–80, 202–3
  quantitative data, 186–92
  research questions on, 11
Teacher-talk, 53, 67, 79, 88, 142, 153–54, 163, 171, 203, 214
  quantitative data, 200
Teacher's guides, 120, 151
Team teaching, 207
Tests, achievement, 5, 17, 205–6
Textbook adoption and use, 207, 219
  Harrison School, 134, 141, 143, 162, 180
  Pine Springs School, 41–42, 75–76, 88, 92, 112, 114–15, 120, 122–23, 220
Time, organizing, 51, 63, 76–77, 86–87
Transition, lesson, 48, 59, 160
Tukey, J., 223
Turns, taking, 97, 102, 135, 163–64, 202, 219

University of Colorado, 6

Virginia. *See* Pine Springs School
Volunteers, school, 38, 117, 131, 143, 207

Waiting time, 87, 135, 163–64, 176
  instructions for rating, 227
  quantitative data, 186–87, 189, 190
Welfare, social, 36, 127
"Withitness," 68, 176
Word problems, 193, 195, 196–98
Writing
  creative, 142, 153, 164
  about research, 26
Wright, E. N., 7, 223